Wait Until Dark

Wait Until Dark: Jazz And The Underworld 1880-1940

Ronald L. Morris

Bowling Green University Popular Press
Bowling Green, Ohio
1980

This book is dedicated to Alan and Klonda, Jeff and Jean, and Willa, for their inspiration and advice.

Contents

Chapter I

They All Wore White Cowboy Hats

Whenever we think of Duke Ellington, Charlie Parker, Louis Armstrong, Bix Beiderbecke and King Oliver we think of musical genius, boundless creativity, and jazz showmen who loved to entertain. So we have come to assume that in a world where such extraordinary musical talent is appreciated, these men, and others like them, rose to prominence on the strength of sheer merit and innovation alone. This is a natural assumption but one quite at odds with the truth. For in their cases, individual success and recognition had little to do with innate talent, technical skill, or, for that matter, their own free will. It had everything to do with the fact that a high value had been placed on the music they played by certain infamous admirers willing to pay handsomely for its performance and who economically determined its sphere of infuence.

The reality of the situation, particularly as it affected jazz musicians between 1880-1940, the period spotlighted by this study, requires that these hitherto unpublicized admirers and well-wishers be discussed for what they were and what they did.

I am referring to that legion of underworld characters known in the Broadway vernacular as mobsters and racketeers. I am also referring to their sponsorship of jazz, an activity without which the artists themselves would have shriveled up and died. Traditional accounts of gangsters are bone-chilling for the average reader, casting these men as rapacious murderers. Jazz journals, following suit, award them little attention, verifying their presence with some mean anecdote or footnote. Yet these uncomplimentary descriptions only muddy historical waters and detract greatly from our study of jazz musicology. Nevertheless, and simply stated, this mercenary band of gangster types marketed, befriended and

1

encouraged many hundreds of jazz performers in attaining an otherwise elusive popularity. It must be remembered that this was a time when society showed no great fondness for black people, let alone their musicians and white imitators, expressing displeasure in a variety of violent and neglectful ways. Bluesman Honeyboy Edwards bemoaned the enormous waste of talent during these years, of men "stuck back in the woods or on the farms who never had a chance."[1]

Despite the fact that most leading jazz entertainers after 1880 were closely allied with racketeers, the social significance of this association, together with the extent of contact and cultural interaction, has been previously overlooked. The purpose of this study is to rectify a bad omission. Doing so finds me contradicting viewpoints normally attached to mobsters about their attitudes and behaviors; their animal vindictiveness, their contempt for the public and their rank, abrasive venality. For the vast majority this inane stereotype is simply untrue. Assuming otherwise, I intend to present a functional and descriptive analysis of how so strange a brotherhood influenced the performance of jazz music and significantly affected artistic creation in the process. These men may not have been as relaxed toward their enemies as the corner grocer, but the extent of their meanness is debatable, while their contribution to jazz should at least earn them our unstinting gratitude.

Jazz musicians hardly make the worst critics. Art Hodes, Max Kaminsky, Duke Ellington, Earl Hines and Mezz Mezzrow pay their respects in the autobiographies they wrote. Bessie Smith characteristically cloaked them in praise when the blues singer exclaimed, "Any bootlegger is a pal of mine."[2] Sonny Greer, drummer for the Ellington orchestra, was more wistful:

I keep hearing about how bad the gangsters were. All I can say is that I wish I was still working for them. Their word was all you needed.[3]

Trombonist Dickie Wells "was always treated well and never bothered"; cornetist Wild Bill Davidson claims they "gave me the greatest job I ever had"; and pianist Willie "The Lion" Smith transcribed how mobsters benefitted musicians who kept to a workable code of ethics carved from the bedrock of slum life they shared in common:

The Big Shots were kind and considerate to the entertainer they liked. You just had to know when to talk, kid, or shut up, and conduct yourself well and you had a chance to get good money and jobs.[4]

Mobsters have been depicted at their most obnoxious during moments of tight-fisted business negotiation. Yet even on this point a musician like Earl Hines disagrees. Writing in 1949, he recalls "relations with gangsters were always cordial."[5] One elderly jazz musician, preferring to remain anonymous, confided to me that in the case of bandsmen this simply was not true. Mobsters were creampuffs:

Those bargaining sessions could be heated affairs. But I always stood up for what I felt I was worth and rarely did the mobs fail to meet my demands. Actually, some just liked to argue, knowing all along they fully intended meeting my price or better, just putting on a show.

Archie Shepp, a contemporary jazz group leader and saxophonist, recognizes their contribution to the night club milieu in which most musicians blossomed:

You can't evaluate a jazz musician without being aware of the factors that shaped his life.... Had there been no Kansas City (and its many organized mobs)—suppose it had been a Mormon society—what would have happened to Charlie Parker?[6]

Sociologists have rarely bothered to examine the socioeconomic aspects of musical production and distribution, much less artistic creation, although Ben Sidran has written on the importance of "gangster night life to innovations in black music" and the Marxist musicologist T.W. Adorno notes that musical trends are subjected to "innumerable processes of social selection and guidance" by a whole range of influences before they reach the masses. Alan Lomax, Jelly Roll Morton's biographer, also admits too little is known about the "extra-musical gangster-control influence" upon jazz of the prohibition years. Professor Stearns, a respected authority on the subject, insists on the importance of the 1920s for the establishment of jazz. Whether this opinion is accepted or the one I maintain—that the critical foundations for all that followed in the presentation of jazz were laid as early as 1880s—on one matter there can be no equivocation: It was the mobsters who succeeded in putting it over the top.

Comparatively speaking, what travel agents and airline promotions dispense as the tonic for the weary worker, known as the "Las Vegas Scene," glittering with night club revues and brassy, lavish entertainment round-the-clock, is but a thin slice of the kind of adult pleasures found in most major cities after 1915. In those days no self-respecting night club could reasonably attract public acclaim without enlisting the services of a hot jazz band. "It wasn't only an innovation," showman Jimmy Durante wrote, "it was a revolution." Clubs and jazz went together like two peas in a pod.

In my effort to assess the grip which racketeers had on the night life of this period, I consulted John Hammond, chief jazz talent scout for over four decades and Vice-President of Columbia Broadcasting System. His rough reckoning, which I later found no reason to dispute, is suggestive of their preeminent control. Hammond believed no fewer than three in every four jazz clubs and cabarets of this distant period were either fronted, backed or in some way managed by Jewish and Sicilian mobsters (an important distinction to which I shall soon return), owners of police records of long-standing. If we conclude that most clubs came to be owned by different syndicates and underworld characters, jazzmen were directly paid from the pockets of these benevolent thugs. Proving this contention shall henceforth be the subject of this study.

The Jewish and Sicilian grifters were in many ways far less powerful politically than the Irish gamblers and saloon-keepers of the 1880s and 1890s whom they emulated. In any event, as high-living spenders, with fast cars, loose women, swank clubs in which to operate, and reckless vivacity, these men circulated a great deal of money in the entertainment business from 1890 to 1940. By so doing they furthered not just jazz, but the era of great Broadway musicals, even, to some degree, the Harlem Renaissance. Economist Werner Sombart explored lengthily what Jews have done as master traders:

As innovators and ready cash men Jews were always ready to finance new commodities, new methods over old, and use gimmicks to attract customers.... They were the first ones to open coffee houses in Germany.[7]

In addition they promoted a cultural and employment boom only the severest of depressions could retard. For once having hired an orchestra, Jewish and Italian mobs spun a protective cocoon around the group, allowing it time to perfect its own brand of music. Orchestras were often hired on an indefinite basis until this was accomplished. Consequently, and fortified with a cosy guarantee of near-perpetual employment, groups developed styles, personalities and showmanship which later carried them to their successes. Such patronage was crucial in the face of an indifferent public, and, as a result, black musicians were treated to the luxury of steady work, steady income and steady appreciation. Considering what had come before, this was indeed something of a minor miracle.

If life under gangster rule can be characterized as rough and uncertain, it was immeasurably better than what most musicians had previously known. Saxophonist Bud Freeman recalls:

The better hotels and restaurants employed violinists and pianists who played...very old fashioned music. We were happy to have a (mobster) place to play the kind of music we loved.[8]

Without this musical matrix, jazz artists would never have escaped the inhuman turpentine mills of the violent, ante-bellum South. Nor would they have survived the hazardous honky-tonks in New York's "jungles" or the drab pit theatres along Chicago's Near South Side. In actual fact, the collective resistance from diverse establishment factions toward both jazzman and his racketeer-supporters who sought entry into the night club business before 1914 has never received adequate attention. Yet the force of their opposition could hardly be taken lightly. Bankers, bordello operators, bar owners, restaurateurs and musicians' unions, each in their own way, staunchly opposed mobster incursions into areas they long enjoyed inviolately. Impressions to the contrary, racketeers had little choice but to accept this challenge in purely legitimate and competitive ways. Kidnapping and strong-arm tactics might be reasonably persuasive when terrifying a rival bootlegger into compliance; they were hardly appropriate against a status quo who could legally snuff them out. Here guile was wanted, and mobsters were not without this attribute.

Nevertheless, and even during the best of times, the placing of jazz before the public was a gamble. Profits were far from calculable, and despite every effort no one could be assured of coming out ahead. Enough examples can be provided, from Atlanta to Dallas, which illustrate the hard business fact that though jazz and the blues were inseparable from the black communities of America, personal and financial rewards accrued to neither artists nor their local backers. A certain urbanized chemistry was required for this to happen. One part black had to be mixed with equal parts Jew and Italian before the music's popularity began its spiral ascent. That these three groups supplied a large immigrational harvest to the Eastern cities between 1890 and 1930 is hardly coincidental to my analysis.

In any case it would be wrong on my part to advance the notion that gangsters promoted jazz exclusively for lucrative reasons, operating cabarets solely to make money. This belief is long in keeping with their supposed predatory natures, a belief I hope to disprove during the course of this study. Affection for the music, combined with an old world style of entertaining, and the sheer enjoyment and camaraderie promised by cabaret ownership offset years of adversity, drudgery, and declining values for marketers of the music. Some stayed in the game just for the music alone. Art Hodes tells us of racketeer Larry Mangano who left the operation of his club to his woman friend just so he could sit by the bandstand and listen to his favorite jazz piece "It's Tight Like That."[9]

Luckily for the musicians, these men were perennial gamblers down to their highly-polished, pointed shoes. For the novice, a label befitting many mobsters, night club ownership was something less than romantic. Durante said that after twenty-five years the only thing he got out of the business was "a Mazda-yellow suntan and round shoulders." Borderline financial operations far outnumbered success stories.

Forestalling failure meant paying close attention to the details of running a club and to being prompt in paying the right bootlegger, cop and politician. Ironically, Sylvester contends that most of them were their own worst enemies and were absolutely incapable of being callous or ruthless even if prosperity depended on it.

Regardless of these qualifications, the negative image of gangsters that Hollywood began promoting in the late 1920s remains virtually unchanged today. Much like the fine art of voodoo, racketeering is deplored by all but its own practitioners. Chicago Judge Lyle, representing the leaden voice of authority, unequivocally detested these men, some of whom appeared before his bench. "The gangsters of the 1920s," he wrote in his account of this period, "reached out like greedy street urchins for all the ripe apples on the tree." Following the box office success of *Underworld* in 1927, Hollywood churned out an ever-increasing number of movies which ridiculed and scoffed at nattily-dressed men who barked out "Okay youse guys, up against de wall," and "Stop wisecrackin' ya mugs, we means biznuss." Nor did people quarrel with the crime reporting sensationalism of Edward D. Sullivan or the assertions of Frank K. Notch in his fashionable *King Mob* (1930), that hoodlums were culturally atavistic, materialistically mad, and terrifyingly destructive, even in their lighter moments.

Racial prejudice introduced fresh distortions. Professor Morroe Berger uncovered but three of 21 articles written in the *New York Times* between 1919-1927 that were less than blatantly hostile toward jazz and its musicians.[10] Bernard Berelson and Patricia J. Salter, in surveying magazine articles published 1937-1943 argue convincingly that Jews and Italians were given the worst roles by writers, sketched with swarthy, brutish faces, funny foreign dialects and a full range of mobster-like mannerisms. Accepted as plausible by the readership, these qualities were subsequently transferred to an entire ethnic group. A 1940 opinion poll discovered from 21% to 51% of the respondents believed Jews to be clannish, ill-mannered, unusually aggressive and unscrupulous in the way they sought control of businesses; features normally associated with the mobs.[11] Academician Daniel Bell labels this a "statistical accident," a public misconception about Italians and Jews which most writers cared little to dispel, although Protestants and native white gangsters had long dominated most illegal activities throughout the country.

Contemporary fiction, always opportunistic to trends, swallowed the bait whole and linked Jews and Italians to that repository of forbidden pleasures, the night clubs, with violence rarely beneath the surface of the story. Scott Fitzgerald, who shared his era's dislike of Jews, was an early adversary. In *The Great Gatsby* (1926) he implicates gambler-restaurateur Meyer Wolfsheim of bootlegging, pimping, extortion and murder. Abie Wise is the vicious, uncrowned "King of Chicago bootleggers" in MacKinley Kantor's potboiler *Diversey* (1928). "Jake the Jew" is the wily night club boss in Elizabeth Jordan's *The Night Club Mystery* (1929), while Angelo Moretti appears as a degenerate Harlem racketeer in Frederic A. Kummer's *Manhattan Masquerade* (1934). Racketeers were not only malicious, they were made to look the part. Cabaret owner and feudal lord of a band of thugs in Edward J. Doherty's *The Broadway Murders: A Night Club Mystery* (1929), Big Joe Carozzo has "eyes like a sewer." The bootlegger in the Grahams' *Whitey* (1931) is described as "six feet of Wop, smooth-shaven, and husky as hell." In *The Trembling Flame* (1931), Louis J. Vance characterizes his cabaret owner as an "American mongrel animal" with "shapeless, thick lips and a negroid outcrop," while the Jewish night club operator in S.S. Van Dine's polished *The Gracie Allen Murder Case* (1938) is "dark and fawning." Finally, Dorine Manners' *Scarlet Patrol* (1937), features the story of night club owner and vicelord Manny Quintero, a man with a "Latin strain that conceals an inherent cruelty that is a natural instinct."[12]

Flying in the teeth of this pejorative legacy from the past which has seen organized crime precede by generations the arrival of Sicilians and Jews in America, I venture forth with an entirely different viewpoint. Let it be said from the outset, my intention is not to subject Jews, Italians or Black Americans to ridicule, for I myself am Jewish. Rather it is to present an opinion unheard before. To my mind these men typified paternalistic loyalty, were generous to a fault, seriously engaged in racial integration when others sought a lynch rope instead, and exhibited remarkable restraint toward employees and customers alike. Interviews I have had with people who rubbed shoulders with racketeers assure me this was generally the case. Hammond, Phoebe Jacobs (promoter for the Rainbow Room in Rockefeller Center), Russ Sanjek (executive for Broadcast Music, Inc.), Ruth Spanier (wife and business agent for trumpeter Muggsy Spanier), and Sam Cohen, a musician who worked for these men, convince me that a gangster's formative years on the streets and inculcation of old world values of respect toward those around him—relatives or associates—advised against precipitating unnecessary disagreements with his staff. Contemporary accounts by various bootleggers, plus the view of reporter Damon Runyan, whom Broadway racketeers considered trustworthy enough to associate with, further endorse these views. Night club bosses displayed a peculiar enlightenment when it came to employment practices, far outdistancing those of most established operations.

To clear the air of any false conceptions I have already promoted, I think it wise at this stage to make a few broad qualifications about my subject. I have, so far, tossed around the terms "racketeers," "gangsters," "mobsters," and the like, with neither definition nor comment. It would thus be a natural tendency on the reader's part to interpret these comments in light of what is usually said about them and think the worse. I use these words less as negative value judgment (inasmuch as I do not believe simple ones could apply), and more for clarity's sake—to keep us all on the same footing. My terms, however, suggest a group of men who while employing questionable business tactics often did so in retaliation against a business world too restrictive and ossified to allow them to practice openly; men whose desire for conformity and acceptance was repulsed by racial and cultural reactions to their very presence; men with criminal, though rarely of violent backgrounds. Opportunists and adventurers to be sure, but most were men whose rules were streetwise and born of unpopular laws, family oriented and designed to protect the group over the individual. Sometimes this came at great cost. Professor W.F. Whyte stresses how the highly-organized, integrated social

system found in Italian neighborhoods he surveyed effectively
moulded future cabaret owners. Habits which emphasized
audacity rather than bloody reprisal, and which shaped
conduct in business relationships, can be traced to this early
period.

Calling gangsters "cut-throats" also misses the mark.
Mobster Vincent Teresa believed writers paid far too much
attention to violence when discussing the mobs, totally
distorting its use and significance.[13] Judging by one urban
study of underworld types, no more than one in five of these
domestic pirates had ever been connected with a violent
crime.[14] Rather, a healthy percentage who entered the night
club field, for instance, and who came to associate with jazz
musicians, turned honest in the bargain, jettisoning mottled
careers of criminality, bootlegging and gambling
notwithstanding. And these were as much a product of bad
laws as profitable lures for unsavory characters. Lengthy
interviews with the racketeer "Angelo" bear this out:[15]

A few bootleggers and operators were into every kind of racket, from women to
whiskey. But most earned their money strictly from gambling and booze. It is
simply unfair to consider the lot of them murderers, bruisers, or even party
spoilers. Few matched this description.

In agreement with sociologists F.A.J. Ianni and William
H. Moore, I found conspiracies between powerful syndicates
and families controlling vast numbers of night clubs and
cabarets to be lacking. This was particularly true for the larger
cities, less so in the case of smaller towns like Atlanta. In the
latter, mob factions were able to centralize with ease, although
there were not many instances where they chose to apply their
control over jazz clubs. Mob development was generaly
dependent upon local conditions, especially in large cities, and
these extended beyond the grasp of any single group, despite
their prestige and bankroll. If anything, the shoe was often on
the other foot.

Walter Lippmann, Moore, Frank Pearce, Walter C.
Reckless, E.H. Lavine and Mark K. Hiller, among others,
represent five decades of academic reproach toward judicial,
political and industrial machines that manipulated the so-

called syndicates to suit their bidding, rather than the other way around. Hiller's article stresses the strong social interrelationship between the underworld, urban machine politics, and local business leaders long before Italian and Jewish incursions, during a time when "boundaries between legal and illegal business were paper thin and seen as such by many."[16]

By way of focusing on the content of the chapters to come, another parenthetical comment on the social aspects of night clubs and cabarets seems appropriate. On one hand it is needless to expound on the importance of commercial achievements in the depersonalized world of capitalism. Our present way of life and the standards we enjoy could not otherwise have occurred. But certainly life does not begin in the marketplace; nor does it end there. There is more to the human animal than attention to merchandising. That is, his or her need for amusement and sources of escapism, for spontaneous release of combustible energy, for the affability and urbanity trapped inside all of us. Philosopher Johan Huizanga described this condition as the "crucial importance of temporarily stepping out of life." The night clubs of the period, no longer regarded as private preserves by the wealthy and aristocratic of the 1900s, were dedicated to this end, and enjoyed by a wide slice of the energetic urban public. In this midst an instant oasis beckoned with mood-enhancing effects to soothe those wishing to suspend anxiety and pain or to invigorate those seeking momentary pleasures. Cabarets bubbled with unanticipated excitement and talented entertainment in an environment purposely devoted to this pursuit. On a more pragmatic level, jazz writer and social critic Nat Hentoff sees them as the setting for "authentic cultural sources," a position which returns us to the subject of this study. For jazz was loud enough and fast enough to stimulate and was an essential ingredient in this highly successful night club scene. In fact, orchestras became famous and attracted followings, not through the sales of records, but by appearing nightly in these arenas. The quintessence of this life for jazz clubs took place in the 1920s, and this is highlighted in the next chapter.

In stark contrast, the musical scene before the popularity

of jazz or the advent of their thuggish benefactors was woefully second rate. Music was only occasionally heard in clubs, and these places resembled musty gymnasiums; it was monopolized by a few indifferent agents; and was completely irrelevant to the swarms of foreign bodies pouring into the seaports. This tawdry tableau is peeled back in Chapter Three. Like a breath of fresh air, the musical program which seemed to come in with Prohibition widened to include contributions from the new migrants, many of whom were starting to assume an active part in its direction. A new kind of music also extended itself into the neighborhoods of these upstart foreigners. The hitherto raucous, non-musical, male-dominated Irish saloon, adequately charted by Jim Marshall, vanished in favor of congenial night spots that featured captivating music for both sexes, all races and a younger crowd—amidst sensual motifs that matured American entertainment overnight.

For the black musician this was an immense step forward. Repudiated and cursed by the mainstream of America's musical entrepreneurs, jazz artists, as portrayed in Chapter Four, had previously been relegated to a wasteland where violence was as common as red beans and rice. Even the respectable members of the black community shunned a virus born from within.

Given the music's limited appeal and the conditions under which its artisans labored, we must therefore ask how sponsorship by the late-arriving Jewish and Sicilian mobsters actually transpired. Hardly coincidentally, all three groups were swept along in the great immigrational tidal wave between 1880 and 1930. It was a time when millions of East Europeans and Southern Blacks exchanged family origins for a few American sanctuaries. Themselves fleeing persecution yet without traditional American bigotry toward blacks, Jews and Sicilians were squeezed into living side by side, or in adjacent neighborhoods, combating identical challenges to their cultural integrity and physical well-being. Jews, blacks and Italians were all unable to penetrate significant segments of the American economy and faced similar patterns of exclusion from the chieftains of industry and finance. Carey McWilliams provides a shrewd analysis of Jews, showing how, as a result of discrimination, they tended to congregate in high-risk, peripheral and new businesses totally lacking in social power and prestige.[17] These were nonetheless subject to whimsies and extortionate demands of the various local power structures. Doubtless a similar conclusion could be made for the other two groups. Chapter Five describes the musical settings and musical attitudes these seemingly unrelated factions shared, and which facilitated the entry of foreign racketeers into the jazz club business. Historically, pride of place for these first meetings belongs to New Orleans.

No less than the princely tyrants whose patronization of painters and sculptors heralded the Renaissance, Italian and Jewish mobsters benefited jazz by introducing their unwritten codes, ambitious motivations, personal interest and innovative schemes. Chapter Six discusses these men on their own terms. It shows how they brought order to the night club scene, how this change greatly aided the performers, and how mobsters were affected by contact with black artists. The question is also raised why night clubs were chosen as receptacles for mob interest. The appeal of jazz was far greater than what one hoodlum told guitarist Eddie Condon was the reason he listened to the music: "It's got guts and it don't make me slobber."

Chapter Seven focuses on the aspects of violence and benevolence which went along with the relationship. My view is strongly on the side of the latter. Benevolence was a far more conspicuous aspect in the personal lives of the musicians than violence and danger, and was not a relative thing as Freeman suggests:

Putting his arm around me, this [underworld night club operator] said 'Buddy, don't ever worry about anybody in this here joint because nobody will hurt you unless he gets paid for it.'[18]

Whatever criminal tendencies their bosses may have shown, few jazzmen were affected to any appreciable degree. Nor were most coaxed into committing criminal acts at the behest of their patrons. Many years on the streets and in the back alleys of life aided musicians in quickly appreciating dangerous situations before they became engulfed. This chapter also examines several important by-products of mobster support for jazz.

The economic nadir for both parties, at least for the years covered in this study, arrived with the 1930s. It was a time of the great economic depression which affected night life. It was also a time of reformism and legal assaults on the mobs by ambitious politicians. Nevertheless, and despite these trends, musicians were still able to avert the depression's worst shockwaves. This was because a few underworld gangs, principally located in Kansas City, wished to keep jazz alive, a policy which brought a tinge of prosperity to a lucky few. But to do so required that most gangsters scale down their ambitions to avoid becoming targets for congressional investigating teams in search of scapegoats to appease a weary public. Consequently, most either fled the Eastern cities for the provinces or developed a hardening of the arteries. Their departure created an unfillable vacuum in the field of jazz club promotion inasmuch as no other prominent groups emerged to accept the baton. Chapter Eight ties these many loose strands together, bringing to a fitful end the collective impact of mobsters and jazz artists.

Today jazz has evolved into a baby's rattle for the avant garde; the masses have been left in the dust. As Phoebe Jacobs suggested to me, the music's danceability has vanished, its happy sounds have faded and musicians no longer find it enjoyable to play. When the gangster contingent removed itself from the floor, or was nudged out by racially-inspired reformers, substitute backers with an "anything goes" attitude failed to materialize in sufficient numbers after 1940. Running a club was a way of life, not simply a business proposition, and too few operators had this gift in the years which followed. This sad state of affairs leads to Chapter Nine which signs off with a quick overview of present conditions. Today, commercial music manipulators, wholly money and recording oriented, have pushed jazz into a corner. Night clubs—the best places to hear this music—have been closing on a continuous basis these past four decades. Impersonal business conglomerates now dominate the trade, and successful musicians and unions alike treat the public arrogantly. It is speculative how many of these factors would have been tolerated by the mobs in their heyday.

Not that they would have machine-gunned their opposition; rather, their personal, familial approach to the presentation of music would have led to different solutions. This, however, is idle chatter. We only know that underworld money has gone elsewhere, very little being reserved for the entertainment world. The mob's departure thus coincides with the closing of a glorious era for jazz music, a time when musicians controlled their product and related to their audience and backers; a time we can never again come to imitate.

*   *   *

Excluding Horatio Alger biographies of bandleaders and sidemen who achieved success, and discounting discographies of recording sessions, we are left with few sociological interpretations of this music. Rare indeed is the study of its creative process or the jazz musician's absolute dependence on his social and economic environments. The way is sprinkled with only a few brief articles published in journals, esoteric and difficult to locate. Musical historians have tended to treat themselves to the easy way out, concentrating on the musician in his own milieu, uncritically suggesting that a limited network of associations—mainly other musicians—influenced his development. Needless to say, the links with underworld characters, for better or worse, are invariably omitted. But to run counter to this movement is to court blank stares and closed doors. Russ Sanjek cautioned me, rightly as it turned out, that superfans and jazz jocks would categorically refuse to discuss sociological topics of an unsavory nature with an outsider since it was in their best interest to avoid rinsing their dirty laundry in public. What information they knew and chose to withhold I never fully learned, for I received the cold-shoulder from writers when the time came for me to begin interviewing. A few told me that gangsters had helped jazz music although they were "very nasty people to know." No elaborations followed and I was left to draw my own stereotypical conclusions. But without substantive material to cement this allegation into fact, I was not prepared to accept such a comment on face value.

Occasionally my efforts met with reward. As when noted

writer Ralph Gleason wrote me agreeing that mobsters were indeed very much linked to jazz musicians. Unfortunately, to Gleason the "details are hazy." In a desire to sweep away this haze I took advice and began reading the spaces between the printed lines in biographies, paying attention to obscure footnotes in academic tracts, and disregarding Donald R. Cressey's claim that it was utterly futile to seek information about these racketeers, their activies or their social alignments.[19]

The most obvious source of information made my task no easier. Musicians subscribed to a time-honored code that views all uninvited inquirers as revenue agents and scandal mongers. As a way of detracting me, they gave me small bits of information, generally enshrouded in myths and mysteries. This saddened me for I knew that most of what I was seeking in the interest of historical research would eventually be buried with the principals. Even when a musician made an acknowledgement, he hedged his bets. Duke Ellington's evasive admissions are a prime example:

Episodes of the gangster era were never healthy subjects for discussion. People would ask me if I knew so and so. "Hell no," I would answer, "I don't know him." But I knew them all because a lot of them used to hang out in the clubs where I was appearing.

Ellington wrote this in 1973 when explanatory details might have been given without the least fear of retaliation from men long dead. And whenever I tried to move the subject onto racial lines, I was met with a stony silence. Louis Prima, bandleader and trumpeter, challenged my remarks as "hearsay." Drummer Shelley Manne claims "In all the time I played on 52nd Street, I don't believe I ever met a big-time hood." Bandleader Benny Goodman was "unaware" of a connection that jazz artist Jimmy McPartland calls "inaccurate."[20] Bandleader Sy Oliver was one of the few to at least offer up a partial explanation for a phenomenon alluded to in countless histories of jazz:

I began my professional life during prohibition. But I was quite young at the time and completely unaware of the sociological aspects in which you are interested. I have never, knowingly, met a bootlegger or gangster. Nor have I ever been aware of any particular involvement of Jews and Italians. This is not to say it wasn't or isn't the way of things—I simply didn't notice.

Playing safe through silence? Holding onto the vestiges of respectability? Fear of the past? Needless to say, respondents seemed uncurious about the past and pretty much preferred to let bygones rest quietly. Such reactions served to waylay my investigations from time to time.

Luckily, I was not completely misdirected. Approximately, half a dozen musicians agreed with my outlook, although they made no amplifications and treated the relationship as an historical oddity. Only bandleader Turk Murphy was willing to admit that mobsters were still firmly entrenched in some aspects of a jazz business they had known for a long time. To my good fortune I eventualy stumbled onto three men and one woman who helped smooth out many jagged edges of my analysis. Three have already been mentioned in passing: "Angelo," the Sicilian gentleman; Sam Cohen, a jazz musician who spent considerable time playing for mobster-owned clubs in New Orleans and Chicago during the 1950s and 1960s; and Ruth Spanier who has a vivid memory of the hilarious times she had with Chicago racketeers in the late 1920s. The final expert is a drummer from Boston, Tom Hall, whose knowledge, while admittedly sparse, throws some light on the distinctions between Irish-owned and Jewish- or Italian-owned clubs, particularly in the Northeast. Their comments I have woven into the narrative at appropriate spots, and I hope they illuminate some of the points I am trying to make. They were extremely helpful since obvious research sources proved quite limited. The jazz library at Tulane University uncovered but two pages of information on this subject from their voluminous files. The libraries at the Chicago Historical Association and Rutgers University and the archives of the Schomburg Collection took me no further.

One final source cropped up and was used sparingly. Contemporary fictional accounts found in hackneyed detective stories offered up a few morsels and were used if authenticated elsewhere. My aim was to establish details that could be verified and corroborated in non-fictional materials. Having ruled out collusion between the various accounts, I felt authors who might have known racketeers intimately could quietly furnish us with useful comments. I do not believe I erred in this course.

Every art has maintained sullied associations during even the briefest of moments. If art history teaches us anything, it is that the public's immediate reactions to new aesthetic forms have frequently been severe and hostile, and driven the artist into the arms of dubious characters for survival. Indeed, one might very well contemplate in horror innumerable works, dating from the Baroque period, which, in the absence of this clientele, would never have been commissioned or performed. In the case of jazz music, the faults and associations of the past, if in fact these can be ascribed, lie less with the content of the music or manners of the men and more with a social and economic climate which made a respectful hearing for black artists virtually impossible.

America has historically shamed and denigrated its ethnic subcultures. Yet ironically if it were not for these groups, that which is seen as most American—in the present study the art of jazz—would have been irretrievably lost in the cul de sacs of time. Without the black musician's Jewish and Sicilian allies, despicable as they may seem, jazz would never have fabricated the crucial staying power to advance. Today the scene has changed. For the black musician, his existence has come full-circle. Alienated and under-subsidized, his position resembles that of his predecessors before the advent of the racketeers. The current entertainment world, which I find to be both arid and wonderless in invention, merely reflects the corresponding business savagery the departure of the underworld patron has created.

Chapter II
At the Top of Their Game

Jazz historian Rudi Blesch reminds us that the public's first serious awareness of jazz began in the 1920s, a time when mobsters themselves were highly popular figures of interest and at the top of their game. So perhaps this period offers a convenient starting point in the study of the unspeakable connection between jazz artists and the underworld. Judging by contemporary accounts, we know the 1920s were gay and sparkling years for dance halls and jazz cabarets and their entertainers. Clubs were thick on the ground, dotting the landscape like anthills, and playing to full houses nightly. Applying sociologist Robert Sommer's interior design criteria, these places were perfectly decorated to appeal to and excite young sophisticates in relatively safe environments. Even the reformist Committee of Fourteen, which investigated 157 night clubs in New York in 1928, came away with the opinion that club interiors had improved vastly from those the Committee had observed in 1902.

Meanwhile, everybody was dancing to jazzy rhythms under gangster auspices (see Appendix A). As early as March 1917 the show business trade journal *Variety* was commenting on the country's shifting moods:

Music is becoming more and more potent and promising among cabaret attractions. Swinging music is what the dancers want and it is even looked for by those who do not dance. Late in the morning the jazzers go to work and dancers hit the floor, to remain there until they topple over, if the band keeps on playing.

Contemporary fiction was equally aroused:

She listened to the jazz band, hidden now behind massed dancers moving on interlacing paths with a certain entity and unity for all their varied characteristics and moods of the couples. They formed one great molecule of

19

electrons and protons, each a universe of mysterious electric energies....

A flight of red-carpeted steps led down under the pavement level of the fashionable East Side club. From below rose the whine and croon of an orchestra beating regularly through a vast discord of party voices....The broad room was overcrowded with table parties, except for a center oval of waxed oak, cleared for dancers. On a low platform at the rear wall, a troupe of boys with pale elderly faces blew and scraped the mumbo jumbo of jazz upon their strings and brass.[1]

A 1925 survey averaged out that over 14% of the men in Manhattan and 10% of its women attended dance halls and cabarets three times weekly; and that the number of dance palaces had increased 60% over those of a few years earlier.[2] Professor Cressey adds another 6% of the adult male population who were convening in the over 100 taxi-dance halls that dotted Manhattan and Brooklyn. By today's standards such figures are an impressive testimonial to live entertainment. Although contemporary barometers of night life for the rest of the country are nowhere near as precise, an acceleration of interest held true for most larger cities.

By 1920 five hundred dance halls were operating in New York City alone. During the next five years, at the crest of the jazz cabaret wave, a further 800 licenses had been granted. And depending on the sources, the estimates for speakeasies, blinds and unlicensed clubs vary from 5000 to 100,000. In his 1931 intimate guide to his city's night life, Rian James calculated 764 dance halls and 150 "reputable" night clubs in Manhattan and Harlem alone, an impressive figure for so soon after the stock market crash. Nils T. Granlund, night club impresario, reckoned that the Broadway district soaked up 20% of the total, the Lower East Side, Greenwich Village and Harlem accounting for what remained. In the case of Harlem, an area far more profligate in jazz clubs than we shall ever know again, the majority of its adult black population frequented nearby spots, legal and otherwise, with no fewer than 500 black-owned or fronted spots standing ready for the bidding.[3] Still and all, these are only estimates.

Vulnerable to 54- and 60-hour work weeks, lower class audiences had never before been treated to so many musical trees from which to pick; nor had such wealth and opportunity been at their fingertips. Clubs remained open all hours, accommodating every trade, taste and temptation. Whatever his or her work schedule, the customer was at least assured of finding some convivial little cellar haunt, described by angry critics as "upholstered sewers," in which to escape and unwind. While for the first time in recorded history middle class listeners and dancers were treated to a full range of nightly pastimes. With just a little bit of hunting, countless clubs, catering to the newly-discovered passion for dancing, stood at one's beck and call. In the case of the wealthy, who have always managed to assuage themselves with diversions, illicit pleasures were unlimited.

Given this demand for excess, many club owners, gamblers in their own right, chanced it with untried musical innovations and special interior decor. Simply stated, the intention was to spice up an evening's hitherto dull entertainment bill. After 1920 cabarets began offering lively cohesive, fast-moving shows with a precision in direction and choreography never before contemplated.

The latest in glazed art deco colors were splashed over club walls; life-sized carvings featured bizarre poses; and futuristic designs washed walls and ceilings in vivid richness. Murals and sconces also began assuming elaborate dimensions, as spirited motifs swept through club interiors, falling on unusual backdrops. Many of these can be seen in the background of photos taken of contemporary jazz bands. Technological devices also served as lures. Dreamland cabaret in Chicago revolutionized dance floors by implanting hundreds of tiny lights to illuminate the areas surrounding a dancer's feet. Murray's niterie in New York introduced the revolving dance floor. And Manhattan's International Casino first highlighted a series of ascending bars which customers reached by moving up an adjacent escalator. These are but a few gangster-inspired improvements.

Typically the jazz club was a smoke-filled basement room or two, with a platform at one end for the band, a smallish space for dancing encircled by flimsy tables, and a bar with stools (where drinks were allegedly cheaper) to one side. Most clubs interwove some common decorative theme which served as its trademark for as long a time, or as short, as the place stayed in business. Service might be expensive, depending on the place, and cover charges were routinely established if revues and bands were to be paid living wages. Most people brought their own booze, thus reducing the profit potential a club hoped to make.

To get around the loss of this potential source of income, the clubs charged seemingly outrageous prices for water setups and carbonated drinks. Narcotics, not altogether illegal in this era, were available in some places and helped cover expenses. A high-living couple might reasonably expect to lay out as much as $250 in 1925 prices (possibly four times that amount in today's currency) in charges and tips for a single evening's worth of musical thrills along Chicago's Southside.

For the jazz musician it was a great time to be alive. By 1920 not only were many clubs offering jazz music as an attraction, but a growing differentiation was appearing between the clubs. Some seemed interested in merely offering hot music with its New Orleans sound intact. Others were developing into what we now think of as jazz cabarets— elegant and sophisticated—such as Chicago's underworld-owned Apex Club where Jimmie Noone's band, featuring Earl Hines on piano, played from 1927 to 1929.

Bands were expected to play not only hot jazz but to mix in a few sweet ballads as well as play behind the shows and dancers. Wellman Braud, bassist for the Creole Band which played the intimate Chicago gangster haven The Deluxe, remembers the excitement and adulation these places generated:

We opened at eight nightly and by ten we didn't even have standing room. I would come down the street and people would say "That's the bass picker from the jazz band."[4]

For the jazz musician the number of opportunities in clubs was mind-boggling. Lyle estimates 12,000 night spots blaring away in the Chicago area alone in 1922, a figure that doubled within four years.

Musicians were given fond memories. Trumpeter Rex Stewart recalls, "During the 1920s, musicians had it so good, you could get fired at 11 p.m. and by midnight be sitting on another bandstand blowing." It was a time when, according to Kansas City pianist Paul Baker, "just two musicians could draw a crowd." Omer Simeon, clarinetist for the Freddie Keppard ensemble, sighed: "Those sure were good times."[5] Duke Ellington paints a colorful picture of the percussive effects activity and demand had on the average jazzman:

The mobster ginmills were wide open at that time, and there weren't any restrictive regulations about closing hours. Nobody went to bed at night, and 'round three or four in the morning you'd find everyone making the rounds, bringing their horns with them.[6]

Surveys of older Southern jazz players indicate they very much approved of these congenial surroundings in which to perform their art, ranking treatment and creative attitudes by management more important than simply earning a lot of money or playing in so-called legitimate (non-underworld operated) clubs.[7] Nevertheless, money had its place, and the younger musicians recognized that with it his social status would improve. Luckily for them, times were right and salaries and tips in these high-flying clubs could be very fat indeed. The Original Dixieland Jazz Band presents an illustration of how earnings might skyrocket overnight for the lucky group. Beginning at $25 a week per man in a small, wayside, independent club in Chicago, they soon went to $150 each after appearing at the mob-owned Casino Gardens, climbing considerably, with the aid of gangster patronage to $1000 weekly by the time they opened in New york in 1922.[8] Other groups realized similar gains.

One obvious promotional factor was the emerging youthful immigrant gangsters, with equally energetic ambitions, then beginning to trickle into the business. Appropriately for these whirlwind times, many of the musicians who later became famous were in their early twenties. More importantly, so too were the active gangsters who figured largely in the music's promotion. A few examples will suffice: In 1925 Legs Diamond was 29, Lucky Luciano, Louis Lepke and Vito Genovese were 28, Al Capone was 26 and Carlo Gambino and Meyer Lansky had just turned 23. Ralph Capone was still a teenager. Willing to confront the older night life power brokers, these gamblers completely transformed a city's club scene by injecting newer values and assuming greater risks. On the heels of the 1919 Act prohibiting sales of liquor in public places, these men, and many others like them, brought their unorthodox techniques before the public at the same moment restaurants and saloons, traditional employers for a small quantity of entertainers, began deleting their alcoholically-oriented musical concessions.

Durante believes this new bunch gave far more value to money than the old crew had; comparative cost estimates seem to bear him out and some of this can be gained from a reading of George Rector's own study of the restaurant business before 1920. Whatever the cause—youthful energy, postwar mobility and prosperity, boredom or even the immigrants' faith in city life—New York and Chicago, under the command of men cut from the same migrational bolt of cloth, acted as twin beacons on how the remainder of the country would behave at night during the next two decades. In the process a larger segment of the urban population than ever before was treated to a good romp.

This chapter cannot begin to adequately detail so extensive a period as the 1920s with its windfall of jazz in various corners of urban America. There can be found as many books written expressly for this purpose as notes in a Charlie Parker chorus. I simply hope to call attention to some of the many links which existed at the time between the two major groups under study as they affected and influenced the night club scene. Jazz musicians found the era the most lucrative and pleasant they would ever collectively experience. In return they dished out to patrons and employers alike many hours of high-charged musical excitement so that historians ever since have conceptualized the entire period as "the jazz age." Only the 1930s spoiled the show and caused the popularity of the music to sag.

Yet in its best days, and under proper guidance, night club jazz encompassed whole districts, fanning out like the fingers of an outstretched hand. Today, and by contrast, only the occasional club, dotted here and there, survives in drab and modified form, alternating a questionable musical policy which features as much jazz in its program as alcohol in its cocktails.

The Chicago Scene

Since the early 1900s a steady stream of jazz musicians had threaded their way up the river routes to Chicago, leaving the Delta Basin behind. Because of prevailing racism and musical conservatism, their initial impact was slight. Black entertainers were welcomed only by carnivals and on remote street corners. Hustling for pennies was commonplace. Nevertheless, and by the end of the war in 1918, this trickle began to assume the proportions of a stream, blending with the flow of other unhappy migrants fleeing the South.

Jazz historian Frederic Ramsey reckons no fewer than forty important New Orleans jazz artists had drifted to Chicago as early as 1914. With an increasing number of Jews and Italians entering the business end of the night club field, the number soon mushroomed. This occurred in both New Orleans and Chicago, which leads to speculation that an informal conduit of communication developed between both factions, exchanging information on promising Southern jazz groups willing to jettison their Southern moorings for better-paying jobs in the Northern clubs.

Linked to the ascendancy of men like racketeer Al Capone, nocturnal gadflies from childhood, jazz acquired the necessary sponsorship and muscle to take hold in Chicago. Earl Hines affectionately remembers Capone:

Scarface got along well with musicians. He liked to come into a club with his henchmen and have the band play his requests. He was very free with $100 tips.[9]

Capone's biographer, John Kobler, describes him as a man who "drank whiskey out of a teacup and was loyal to those musicians he liked, visiting them two and three times a week." As steady customers, Capone and his customers visited the Four Deuces Club on State Street, a ratty little dive where musicians congregated for early morning jam sessions.

One source has it that Capone was quite expert in

appreciating good from bad jazz and can be credited with
employing and subsidizing "most of the earlier Chicago
jazzmen...without a bit of trouble."[10] His respectfulness
toward performers forms the basis for countless anecdotes.
Ethel Waters, popular jazz singer, recalls meeting him, his
brother Ralph, and their criminal entourage in the early 1930s,
and her book recounts her pleasant encounters with them,
where she considered herself "treated ...with respect,
applause, deference and paid in full." She was quite astonished
when despite her youthfulness this same group aided her in
securing a well-paying engagement in New York's Cotton
Club.

Chicago was a marvelous place during these years. Night
club regular Leo Walker reports that by 1925 Chicago and its
suburbs had as many, if not more, black bands employed
steadily as in any other city outside New York. Orchestras such
as Sammy Stewart, Al Wynn's Paradise Cafe Night Owls, Tig
Chambers, Johnny Dodds, Joe Jordan's Sharps and Flats,
Bernie Young and Bobby Williams were earning their daily
bread in gangster-run clubs. So too were Charles Elgar, King
Oliver, Carroll Dickinson, Jimmy Wade's Syncopaters (a band
employed faithfully by the Fountain Inn since 1912), Earl
Hines, Dave Peyton, Punch Miller, and John Wycliffe. White
bands sponsored by the underworld included New Orleans
Rhythm Kings, Coon-Saunders, the Blue Friars, the Brunis
group at The Valentino Inn, Isham Jones, Art Kassell and Ben
Pollack's Chicago Rhythm Kings.

State Street was heavily sprinkled with Sicilian-owned
clubs and cabarets, setting the tone with no fewer than a dozen
competing with one another with the latest revues and jazz
bands. Writer Langston Hughes, a visitor to the Street in 1918,
was dazzled by its Turkish bazaar atmosphere:

A teeming Negro street with crowded theatres, restaurants and cabarets and
excitement from noon to noon. Midnight was like day...for neither love nor
money could I find a decent place to live. Profiteers, thugs, and gangsters were
coming into their own.

Eddie Condon recalls that the "midnight air on State Street
was so full of music that if you held up an instrument the breeze

would play it." "In the case of jazz," voiced another performer, "the worst places on State Street always had the best music."[11] Even amateur musicians came, catching the frenzy on the customer-side of the bandstand. Bohemian Elliot Paul claims that many a club manager winked underage artists in, waiving the cover charges and other minimum expenses as a sort of scholarship in their blossoming musical development.

Police and high-ranking officials rarely bothered these places except in the role of off-duty patrons. The mob-owned Sunset Cafe, known as the "cream of the Chicago clubs," was so popular with officials that liquor was openly served for years without the least fear of raid. Its sumptuous floor show included the best available black acts, and more money was reputedly spent for its revues than in New York's famed Cotton Club.

Dancers found the atmosphere intriguing. Hanging directly overhead was an enormous crystal ball radiating thousands of tiny particles of colored light onto the dancers, while off to the side artificial maple leaves, suspended from a low ceiling, exuded a hint of sylvan intimacy. Louis Armstrong's band was the lead group for many years. During his long engagement, the house limit of 600 was invariably reached long before midnight, when extra shows were presented and the band itself introduced the latest in dance steps. Sparing no expense, manager Joe Glaser was said to have hired the Sammy Stewart Orchestra from Columbus, Ohio, for $3600 weekly merely as backup for Armstrong's successful and innovative Friday Night Charleston Contests. Glaser was also promoter for one of the truly memorable band wars of the era when he pitted Armstrong's house band against an equally thrilling Fletcher Henderson group from New York in the summer of 1927, an event that required complete interior redesign to support the overflow crowds.

Another popular mobster club was the Lincoln Gardens, a cavernous barn situated in the Black Belt. Armstrong himself was impressed by the extent and variety of talent displayed in the half-dozen acts set alongside King Oliver's band after 1922. The Gardens prided itself on seating 1000 people in comfortable surroundings and featured an outdoor dance

pavilion that was particularly attractive on hot, sticky
Chicago summer nights. The club was easily identified from
the street by its enormous, block-long canvas canopy that
stretched from curbside to lobby, advertising the various
orchestras to passersby. Typical of many clubs which had been
theatres before the war, the Gardens had a balcony filled with
excitable amateur musicians who wildly shouted
encouragement to the band members below. One authority has
it that:

King Oliver often stared out at the sea of dancers, ringed with fifty or more
young, defiant musicians clustered in front, trying to memorize every note
played.[12]

Mobster-owned or fronted places could just as easily be
found elsewhere. Sociologist Harvey W. Zorbaugh conducted a
five-block survey on North Clark Street, in the heart of the
tenderloin, and commented on the tight fistful of mobster jazz
clubs. Another splendid location was at the corner of 35th
Street and Calumet. In the mid-1920s this crossroad laid claim
to being America's jazz mecca, a claim based on the presence of
Armstrong at the Sunset, Jimmy Noone at the Nest and King
Oliver at the Plantation—all three owned by underworld
figures. "The battle of the bands was so loud," recalls
Armstrong's pianist Buck Washington, "people simply opened
their windows and let the excitement in."[13]

Close at hand was the underworld rendezvous The Three
Deuces where jam sessions by its principally white musicians
were conducted in the dark confines of its basement room. "The
boys that hung out there," says Benny Goodman, "were
terrifically talented guys."[14] Another mob club was Friar's
Inn, a basement joint with undraped tables, pseudo-leather
seats, a marble dance floor and an abundance of food and
millionaires. Ruth Spanier had but one distinct memory of that
place: "It smelled awful." The cabaret boasted an atmosphere
which prompted considerable merriment from the musicians
and sufficient business to demand three bands, alternating
between 3 p.m. and 6 a.m.

Other wide-open dives included The Panama Club,

Fiume's, The Fountain Inn, The Sparkling Inn, Derby, Erie Cafe, 606 Club, The Poodle Dog, Elites 1 and 2 (both owned by black gangsters), The Deluxe Cafe, Rainbow Cafe, The Midway Gardens (which Ruth Spanier recalls had beautiful Gothic architecture which rivalled many buildings at the University of Chicago), Midnight Frolics, My Cellar, The Valentino Inn and the Royal Gardens, home for 1000 patrons and a dozen energetic acts. There was also the Liberty Inn, one of the few remaining Irish-owned places. Hodes recalls many brawls and much bloodshed taking place with the McGovern clan presiding as management and chief scrappers. White bands were employed exclusively, and drinks were practically free to the hired help.[15] Many of these places were very difficult to locate from the outside. Charlie's, for example, lived in an old stone building in a bombed-out district. Once inside, however, the customer was treated to very posh surroundings, an exclusive restaurant, a beautifully polished bar a half-block long, lovely wall furnishings, a dance floor and the main attraction: the Bud Freeman-Dave Tough Quintet.

Using these places as stomping grounds, gangsters and their assistants booked jazz groups, hoping for lively music while giving jazzmen an opportunity to learn the ropes and cater to each club's distinctive clientele. It is not important for the moment to know why the mobsters did this, or what the music served to cover up; discussion of these topics will come later. Musicians who learned their lessons well, however, could expect further boosts from men whose employable influence was often considerable. The fact that gangsters might be part-owners, regular patrons, alcohol suppliers, or merely related to management, with contacts spread far afield, offered ready-made informal channels for bringing club owners with jobs and jazz artists together. A man of Capone's caliber maintained ties with so many niteries, including his favorite one which was in New Orleans (The Midnight Frolics), booking arrangements was child's play.

Jazz historian Thomas J. Hennessey claims that black artists had every reason to appreciate boosts and opportunities given by Chicago mobsters. In an article he describes four possible outlets for jazzmen during these years—ballrooms, vaudeville theatres-turned-cinemas, eating establishments and cabarets—although only the latter promised steady work and seemed enthusiastic about hiring black musicians. Sicilians made up the majority of this group. Hennessey goes on to summarize the oppositional forces: Irish mobsters who owned clubs along the loop and in the Northside but whose attitude toward music was one of disinterest if not hostility; legitimate theater, cinema and restaurant owners who stayed away in droves; and dozens of respectable ballrooms, of whom Hennessey comments that their dislike of jazz was so widespread that "black bands never held more than five jobs at any one time."[16]

The New York Scene

If night life in Chicago was abundant, New York's was overwhelming. Numerally larger, more sophisticated and wealthier clientele were attracted to clubs which spoke to this greater diversity. And unlike Chicago, nearly every neighborhood seemed capable of supporting jazz outlets. Black people themselves were more diffusely located than in Chicago by 1910. Together with broader exposure available through the media, and a greater acceptance by the city's larger celebrity population, money was spent hand over fist, lifting the music onto a plateau of popularity never since duplicated. In an era when speakeasies resorted to gimmicks to attract crowds, from revolving bars to telephone tables and kissing rooms, jazz cabarets were content merely to hype the "eroticism of black music."

This eroticism might very well have been attached to such local orchestras as Luis Russell, Mamie Smith and her Jazz Hounds, Lockwood Lewis and his "Oh" Boys, the Harlem Rounders, Duke Ellington, the Santo Domingo Serenaders, Sam Wooding, The Missourians, Billy Fowler, Fess Williams and his Royal Flush Orchestra, Johnny Dunn, Louis Armstrong (after 1928), the bluesy but solid band of Cecil Scott, Bubber Miley, Don Redman, Earl Jackson's Musical Champions, Charlie Johnson, Cliff Johnson and his Krazy Kats, Fletcher Henderson, William McKinney and Elmer Snowden. All of these groups played for the underworld clubs as did some of their white counterparts, including Ted Lewis, Paul Specht and his Georgians, Miff Mole and Red Nichols.

A Harlem which has since passed into legend was mecca for a phenomenal number of attractively priced clubs simply bristling with hot music for their fans. Singer Lena Horne remarked how ironic it all was "having expensive, expansive, and mind-boggling shows in the middle of Harlem." Sylvester believed most of them were "scaled down to fit the pocket of the ordinary man." Popular novelist Carl Van Vechten and his party-goer friends made a career shouting "Let's go up to Harlem." and reporter William Dufty counted the limousines and minks which made the trek to clubs that the Grahams claim didn't disgorge their customers until just before dawn.

According to local press accounts, by 1929 no fewer than eleven premier black and white places were available (a contrast to the single club, the Cotton Club—the newest version—currently filling the bill). In addition, resident jazz-goers were treated to fifteen major orchestras and hundreds of smaller competitors actively engaged on a nightly basis.[17] As was the case in Chicago, not only were most of these places run with money invested by independent, as opposed to syndicated, mobsters, but some of the best music was found in clubs clustering together in a small area for customer ease and satisfaction. In Chicago it was State Street. In New York it was Seventh Avenue, as described by Rudolph Fisher in his novel *The Walls of Jerico*:

...a land for tumultuous traffic, the avenue of a thousand enterprises...Seventh Avenue remains for six nights a carnival, bright with the lights of theatres and night clubs, alive with darting cabs, with couples moving from house party to cabaret, with loiterers idling and ogling on the curb, with music wafted from mysterious sources, with gay talk and loud Afric laughter.

The musician Volly DeFaut recalls a "turf center" at 135th Street, between Lenox and Fifth Avenues, vicinity of the Rhythm Club (famous for its cutting sessions and owned by the black gambler and musician Bert Hall), The Green Parrot, LeRoys, Small's, the Sugar Cane Club (the first Harlem cellar club with jive waiters, and popular with whites[18]), and Edmond's Cellar. Another famous place was Connor's, a basement joint that Fisher found by walking down a narrow headlong stairway to the strains of the Bubber Miley band, a club that was "very lively and easier to breathe in" than most places.[19] There was also the famous "jungle alley" along 133rd Street, a strip of clubs which demanded passwords and these included appropriate counter signs for access and were highly selective on which, whites, if any, could gain entry.

Some of these included The Nest (home for Luis Russell), Spider Webb's, the Shim Sham, Basement Brownie's (with the omnipresent 300-pound Brown at the door), the 101 Ranch, the Catagonia, the Orient, Livia's Blue Club, the Green Cat, The Paradise Inn, the Bamboo, Garden of Joy ("where wild little bands were defying all musical conventions,[20] and the house band was Mamie Smith's), the Clam House, Club Swanee, Bucket of Blood (Sam Nanton's wonderful mob presiding), the Baltimore (whose black gambler-owner maintained good relations with the local Democratic party for years), the Hole in the Wall, the Congo (no whites admitted into this club's jungly atmosphere), Dickie Well's, the Lenox Club (with Cliff Johnson), Saratoga (the second home for Luis Russell's group), Yeah Man, the Log Cabin, the Alhambra, and The Oriental which caught Fisher's attention with its black Jewish manager presiding over a three-story club having excellent food, 1000 linen-clad tables and noiseless, velvety floors.[21]

Such evocative names suggest only a few of the secondary but nonetheless illustrious night clubs dotting the Harlem landscape in the 1920s. One black musician writes that these clubs were "run by big-time mobs not tramps. . . who had a way of running them better than anyone else."[22] Musician Max Kaminsky offers his explanation for the tolerant treatment whites received in these clubs:

In this stage of their struggle, the people of Harlem were not only cheered and elated at the idea that they had something the white folks admired, they naturally welcomed the nightly flood of cash customers the music attracted.... The Harlem musicians who took special joy in atonishing white musicians, used to swing so hard that smoke almost came out of their horns.

Lumped together these niteries offered superb musical activity. Blacks may have maintained a disporportionately smaller share of the action than their numbers suggested, but they did do well, and their control, status and earning power placed them on a footing few other blacks could match.[23] Casper Holstein, Richard Morgan, Bert Hall and Barron Wilkins, unchallenged black racketeers, bootleggers and consummate politicians, owned important local clubs that awarded them enormous respect. They, together with their white underworld allies, kept the peace and brought street safety to the areas surrounding their places of operation. One musical historian has gone on record declaring Harlem of this period as less violent, and its clubs less unethical, than was to be found anywhere else in the city.[24]

It is rather pointless to chronicle the life of every club, a subject which warrants separate attention and research. To some degree the task is impossible inasmuch as many roamed the area like nomadic tribes of bedouins, settling here and there, opening and closing at will (or when padlocked by the police), changing names and ownership like suits of clothing. But by examining a few of the primary, important night clubs we can gain some idea of the mobsters' contribution to the scene and assess how much we have lost over the succeeding years.

A few important places are worth remembering. There was the intimate Mexico's, a tidy after-hours place with good booze and friendly faces. Ellington believed its Sunday morning jam sessions, particularly those after 7 a.m. created "lots of noise and lots of heat...you floated rather than danced."[25] Minutes away was Monroe's Uptown House, a cabaret where jamming was encouraged and jazzmen split a nights' pay after passing a hat through the room. Financialy rewarding nights popped up, according to Arnold Shaw, whenever "the numbers men of Harlem dropped into the club; then musicians' money shares increased appreciably." The Kit Kat never opened before 2 a.m. and stayed open until the following noon. Preston's, on 133rd Street, crowded upwards of 100 people into space partly occupied by 25 tables, with standing room for another 30. Owned by a jaunty black gambler whose associations with local mobs predated Prohibition, Preston's featured some of the best names in jazz history, giving trial runs to such performers as Billie Holliday, Rex Stewart, Fletcher Henderson, Luckey Roberts and Fats Waller.

Cecil Scott's popular band was quartered in the Capitol Palace, an immense basement with a seating capacity of 1000. It was a club known for its ties with several local black mobsters and a place whose racketeer-owner kept the price of an evening's entertainment, its good fried chicken and its "gin that tasted like perfume" well within range of the pocketbook of its ostensibly working class clientele.[26]

One of the truly elegant spots was Connie's Inn on 132nd Street. Owned by the Immerman Brothers, its connection with various mobs and Owney Madden was apparent from the makeup of its nightly audiences. Connie's specialized in black jazz for the horsey set, so its prices were steeper. Cover charge was $2.50 a couple, and a bowl of ice fetched $1.00, as did four bottles of ginger ale. Tables were arranged in the usual intimate configuration while low ceilings dipped onto a cavelike ornamentation. Lining the walls in art deco style were tiny villages of bungalows, their speckled lights twinkling from miniature window apertures. Louis Armstrong was of the opinion the club reeked with atmosphere and by the time he got to Connie's he was a good judge of what it took to be stimulating. By the late 1920s the Inn had become specialists in presenting masterly revues with as many as 30 dancers, backed by Armstrong's torrid band. Jazzmen were beneficiaries of the mob-backed showplace. Bandleader Lois Deppe recalls:

I went to work at Connie's Inn in Harlem. They had two shows a year there, and for each six months they'd get themselves a new band. While I was around they had Armstrong, Henderson, Russell, Wooding, Luis Russell, Don Redman and Fats Waller.... Duke once tried to talk me into leaving Connie's and going into the Cotton Club but I told him I was satisfied where I was.[27]

Deppe's remarks about the Inn's biggest rival, the Cotton Club, conjure up the name of one of the leading jazz palaces of all time, a club which has just recently received attention in the form of its own biography. It, too, like the others already mentioned, was a mob-catered affair, standing on Lenox Avenue and 142nd Street. Its interior detailed a plantation-setting shaped into a horseshoe. This legendary club seated 800 into booths lining the walls and behind small tables ringing two tiers. Although former heavyweight champion Jack Johnson was part owner and honorary greeter, only the rare black celebrity dared, or could afford, entry into this expensive showplace. Lena Horne worked there as a showgirl in the mid-1930s and her reason for the sparse attendance by blacks is as good as any: they simply felt awkward and irritated in the presence of high society snobs and exploited by prices which ranged from a stiff $3.00 cover charge to $15.00 for a pint of dubious liquor.

Manager and talent scout Herman Stark was typical of many men in his field. Stark, a portly, cigar-chewing friend to jazz bands, was forever nosing around in his search for talented groups to fill the club's large entertainment bill. The Cotton Club, with almost three times the weekly budget of Connie's, (or nearly $4000 in its salad days,) delivered spectacles seven nights weekly. Its fashionable posters flooded the city, promising dozens of beautiful women dancers, comedians and other eccentric acts, in addition to its chief pearly magnet, Duke Ellington, "the aristocrat of Harlem," and his high-priced orchestra. Many of the shows hummed along to songs and lyrics by Jimmy McHugh, Harold Arlen and Dorothy Fields, to name a few of the songwriters whose exclusive materials found their way into the almost inexhaustible number of dazzling revues. Ellington admitted audience reponsiveness and the mood of the club itself exerted a powerful influence on the musical style and direction of his orchestra.[28]

Other places included Small's Paradise (owned by a white and black mobster consortium), where singing waiters twirling silver trays and the Jimmy Harrison Orchestra carried on a lively patter until the place closed at 6 a.m.; Bamville, with earthy black torch singers ambling through the club during their acts; and The Lenox Club. The last named was another place patronized by black racketeers who came to hear jazz. Attendance was 90% black, crowding into a room seating 400. Whites, generally showpeople, were well-screened at the door before the doorman allowed the lucky few to filter in. The dance floor was large and usually packed, attracted by the good jazz bands and the musical revues. The club's special event was its Monday Breakfast Dances which began at 3.30 a.m. and, by all reports, did a lively business.[29]

Singer Ethel Waters rounds out this night club panorama with a tantalizing vignette of Edmond's Cellar, where she worked for some time, a club Fisher called the "social center of black Harlem." Edmond's represented a whole stratum of lower class places located throughout Harlem between 1927-1934. Waters describes this honky-tonk with fondness and suggests it was a kind of underworld Shangri-La. Many of its customers came from the ranks of fashionable crooks and musically-inclined mobsters who filled the place during her long engagement. The club's interior was mindful of so many: low ceilings, walls gaily festooned with artificial flowers and with recurring if tattered and aging photographs of long-since retired stars of black theater and sports peering back from every nook and cranny. As in most Harlem joints, set hours were non-existent. "Although you worked until you were unconscious," writes Waters, "it was the happiest time of my life."

Scattered throughout the city were many other clubs. They have have been less inventive, less colorful and lacking the musical talent found in the Harlem joints, but they nevertheless offered havens and job opportunities to countless wandering musicians. Unfortunately, because the clubs pushed publicity less and wad-packing patrons were less inclined to visit, they summoned up less interest for writers and musicians of the period. Thus our insiders' view is blocked almost entirely.

Durante claims Brooklyn had its share of clubs as did the Bowery or Coney Island during the summertime. Also roadhouses above the Bronx and deep within Long Island, and a few cabarets in the West 50s rewarded the patient jazz explorer. The Greenwich Village area was mainly for the college bohemian crowd and only the Hot Feet Club comes to mind. This place was run by gangsters whose musical interest led to the hiring of Fats Waller, Elmer Snowden and Chick Webb, and their bands were aided by the radio airchecks beaming from the club at the odd hour of 1 a.m.

Elsewhere Less Razzle Dazzle

Every American city and town was to some degree transformed by the events brought on by the war and Prohibition. Thus one might reasonably assume that most of these areas were likewise affected by the new, energetic sounds and rhythms already noted. He might also assume that these towns acted as hosts for musical incubation. Alas, such assumptions would be erroneous. Pianist Earl Hines told historian Stanley Dance how cheated he felt by the lack of opportunity provided by his hometown, Pittsburgh. Sadly few young musicians were adventurous enough to explore other areas. So for the majority, they simply exchanged their musical aspirations for other vocations in their own home setting.

Certain cities offered more to the musically-inclined. Admittedly the thesis of this study rests on the notion that places successful for the pursuit of jazz occurred primarily because underworld types in principal cities appreciated the music and had the collective muscle to subdue parochial restrictions against its being played. In fact, racketeers in select cities were solely responsible for the fact that many black musicians, and some whites too, travelled and played where they did and as frequently. The importance of such sponsorship lies in knowing the flip side of the musical coin. Albertson reminds us that the 1910s and 1920s were bad periods for public acceptance of black performers. One shudders to imagine the outcome for jazz artists without their widespread mobster support.

The base of operations was crucial. Cities had to have been cosmopolitan, (being a mixture of different peoples) and— tolerant. They had to have created an artistic stimulation of some sort and have been willing to reward it though this is hard to measure on a broad basis. But we know the years of European domination in New Orleans left an aesthetic heritage that shaped much of its later life; the same holds true for New York, slightly less so in the case of Chicago. While blacks clearly authored the music, racist practices choked almost completely the opportunity by black people to adequately finance, show-case and sponsor their own art forms.

The dominant Protestant ethic and, for the larger Eastern cities, reigning Irish culture in political circles, significantly opposed black expansion, much less black music. So it was that only in cities which played host to hundreds of nationalities after 1880, especially accepting Jewish, Italian and black migrants, were seeds of interest planted. Grudgingly, these areas, which to a lesser extent included Memphis, Detroit and New Orleans were transformed into leading jazz centers (see Appendix B).

Harlem was mecca. And mob-owned clubs in Harlem were its religious sanctuaries. They set the tone, particularly after 1923, in how the art form would be presented elsewhere. Even New Orleans, birthplace for much of the music's traits, bowed submissively:

The Negro night clubs of New Orleans were patterned after those of Harlem. The proprietors visit Harlem to study the color schemes and acquire the atmosphere of night clubs because "it serves well along publicity lines." Even the music and floor shows are handled in the Harlem manner—nothing less than red hot.[30]

Kansas City (mentioned at length elsewhere in this study) and Memphis before 1925, with its highly touted Beale Street district, appropriately fit the mould. So too did Detroit during the time of the Purple Gang of Jews and the Italian bootleggers who ran jazz joints in competition with the respectable hotels. Mezzrow writes of Luigi's Cafe, operated by an Italian/Jewish combine for the city's smart set:

I don't know if those upper crust Green Pointers ever appreciated it or not, but under the auspices of Louis the Wop they were treated to jazz sessions night after night by practically all the top-notch musicians who made jazz history in this country.

Responsive haunts and playgrounds like Luigi's were few and far between in most towns. Bandleader Artie Shaw called Cleveland "drab" for jazz and was equally critical of suburban-ruled Boston, a city Kaminsky said was "hopeless." Denver drew the ire of reporter Robert Allen: "People fear change more than they hope for betterment...and roll up the sidewalks at 11 p.m." Songwriter Hoagy Carmichael wrote me that Indiana was one place where "outside influences were not considered." And of jazz in Philadelphia, one correspondent for the *Jazz Record* noted: "It just ain't."[31]

Ridiculously low-paying work in obscure cities like St. Louis, Columbus, Baltimore and Milwaukee drove out the sizzling bands of Cab Calloway and the Missourians Sammy Stewart, Chick Webb and Earl Hines, respectively, to Chicago and New York for survival. Jimmy Lunceford's crack band left the South for the same reason, fled Buffalo and its low wages, and "nearly starved to death for lack of work in Cleveland."[32] Backwater areas posed insurmountable problems for most musicians, and no biography is complete without mention of some horrendous hassle that musician and his band encountered outside the few major cities open to them.

Radio programs piped in popular jazz music, and only the most rural outposts could escape the invasion. But this improved the careers of out-of-town groups mainly. Drummer Jo Jones considered Louisville beneficial but for one reason: It was a musical marketplace, a catchment area, where orchestra leaders could locate and hire and take up North talented musicians trying to flee the South.[33] For in most Southern towns, jazz was relegated to the most dismal parts of town, a restriction that put off all but the most dedicated listener. British blues writer Giles Oakley presents a grimly vivid account of Fanin Street in Shreveport, Louisiana, reminiscent of streets found in other small towns throughout the South as late as 1945. Here jazz survived in crummy honky tonks, cheap hotels, gin mills and cathouses—themselves allocated into the excitable black district where violence was sleazy and abrupt. Beyond were the rural and countrified regions where new music was non-existent and a musician's staple fare was the ancient rag and simple breakdown sound, with techniques almost unchanged from his grandfather's time.

Soil on the West Coast was almost as infertile. Prominent jazz artists like King Oliver, Jelly Roll Morton and Ben Pollack, each in his own way, had tried to make a go of it but to little avail. San Francisco clubs considered jazz a novelty, and local women's clubs saw a danger in black musicians. Black orchestras were circumscribed into a small area of the city and shortchanged when it came time to secure dance permits.[34] In fact so sparse is the musical history for San Francisco that the visitor to the local jazz museum (two small rooms operated by an investment firm) can find no reference to groups predating 1940. Los Angeles provided no more pleasant a setting. Black novelist Wallace Thurmond's caricature of the city in the 1920s as a "small town mentally, peopled by mentally small Southern Negroes" augurs poorly in our considering it as a jazz center. The town supplied few sounds, and clubs like Sebastiani's Cotton Club in Culver City and the Paradise, in the city's Black Belt, kept the torch lit in an area lacking sufficient mob activity in the earlier years to provide much foundation for those that came later.

So it was that most of the better groups in the provinces either headed for the underworld capitals, or meekly accepted the rewards of obscurity. Some bands probably enjoyed crisscrossing the country's wasteland circuits; others were no doubt frightened into immobility by the sheer thought of success. Misguided management and individual laziness took their toll as well. Eschewing cities where mobs ruled the roost and were willing to patronize a band decidedly retarded an orchestra's potential, if not growth and fame. Herein lies a certain sadness for jazz musicologists. For they shall never be in a position to properly judge the talents of the unknowns, let alone fully appreciate the tantalizing possibilities found in those rarely heard and recorded bands of Grant Moore and his Dakota Black Devils, J. Neal Montgomery and his Atlanta-based band, Zach Whyte's Chocolate Beau Brummels of Ohio or Lloyd Hunter and his Omaha Serenaders.

Top Left. Ralph Capone owned several suburban Chicago niteries and was an avid jazz fan. He was very popular with musicians and was especially friendly with Lucky Millinder.

Top Right. Mitzi Capone, a youngest brother of the Capones was a regular visitor to jazz clubs and knew Earl Hines well.

Opposite. Al Capone. His syndicate ran the sleek Grand Terrace, the number one jazz spot in the 1930s; a very bountiful man toward jazz artists since 1913.

Legs Diamond. Part of the Cotton Club mob. He once tipped Duke Ellington $2000 to play "St. Louis Blues", a typical gesture of mobsters towards musicians in the 1920s and 30s.

Night club bombings were very infrequent, as was club violence generally, but always received full media attention when they did occur, as in this late 1920s Chicago photo.

George "Frenchie" DeMange, an underworld figure whose face and tipping policy were well known to Harlem musicians.

Owney Madden was part of the Cotton Club syndicate which gave not only fabulous revues but after hours' gala parties for racketeers, musicians, and plenty of chorus girls.

1930 Hollywood set depicting a typical 1900 lower class saloon. Here gritty floor, grimy furniture and inelegant decor could be found any number of volatile customers and what purported to be entertainment.

1932 set from the Hollywood movie "The Crooner". Note the smartly-styled, urbane environment which was far more musical and a good deal safer, thanks to the underworld owners and managers, than would be found in the previous photo.

Chapter III

Early Entertainment and Night Club Life

Small or Nothing at All

Like urban renewal, the best way of appreciating the combined efforts of jazzmen and mobsters is by scanning the delapidated worlds of entertainment and night club life prior to their arrival. Before 1900 we have it on good authority that countless performers suffered quietly, going a lifetime with neither recognition nor reward. In many ways they paralleled the lives of Southern black musicians minus the heavy barrage of racial and economic degradation. Not only were they unimportant beyond the narrow confines of the places in which they appeared, but they were virtually without protection when it came to their own individually-contoured acts. Plagiarism and thievery hung heavily over the field, and the onrush for quick profits set a dazzling pace. Patents and copyrights of songs had little meaning; and theatrical and musical presentations, if they were any good, faced theft without remorse. The public, while all this was taking place, stood by indifferently.

Musical styles of the period were crude and simplistic, and lacked singular distinction. Indeed a thick veneer of puritanism spread across whatever music could be had in polite company, leaving only music hall revues as the people's choice in nightly amusements before 1900. And Durante claims these were "lousy but with no dramatic critics in the audience, nobody knew the difference." Progammed with six or eight song and dance routines, and climaxed with a whirling dervish gypsy violinist, the card was unceremoniously, repetitiously dull. In the words of New York journalist of the era, Jack Kofoed:

46

It was a time when dog and pony acts were considered big time, and deep-voiced ballad singers could stop the show.[1]

Lower down the social scale, minstrel shows provided crowds with musical scapegoats, such as lazy, brashly-dressed blacks who spoke like college professors when raiding a chicken coop. Irving Zeidman's history of this brand of lower class show business sparkles with stories of female impersonators, overstuffed hoochy-coochy dancers, and the excessive number of slapstick comics who ridiculed the various new ethnic migrants with pantaloon and floppy shoe costumes.

It was a time when the narrative ballad ruled the island of popular song. Tunes like "Daddy Wouldn't Buy Me a Bow Wow," "Piff, Paff, Pouf," "Down Where the Wurzburger Flows," "I'm Not Pretty But I'm Good to My Family," and "There are Fairies in the Bottom of My Garden" somehow caught the popular mood. Many were exceedingly intricate, written for popular piano, and impossible to orchestrate for dancing.

In any event, the problem was fairly academic as there were very few orchestras capable of coming together, much less playing together. Since conditions were appalling and demand insufficient, few hung around to starve. The lucky ones had to be vigilant and create their own summons by hiring out for circus parades, cigar store openings, and election campaigns. The occasional society ball was a bonus but only those in-the-know ever received a call.

Pianists, on the other hand, were better situated. For them there was always some desolate saloon which would keep them in beer and skittles, if not furnish a decent livelihood. "Work was irregular," recalls one hardy soul, "and simple music was the order of the day."[2] Those who chose to hire bands were not always satisfied with the result, as restaurateur George Rector suggests:

Our first orchestra was famous for its endurance and volume.... We had four orchestras playing in relays and they all played like mechanics repairing a locomotive.

Students of serious music fared little better. Musicologist

Paul is very critical when he writes "classical music had about as much appeal as polo." Grand opera was repressed for its licentious and violent themes, and most symphonic orchestras were hothouse flowers for the wealthy who rarely allowed them to play for more than a handful. And these, the social critic H.L. Mencken despaired, were third-rate.[3]

It was a bad time to be young. Little could be found to do at night, unless one gives consideration to "learning the facts about life" quickly and sordidly. Young women were even less blessed. Their lives spent after dusk were overwhelmingly protected and might just as well have been hacked away for all the good it did them. Functions at big hotels and country clubs came around now and then, especially during the big holidays, but the chief purpose was less to be entertained than to locate a suitable marriage mate or business partner.

Before 1910 dancing sparked tremendous opposition. The respectable class allowed itself only an occasional fling, and these were pompous and well-chaperoned, conducted in fraternal halls where lemonade, warped dance floors and early closings were foregone conclusions. Counterparts on the other end of the social spectrum were just as gloomy. Here the nonconformist or deviant, devoid of other outlets for rejoicing, could partake of unsavoury, grotty places in the slums which attracted a dangerous, besotted element. Rules and decorum were afterthoughts in such dance halls, and the climate could heat up at the drop of a statement. Herbert Asbury's study of San Francisco's Barbary Coast, and showman William A. Brady provided two perspectives that claim the wise slummer never visited these places without being well-armed.

Presiding over this dreary scenario were several groups. It was they who watched nightlife and controlled its character, although they were hardly a brotherhood in temperament. Rather they suggested a loose consortium of allied interests and cultural concerns aimed at opposing encroachment from whatever quarter. Strikingly, the methods, if not the manners, of these protectors and planners of a city's night life, strongly suggest the gangsterism associated with the 1920s. Knit together by racial affinity, these mainly Northern Europeans employed monopoly tactics, trickery, violence and deception against newer groups seeking entry. Tied to political and legal agencies, they could always summon up police reaction to harass the newcomers.[4]

John Higham, their biographer, writing of this jingoistic age, entitles them "patricians on the defensive." Who used every means at their disposal to prevent job competition they suspected would only dilute an elegance they had established in conducting business. Higham continues:

At the outset Anglo-Saxon nativism vaguely indicted the whole foreign influx.... They worshipped tradition in a deeply conservative spirit, and in the tumult of the 1890s it seemed to them that everything fixed and sacred was threatened with dissolution from these South and East European immigrants.

Foremost against the dark onslaught were the Irish, German and other Protestant restaurateurs and gourmands, occasional employers of musicians. George Rector lists himself amongst a broad front of allies that included Captain James Churchill, John Kelly, George Considine, Davy Johnson, Louis Sherry, the Shanley Brothers and John Dunstan. This proved a stiff wall of resistance for encroachers in the New York area. Other cities had similar coteries. Many of these men were adamant about competing with swarthy Italians and Jews who lay emphasis in their niteries on music and dancing—loathesome activities that could only boost operating expenses. Snobbish contempt set the tone. Rector claimed the dancing element which ushered in the "jazz age" ruined the fine art of dining and conversation and demolished the tastefully subdued atmosphere the older establishments had striven to maintain for their wealthy diners. He was certainly correct about the cost factor. Adding revues and bright orchestras would force up overhead costs the older places had always managed to keep notoriously low, in that practically the entire staff worked solely for tips, some even, in the better places, having to pay managements for the privilege.[5]

Restaurateurs were not the only ones at the barricades. The "theatrical trust," a band of seven Anglo-Saxon monopolists led by A.L. Erzlanger and M. Klaw dominated the Broadway stage for decades while a similar monopoly, under the Keith imprint, controlled the burlesque circuits. Gentlemen gamblers and bordello madams in the Eastern vice districts also opposed interruption. Contrary to this same element which had done so much to support jazz in New Orleans, French Emma (inventor of all-mirror rooms), Zoe Willard, Aimlee Leslie, Dink McKenna, Mike McDonald, Georgie Spencer, Big Jim O'Leary and the Everleigh Sisters of Chicago declared the music unfit for their clientele. Bankers and other traditional money lenders were no less resistant. Loans were categorically refused to men who also faced extortion from police and resistance by local musicians' unions.

These collusive practices guaranteed that the unaffiliated, these and the unprotected immigrant, tinkering around with legitimate business tactics, would never rise above the level of pushcart management. So it was that the entertainment operators ushered in after 1910 were a strange and aggressive bunch of mavericks—Irving Wexler, Jack Diamond, Jakey Shapiro, Frankie Marlowe, Arnold Rothstein, Augie Carfano, Larry Fay and Lucky Luciano—all possessing skills and aggressive desire that ran sharply counter to the the desires of the older night club school.

Night Club Life of the 19th Century

One simply cannot appreciate the advances made in musical expression or realize the debt owed the underworld club owners of the 1920s without first studying the social blights they eventually plowed under. Saloons, dives and dance halls of the earliest period were often tasteless, mirthless and inspirationless. How else to evaluate an era when many saloons began business as early as 5.30 a.m., with customers lined up outside ready for a day's hard drinking? Brady believed variety houses and music halls of the 1890s deliberately sandwiched themselves between saloons offering a quick guzzle to actors and musicians who drank their careers away. Some booze factories never closed, and for some there was no need to forge keys and locks.

It is worth mentioning five major criticisms of these turn-of-the-century boozeries, which strip away any attempts at sentimentalizing them. There were far too many of them; violence was rampant; their orientation was along strictly ethnic lines; any possible charm was washed away by filthy conditions; and they promoted sexual bias. In all, they fail to measure up to their counterparts of the flapper era.

Elsie Lathrop's detailed study indicates that taverns and saloons were prolific in 1776; Asbury was dismayed by the ensuing heritage:

In the 19th century there were always from three to five times as many saloons in the U.S. as were necessary to satisfy the legitimate demand for liquor at retail. On some streets in the large cities during pre-prohibition times, there was a saloon on every corner and often 2 or 3 in the middle of the block.[6]

According to tavern historian Jim Marshall, 42 blocks in New York's Bowery district in 1897 mirrored the country's penchant for drinking: 50 times more saloons than religious houses for an area fast filling up with orthodox religious people from the Old World.[7] and even as tavern life in the East was indeed blossoming at this time, such drunk tanks were outnumbered perhaps three to one, on a per capita basis, by similar drinking spas in Marshall's West.

The ready availability of such social beacons, "the poor man's hall of oratory," together with the increasing tensions and urban blight which surrounded the characters that made up the patronage, led to scenes of wholesale, almost indescribable violence. "Public taste in this period," recollects one battler, "seemed to demand the spectacular and the dangerous."[8] Danger always seemed to be lurking, as evidenced by the artist Thomas Hart Benton's view of provincial Missouri:

Nighttime gaiety was pretty boisterous and loud, as if to make up for the silent misery (nearby). It lasted late and though I saw but one actual fight they seemed to be always in the making.

By 1895 unkempt, sinister-looking clubs, affectionately termed "dives" and "gyp joints" by those who knew them well, were the most numerous saloons found in larger cities. In 1898 a New York City police inquiry assessed 100 of these joints in lower Manhattan, certifying a mere 10% as safe for the average bar wanderer. Twenty years later a New York *Herald* survey believed an even smaller percentage was worthy of cash customers.

These joints not only meant a second home to the workers who frequented them, but provided congenial surroundings for hoodlums, robbers and questionable politicians. Strange and mischievous intrigues were forever being hatched. Asbury notes in his study of New York gangs how intricate and historical were the associations maintained by Irish mobsters and the saloonkeepers of lower Manhattan. Barkeeps and their waiters were only too-willing accomplices for owners who loaned out their infamous "backrooms" for nefarious purposes. Opium dens, robbers' lairs, gambling casinos, cribs and clearing houses for stolen goods are examples of some of the possibilities these places offered the opportunist saloonman. By 1930 many of these money-makers were no longer a part of the night club scene.

Gyp joints could be murderous to a customer's health. As much danger could be found inside a club as in the streets beyond, and gun battles were frequent. Marshall points out that the Bowery clubs during the 1870s averaged no fewer than 100 murders a year over a long stretch. For safeguards, smart owners, hired bartenders built like gorillas, installed iron-plating in the doors and lined bars and mirrors with boiler plate against the eventuality of ricocheting bullets. Names suggested what might lie inside: The Rat Pit, The Hole in the Wall, The Graveyard, Bucket of Blood, The Morgue. Durante remembers the many prostitutes who were controlled from the bar by the waiters; another writer recalls all the varieties of swindler and robber to be found within.[9]

Pickpockets milled around in clusters at the Chatham Club on the Lower East Side until 7 a.m., when they dispersed to prey upon their fellow worker heading for the subways. The Windsor House enjoyed the reputation of always short-changing its patrons while speculation has it the number of people robbed inside McGurk's Suicide Hall was in the thousands. Only one rule operated in McGurk's: anyone could rob anybody else—customers, waiters, prostitutes—just don't get caught! If so, all proceeds had to be surrendered to McGurk. Some places were so tough, as in The Crystal Palace, that the piano player was urged to wear boxing gloves for protection when he played. Of Maxine's in Brooklyn, Durante warns, "That place was so tough if you took your hat off you was a sissy."

Some clubs were so violent spiders were welcome additions to an otherwise dismal interior and local game laws were passed to protect them. For their webs were useful as a hemostatic to absorb blood flowing from the daily bashings, stabbings and shootings. One account has it that a club manager, striving for the "worst dive in the world" title, collected human ears and noses bitten off in his club's brawls, pickled in alcohol, before submitting his claim.[10]

Today countless pubs and "body shops" attract a riot of color and nationality, befitting an age of blurring ethnic conceptions. Not so in 1900. Our second criticism of early club life points to their conducting of business along exclusive ethnic and racial lines, all strictly enforced. Sons followed in the footsteps of fathers, as if by hereditary transmission, adhering closely to a unilateral compact of racial rules demanded by each saloonkeeper. Within walking distance of a customer's hovel, taverns catered to a clientele where nearly everyone looked and dressed alike and shared similar national origins. While a case can be made for heterogeneity in the squalid parts of town, dismal sectors degrading all men equally, in the quiet shadows of the respectable districts it was different. Origins mattered. So it was that a would-be drinker, be he Irish, black, Anglo or German, knew his place. Disregarding such a code by walking into a strange saloon opened a customer to severe scrutiny, if not worse treatment. Some indeed took their lives into their hands. At best it was a risky venture.

By and large, these places oriented themselves toward a clannish Irish patron whose numbers, volatility and penchant for booze comprised the backbone of the drinking class in the late 19th century. It also made an evening's entertainmnt unpredictable and wild.[11] Yet owing to the commonality of

background which policeman and saloonkeeper often shared—
and in the Eastern cities this was Irish—violence and other
irregularities were tolerated, dismissed or ignored. It was a
casual attitude which underwent a marked change when the
next generation of barkeeps and cabaret owners included a
healthy percentage of Sicilians and Jews.

The rich have always been able to afford refined
entertainment. The same was true when it came to clubs in
1900. Waterholes for the wealthy might offer vintage wines
and fancy cocktails from behind dark mahogany bars,
catering to a select membership. New York's Old Waldorf Bar,
for instance, with bartenders advertised to know "491 different
ways to mix drinks," constituted a male sanctuary of leading
financiers and politicians. Women were invariably barred.
Chamber music concerts alternated with bawdy theatricals in
an atmosphere of elks heads and pictures of "arty" ballet
dancers spread across highly-stained walls.[12] These clubs
controlled profit margins like medieval robbers and Rector
claims enormous markups, far exceeding anything
contemplated in the 1920s, were standard for both booze and
food.

As the peripatetic saloon visitor descended the social
ladder, he discovered that the hours which people devoted to
drinking widened as the levels of noise, filth and
unpleasantness expanded. In most instances these places were
blots on the local landscape. As part of the hobo floating
population around 1910, author Jim Tully recalls one Chicago
saloon where:

the place reeked with the filthy clothes and bodies and broken, wasted derelicts
made it their daily headquarters.

The majority of these taverns catered to people for whom
amenities were irrelevant to the important business at hand—
drinking.

Atmospheres reflected this indifference. It was not
uncommon for a visitor's sense of smell to be as much attacked
by walking past the double doors as by his sense of sight or
social awareness. Sanitary facilities resembled the hulls of old

China tea clippers; sawdust floors, tables hacked up by constant torture from knives, and lighting that was dim and full of gas fumes complete the picture. Harlow has described Geoghgan's Bar (pronounced 'Gagan'), a cheap Bowery dive with gangster owners, as commonplace between 1870 and 1910:

Inside. . . a round of drinks brought the privilege of staying the rest of the night in a chair, on a stool, slumped forward on a table, or on the unspeakably filthy floor, where one was in danger of being eaten by rats.

Durante remembers playing piano for an uptown club, The Alamo, before 1914. He found it dank, murky, noisy and unfit for a performer; like most places of its kind, "no class and little overhead". Durante notes that the "only fresh air to be had was what the customers brought in on their clothes."[13]

Early clubs were cheerless places that could hardly be told apart. Until 1915 cafes and saloons, excluding those willing to circumvent the laws (an enticement that usually brought in underworld types), were prohibited from having orchestras, and dancing was illegal beyond the confines of public dance halls. In these Victorian laws was the signature of traditional niteries hoping to keep overhead costs as low as possible. One Kansas City ordinance of 1894 extended this prohibition to infinity:

The playing of any musical instrument or instruments, or the making of any unusual noise or disturbance, or the singing of any person or persons, or the keeping of any parrot, quail, monkey, squirrel, or other bird or any animal in any saloon, or tippling house or dramshop is hereby prohibited.[14]

Consequently musical offerings were for the most part unorganized affairs that came and went. Drunken patrons were left to double as singers and dancers, depending on their mood. On occasion a place might provide singing waiters but here a patron was advised to be especially wary. For the waiters had management's green light to wander through the crowd and pick the pockets of boozers fast asleep and unaware. The small musical band was a rare treat and found in places willing to violate the law or in areas where the law paid little attention to what was taking place. Bands might range from five-piece destroyers of the classics to a tormented pianist pounding out nostalgic weepers. Bandstands and platforms were tucked away in a corner and generally ignored by the drinking brigade which outnumbered listeners ten-to-one. Musicians might just as well have put down their instruments and played cards, for as one reminiscer tells it, "few people listened with any attention to the music."[15] Irish songs were a great favorite. Journalist Joseph Mitchell provides a peek at a typical lower class gin mill in New York around 1905:

A beery old saloon musician would show up with an accordian and a mob of maudlin rummies would surround him to sing hymns and Irish songs....Dancers would grind peanut shells under their shoes, making a strange, scratchy noise while they danced.

Al Jennings, the confidant of short story writer O. Henry, writes of the time the two of them visited a Lower East Side dance hall in the 1900s. Men lined the lengthy bar while garishly-dressed women sized-up each new prospect from their vantage point at the tables. O. Henry beckoned to a pair, and Jennings continued:

The girls came over and sat at our table. It was the cheapest kind of dance hall in a basement under a saloon. A fellow with an accordion was pounding a tune with an old rattle-bang piano; a few tawdry-looking couples moved with grotesque rhythm in the middle of the floor. At the tables about a score of men sat erect and stupid—some of them were half-drunk; others bawling out harsh snatches of songs. The noisy guffaw of the place was more disturbing than the reeking exhalation of its breath.

Lastly these clubs stand accused of sexual bias. Women were categorically barred from what was seen as a man's bastion. Men gathered in saloons simply because they were the only places they could come together with grime still caked on their faces, and without females to disturb the flow of conversation, ribald or political, as the case might be. The presence of women might even upset their favorite pastime after that of guzzling: fights and punch-ups which followed close behind the interminable bouts of drinking.

Occassionally, prostitutes, women bartenders and degenerate females were accepted in the worst places and nice ladies permitted a dainty drink in one of the specially-designated rooms in middle class taverns, but these were exceptions. According to Marshall, a competent historian of his subject, in some saloons it was customary to station a look-out at the door or window to detect approaching feminine trouble. In the event she actually made a direct course for the saloon, the look-out's responsibility was to flash a signal at which time the rowdier customers would emit an appropriate torrent of vulgarities which dissuaded even the most determined woman from entering.

Chicago: Prelude to the Roaring 20s

Chicago in the late 19th century was very much like most cities, sporting a terrific corridor of sin and vice. Within the specified territory something of a boom-town atmosphere prevailed as 1precgo, in some ways, made a special effort at catering to night life. Its first building in 1831 housed a tavern and the first reported crime occurred in a saloon. Legend has it that gambling preceded women to the city. By 1835 a vice corridor had developed to appease the local Irishman's appetite for drinking and betting. This was located along the city's South Side and had, by 1885, acquired the name "The Levee." Most of Chicago's roustabouts could be found here as well as the underworld syndicates and employees "who were so intensely Irish."[16] Their neighborhoods were unmeant for the faint-hearted tourist: "Little Hell," "The Black Hole," "Satan's Mile," "Hell's Half-Acre" and "Dead Man's Alley."

Chicago School of Sociologists John Landesco, Walter Reckless, Harvey Zorbaugh and Paul G. Cressey have surveyed these districts and the Irish gentlemen gamblers and racketeers who controlled them from City Hall, establishing precedents for the many non-Irish gangs that followed. Their literature indeed suggests this early underworld were paragons of power to dominate that far outdistanced their later counterparts. In turn the amount of protection garnished by politicians on these earlier buccaneers was of an order which the later arrivals could only dream about. To a large extent ethnic similarity made the going easier and more pleasant. Professor Hiller overlaps the workings of men such as John Loughlin, Dink Kenna, Timothy D. Murphy, M.B. Madden and Mike McDonald with the worlds of politics, law enforcement and the judiciary—areas they regulated to regulate to suit themselves. John Kobler and Daniel Bell remind us the night life over which they presided was far faster than we have given them credit for, although nothing like the one later offered by Jews and Italians.

This Irish-dominated night club scene remained in effect without major revisions for almost five decades after 1865. Stephen Longstreet estimated over 200 bordellos and ten times that number in dangerous bars along The Levee before 1900. It was an exclusive preserve that lasted until Jewish and Italian underworld figures began poaching with a muscle approximate to that of the Irish groups. This was surely the case after 1910 when the city began to be chopped up into little suzerainties by the various competing ethnic syndicates.

The approach and style of the newcomers was wholly different from the Irish. John Kobler notes the steady increase in cellar night clubs rented by the Jewish and Italian mobs and where they indulged in "drinking and dancing to their heart's delight." By so doing they were anticipating the changes which grew out of the 1914-1918 War. Afterwards, a new kind of night life seemed to be demanded by America's youth—one that was brighter, livelier, with more attention given to exuberant music, the congealing of races and sexes, and better amenities for the night-lifer's dollar. In this the Jews and Italians were happily placed to perform such important middleman functions.

Much like their counterparts in New York, New Orleans and Memphis (to be discussed in later chapters), Jews, blacks and Italians were numerically significant in Chicago yet corralled by reasons of poverty into residential pockets close by or in The Levee. The immediacy which their environments pushed on one another, together with a resentful and cynical approach these tough areas required them to adopt, were not lost on street people who noticed how willingly police accepted appropriate payoffs from the more flamboyant and politically adroit Irish criminals.[17]

How then did these newcomers revolutionize the night club world? First, they specialized less in the gambling and liquor tax evasion of the old school—which seemed not to appeal to the younger crowd—and far more in developing a fashionable network of cabarets, highlighting new forms of danceable music. In this sense they were admirably positioned in that their adolescent years had been spent at this very activity. Socialites and celebrities were not slow in appreciating the escapism and publicity aspects such places might provide, and many began attending on a nightly basis. It was not accidental that many performers and show people were Jews and Italians who felt comfortable in the new clubs.

Thanks to the musical upswing the newer racketeers fostered, a great reign of night life descended on Chicago by 1915. Nearly 300 dance halls (most of them totally ignored the black bands) hived off a trend made acceptable in the over 100 cabarets (that did most of the hiring). Far and away, Jews and Italians comprised the majority of the new operators, including the Weiss Brothers, Ike Bloom, Joe Saltis, Jakie Adler, Solly Friedman, the Guzik brothers, Johnny Torrio, Charlie Maibaum, James Colisimo and "Jew Kid" Grabiner. In addition there were the black owners Henry Jones (who had several outlets), Robert Motts, Dan Jackson and Roy Jones.

Secondly, these men enlisted new sounds for their enterprises. Evidence cannot be found to confirm just how early this took place with any degree of regularity, but I believe sometime after 1910 jazz groups were being injected into club entertainment packages. In all probability the first New Orleans white jazz band to Chicago, Tom Brown's Syncopated Novelty Orchestra, was hired after 1910 by one of the leaders of the new mobs, Jim Colisimo, for his South Side cabaret and club.

Thirdly, by paying off local police, the Italian and Jewish club owners assured longevity for the black and tan clubs which they began buying up. Originally known as "black and whites," clubs of this genre featured black and integrated musical attractions. A study of their origins is certainly demanded, for we have no idea when they first appeared or where. But black ownership made them a novelty and certainly worth researching. Racial and sexual tolerance was shockingly loose for the times, causing the average beat cop to take matters into his own hands and clear the joints, as Walling notes, whenever his own morality against sexual integration was visibly challenged.

Small and jumpy bands may also have been present, particularly wherever black laborers and stevedores congregated; they may have even furnished the bulk of the audience. We can only speculate that Jewish and Italian mobsters visited these places while kids since they lived in adjacent neighborhoods around 1914. Whatever the possibilities, it was only after the Jews and Italians started protecting these niteries that their value improved as investments. Before the war it was highly unlikely that clubs of this calibre would derive much income from the white slummers drawn like moths to light before the spectre of black men dancing with white women. Night club historian Stanley Walker discusses the mobster contribution to their survival:

They banded the proprietors of the clubs or dance halls together for survival, wherever black musicians or black and tan operations were in effect. At the time police had the choice of harassing in particular these places with regulations developed under reformist regimes. To avoid police intrusion, the mobsters realized that strangers needed extra protection while in the clubs lest police close them down solely on grounds of being clip joints.

Fourthly, amenities were added and an exhilerating ambience introduced. During the war, with land values rising, the new recruits began the practice of buying up older cafes and theaters whose patronage was dwindling rather than building new places at alarming costs. By gutting and renovating the interiors of what writer Jerry Stagg calls "Moorish nightmares," the new owners created enlarged premises which permitted the presentation of broader entertainment revues for jazz and dance.

The Pekin Cafe and The Casino Gardens represent two of

the period's archetypal gangster-owned clubs. Originally a roomy theater on 26th Street and State, the Pekin had long been the only black theater in Chicago. In 1905 the black gambling lord of the South Side, Robert Motts, converted an insignificant backroom into a beer garden, ushering in a musical policy that pleased the black and white customers as well as the performers. After 1906 the immortal Tony Jackson, ragtime pianist and orchestra leader from New Orleans, was musical director. Unwilling to make alterations, Motts sold the place during the war, and the new Italian and Jewish owners immediately went into redesigning the balconies to conform to a night club setting. Linens, carpeting and various concessions were added, and a regular policy of featuring jazz bands pushed the club into its glory years. Louis Armstrong and King Joe Oliver received their first Northern exposure in a club whose very late hours of operation imitated the hot and spicy all-night jazz joints of Memphis and New Orleans.

The Casino Gardens was located just outside the Loop on Kinzie and North Clark Streets. Another beer hall on the skids, the Gardens, was purchased by gangsters from bootleg profits during the war. Its walls were flattened, dining room space extended, and more tables inserted. Billed as the "theatrical profession's most popular rendezvous," it attracted some of New York's more fabled personalities who came to hear the latest jazz sounds. Beginning in 1916 with the Original Dixieland Jazz Band, the house inaugurated a regular policy of employing jazz groups to turnaway business.[18]

Lastly, under this new ownership, the presence of women became acceptable. In fact, furnishings and ambience were planned to attract the woman's eye and appeal to her aesthetic judgment. A nation fast becoming urbanized after the war, and certainly more conscious of its varied racial components, sought a musical expression more related to this mood. Male-dominated Gaelic ballads, German lieders and the insipid songs of the Victorians were much too inappropriate to be entertaining. It is to the credit of the immigrant mobsters that they became catalysts in this changing taste for music.

But to promote jazz meant facing the glaring prejudices and hostilities which black musicians had been forced to endure from time immemorial. The extent of this hardship on the musicians is worth examining so as to more fully appreciate their mutual achievement.

Chapter IV

The Life of the Early Jazz Musician

Prefactory Speculation

Whether jazz music, as it came to be known after 1890, flourished in the South because of the presence of gangster support or in spite it will forever remain a mystery. Lacking adequate archival resources, any answer would be inconclusive. It is also pure guesswork what Southern jazzmen would have achieved in an environment completely devoid of the underworld. On the plus side of the ledger we at least have some rough idea of how jazz musicians fared by examining areas where mobs were rife and where they were non-existent. A useful time frame is the last thirty years of the 19th century, when much of what was to hatch by the 1920s was still in an incubator phase. During this interval there is evidence enough to suggest that wherever jazz was profitable to musician and entrepreneur, as in New Orleans and up-river in Memphis, the image of the underworld backer looms very large. In such settings the climate for gangsterism was pervasive, enabling artists to ply their trade with relative ease. The flip side of the coin was also true: places lacking mobs failed to sustain the music.

Furthermore, the collective misery of black people at this time was so great that any external support, regardless of the source, helped reverse the prevailing economic blahs. New Orleans sporting life tells us that creativity and musical invention improved in direct relationship to available opportunities, and these were thrown open by expansion of the underworld mobs themselves. In this assessment we are aided by Peter Burke's study of artistic developoment coinciding with support bestowed upon artists by the tyrants of the Italian Renaissance. Burke adds that:

Social forces cannot produce great artists but can frustrate them. Art and
literature flourish in the times and places in which abilities are frustrated least.

This chapter surveys a few of the limitations imposed on
the average Southern black musician after 1870 was
considerably ham-strung and repressed. In locations where
mobsters were fewest, musicians were kept well within a
narrow social radius or exposure, playing before listeners
whose similar plantation backgrounds could do little to alter
primitive technique or assure stardom. Under these conditions,
the impact of these players was limited. Simple survival
preoccupied the lives of most, and little room was left for
musical time-outs, much less merry-making. So it was that if
any sharp break of traditional patterns of constraint was
going to take place, it would have to originate beyond the black
community. By 1870 and seen in the guise of Italian and
Jewish foreigners, that cultural assistance was near at hand.
The arrival of this uncommitted faction, focusing on the
Italian underworld in New Orleans night life, and the immense
improvement they made on the lot of jazz musicians, must be
discussed on its own terms. But for the moment it is necessary
to consider what life was like for musicians beyond the mob-
influenced cities of the day.

The Black Existence

Life for black people after Reconstruction has never been
seen as a "bed of roses," however one views emancipation. The
period is perhaps best characterized as having fewer barbaric
excesses than what had come before, but one is hard put to
imagine emancipated life under more stifling conditions. By
1891 Southern blacks had fallen heir to complete political
disenfranchisement and total educational discrimination. The
vicious Jim Crow ordinances assaulted nearly every aspect of
black social and vocational life. Even the criminal statues were
elevated to a new degree of racist cunning.Blacks who ran
afoul of the system, and this included wandering troubadors,
found themselves physically immersed in the notorious
convict lease and county chain gang projects that have since

been immortalized in the annals of correctional tyranny. As late as 1905, W.A. Sinclair was writing:

This system is carried on year after year, and the colored man never gets ahead and so cannot leave his plantation prison-pen.

Racial hostility was adroitly managed by those who had most to gain from its vindictiveness. Aristocratic landlords of a dying world played upon the cutting edge of raw competition between poor white and black labor and beamed with ill-placed self confidence:

It is an aphorism that you can tell a "nigger's place" by its dirt and dilapidation. Poverty, ignorance, and lack of pride or ambition are general among the colored people. They simply exist, and the amenities of life are nearly altogether disregarded.[1]

Contempt of this magnitude prompted evil so lurid and hair-raising as to defy description. Walter White's accounts of this period attest to what life meant, and how horribly it ended for the black and defiant. Over 3500 blacks, nearly all males, suffered indignities and grisly brutalism before being lynched by frenzied white vigilantes between 1882 and 1927, mainly in Southern states and border allies. To this figure might be added tens of thousands of persons intimidated and cowed into utter submission; also the many pitiful cases where no tracks or records were ever made of their final demise. Such violence—which in no way can be attributed to the various underworlds—had a way of infecting black attitudes toward each other. Consequently, homicide rates for black people were five and six times higher than among Southern whites, themselves capable of initiating more bloodshed than anything witnessed during the mobster heyday for murder in the 1920s and 1930s.[2]

It was a demanding and wearisome life during the best of times. Scott Nearing's photographs taken before 1910 vividly recapture the anguishes specter of a countryside laid waste by the ravages of governmental neglect; of rickety shacks overrun with ill-clad children; of hastily improvised, inadequate health facilities; of unpaved roads leading nowhere amidst bare and drab surroundings; and of the endlessly recurring scenes of listless, forsaken young people, like war refugees, huddling together for warmth and comfort. Of all the age groups, these suffered the most. They had been born into an austere upcountry environment whose institutions deprived them of childhood, education and opportunity. In the fields and along the levees, their presence guaranteed an abundance of human twigs meant for exploitation.

Danger was always near at hand. Trombonist Trummy Young told an inquiring Stanley Dance (in the study of Earl Hines), his father, a railway worker, although severely injured from a boiler explosion, was steadfastly refused compensation, nor was the family aided in any way by a company indifferent to their needs. Such mishaps, and the inevitable company disregard, were all too common events. Even when intentions were good, violence to young people by concerned relatives was a regular event. Whipping of sons by fathers, ostensibly to instill vigilance during hazardous duty which most children encountered early in life, did little to soothe the psyche and promote tranquility. Such actions contributed greatly to the "predisposition to lethal violence" that has been an historical force in Southern regional culture.[3]

Surrounded by an array of social and economic constraints, many black youth had few pleasurable outlets. Inasmuch as sporting activities retarded a child's production quotient, these were hedged with taboos. Little wonder, then, that diversions, including drinking, dancing, even the playing of music of a non-religious nature, were discountenanced by the elders all the while youthful dissidents shaped these actions into approved avenues of protest. Seen as forbidden fruit, taverns, juke joints and other places that eventually began featuring high-spirited music were prolific in many Southern areas. The fact that itinerant musicians who were hired to perform exhibited a migratory recklessness toward traditional black life was not lost on young, adventurous listeners quick to imitate their rebellious and shady idols.

Whatever the economic and political reasons, many of which require lengthy historical explanation found elsewhere, thousands of blacks heeded the call of nature and packed up, heading Northward, before 1914. In 1890 nineteen percent of

Black America lived in the cities. By 1920 this figure had swollen to a third. And between 1915-1923, almost one million people had moved into the industrialized North, many abandoning crops still ripening in the fields. By 1925, Pittsburgh and Detroit, to name two such cities, virtually lily-white a few years earlier, could count on a labor force now 25% black. In the decade after 1910, black resettlement outnumbered its white counterpart by almost 300% in Cleveland, 50% in St. Louis and New York. Other cities from Philadelphia to Akron and Los Angeles witnessed equally vigorous surges during these years.[4]

The result was a tremendous demand for any cultural traces recalling the life left behind. Music and dancing, as well as gambling and drinking, figure largely here. For not only did they best express a former life, they suggest a hard rock of rebelliousness that underscored the intentions of the migrants themselves. Saturday nights had always been scenes of abrupt festivity and temporary musical relaxation. Moving North did little to abate this thirst. And racial oppression was still unrelenting, as seen by A. Epstein's 1915 portrait of black life in Pittsburgh.

To appease a seemingly insatiable urge, night clubs sprang up wherever space permitted. Ownership in the early days might be black or white, mob-owned or not, but they traded on the presence of many people living in nearby districts whose work weeks were considerably less than they had known in the South. Thus clubs remained open for very long hours. Since the clientele was mainly poor black, a group that had long disregarded the stiff Southern restrictions on drinking and had dabbled in petty illegal acts, there is little reason to think they cared who, or from what element, comprised night club ownership. It mattered little if underworld characters, much as they had known in Dixie,in time, came to achieve a preeminence in club management so long as the exuberant music from the South was exposed. Middle class audiences were further behind in this attitude.

The Early Black Magician

The first generation of post-Civil War black musical vagabonds burst forth on the scene like quail flushed from a thicket. Giles Oakley likens them to a "fluctuating community," travelling from this plantation to anon, garnering what few crumbs there might be, especially around harvest time when entertainment was in order. Ominously, the release from bondage meant not only awkward mobility for these men, but an urgent need to become self-sufficient, whatever the cost. With most districts devastated by war, implicit was a continual moving on, and many starved along the way. There is no reason to believe that the drop-out rate of these artists was any fewer than nine in every ten.

Lacking income that would enable them to visit even the most modest of towns, towns scarcely able to support their own motley collection of entertainers, these simple strollers performed to very restricted acclaim. Goats and pigs might outnumber paying customers. Black musicians followed railway tracks weaving behind backwoods communities, oblivious to bystanders or wardships alike.

Hostile environments forced artists to adopt various ways of escaping although these might be just as ruinous. Blues singer Bessie Smith, whose life experiences were by no means exceptional for the contemporary black artist, emerged from conditions of bone-crunching poverty to be discovered in a rough gin-mill in a no-less dismal section of Selma, Alabama. Her biographer, Chris Albertson, plainly writes that the conditioning she received in the dangerous places where she toiled led to excesses of alcohol which prematurely cut short her life. Paul Oliver's inventive study of other blues musicians reveals a dreary repetition of such stories. He notes the brutish environment which severely hampered musical development:

Many barrelhouse and blues pianists played in the company towns of the levee, turpentine and sawmill camps of the forest belt.... It was hard, dangerous, dirty work...rough and beyond the law.

Interviewed by the BBC, bluesman Little Brother spoke of his observations in the honky tonks of the logging camps:

Those were rough places....Most fellows carried German Lugers. They'd kill somebody and then stand on them and keep gambling.[5]

Black anthropologist Zora Neale Hurston noted how lax were the laws in these remote encampments and how rampant the resulting crime. Anything might happen in such unprotected areas:

All of these places have plenty of men and women who are fugitives from justice. The management asks no questions. They need help. . . . In some places the "law" is forbidden to come on the premises to hunt for malefactors. . . . The wheels of industry must move, and if these men don't do the work, who is there to do it?

The successful musician was the one best able to translate his skills into everyday labor. This meant setting aside his instrument until the opportunity to play presented itself. This might not come often. And non-musical work could be back-breaking field labor or drudgery in the timber camps and along the railways, with all the dangerous elements just mentioned. Even in these cases money was hard to come by and most artists depended solely on "throw money," or coins tossed at them by their equally-poor audience. Some believed hard work aided in playing. Guitarist Leadbelly held great store by field work since "working in the fields gave the musician the rhythm he needed for his music."[6] Few, however, shared his enthusiasm. Brownie McGhee, blues singer from Tennessee, recollects how the fingers and hands of a musician were easily ruined beyond recovery by performing common labor, logging or sharecropping. Not to mention loss of life. Singer Homesick James spoke for hundreds of colleagues who fled this shattering domestication:

With that hot Tennessee sun out there in the fields, I wasn't going to stay out there and get baked. That's the reason I left home. . .[if I wanted] to play the guitar.[7]

Weary, impoverished, dirty and without prospects, these strollers trudged from one work site to another in search of jobs. They certainly brought relief to tension-edged laborers, although the hours were long, the audiences not always appreciative, and the risk of falling victim to the wrath of white management was high. Violence was rife and affected everyone. Tyrannical white overseers, deciding as they did who might play, when and for how long, were known to contradict their own orders with unpardonable rage. R.J. Lockwood recalls his experience with a Mississippi plantation owner who gave his consent to play a barnyard dance only to suddenly whip around and ban the party, bust Lockwood's guitar and toss him off the property in a fit of overpreening authority.[8]

Far from main towns and brightly-lit saloons, scores of musicians chose the unrewarding life of the small but familial variety caravan, rodeo or medicine show. Jazz musicians such as Gene Sedric, Lester Young, Thelonious Monk and Zue Robertson (trombonist for the Kit Carson Troupe) graduated from shows that wound their way into the dark regions. Veteran drummer Jo Jones claims it was a life replete with everything but redeeming features. Stifling heat offset bitter cold, dangerously strong alcohol mixed with questionable food, while violence and unexpectedly poor road conditions placed every trouper's life in daily peril.[9]

The patient and the persevering who refused to jettison their careers could always stand on street corners and road beds in the hopes of attracting attention and getting something to eat. Drinks and party engagements might also be had but the price in terms of sheer dogged endurance was rarely cheap. As late as 1929 (if in fact not much later), musicians were still playing in the streets in the hope of locating work. Clifford Hayes' Stompers serves as an example. Their outdoors performances in Louisville were free for the listening, but they served as advertisement for social directors of liquor stores who roamed the streets ready to hire a band cheaply for the evening.[10] Some promoters gave the men alcohol and food while taking 40% or more of whatever the band was paid.[11]

Every town had its own circumscribed "darktown." Here the gambling tsars ruled nasacent night life with an iron claw that throttled unacceptable styles of music. Oakley provides excellent glimpses of this firmness in action for cities like

Dallas, Memphis and Atlanta. Musical success, even where the climate was agreeable, still fell within narrow perimeters.

The atmosphere inside a Southern juke joint can only be likened to a scene from Dante's *Inferno*. Broken-down food stands, barnyard taverns, lean-tos and fly-ridden cafes doubled as joints where on a hot and humid evening the internal frenzy sapped every patron's intelligence. Hurston visited many of these eyesores during her Florida peregrinations in the early 1930s, commenting:

After dark the jooks came into people's lives. Songs are born out of feelings with an old beat-up piano, or a guitar for a midwife...and paynight rocks with music and laughter and dancing and fights.

The general mood balanced on the edge of a knife, and this was used often. Opinion has it that as late as 1900 one might look in vain for a safe and decent night spot throughout the lower Southern states, from Atlanta to Galveston, excluding New Orleans.[12] Many stories document the rash of fights and homicides and the flurry of lovers' quarrels that led to tragedy. One such weekend dance ended in disaster, as seen in this 1931 press headline:

Dance hall is scene of killing Saturday night. One dead and two injured as Negro ex-convict runs wild with knife.[13]

Grievances and pent-up frustrations boiled over under the pressure valve release caused by over-drinking. The presence of women added the final touch for whirlwind finishes in the early morning hours. It is a sad commentary on local life generally that musicians, already pictured as castoffs and unfortunates, were seen by women as passports to fame, travel and fortune, thereby invoking the anger of male friends and husbands who felt little compunction about slicing a musician's throat. In fact, the bandstands upon which the entertainers worked made them perfect targets for assault. Knifings and razor cuts, flying bottles, even bullets, ended (in one form or another) the playing nights of more than a few rural performers. In these arenas even innocence could be fatal. While doing her cultural research, Hurston found herself interviewing a local guitarist only to evade death by inches from his knife-toting girl-friend who had viewed the researcher as competition.

Many customers believed entertainment could only be had at someone else's expense and set about a night's pleasure accordingly. Thus clubs were forced to protect their bands. Some did this with chicken wire, stringing a canopy above the dais to shield performers from overhead bombardment. This wire served perfectly in entangling large pieces of glassware but there was always risk of injury from small splinters. Shards of glass made ideal weapons and nobody on either side of a bandstand was truly safe. Killings were so common in the Memphis Monarch Cafe, Oakley reports, that bodies were simply dumped outside to be collected by undertakers making late-night runs. Oakley claims it was a club which easily earned its sobriquet, "The Castle of Missing Men." Of the Atlanta clubs one blues musician writes:

It was a tame Saturday night on Decatur Street if there were only six razor operations performed and if only four persons were found in the morgue on Sunday morning.[14]

Some places were so rough that beer had to be served up in discrete little paper cups. Louis Armstrong recalls his early playing days in the clubs just outside New Orleans. Here Saturday nights were synonymous with mayhem as unruly levee workers bounced beer mugs off one another's heads. Armstrong claims every form of vice was on brilliant display by men and women who cared little what happened. Hardly recipient to the adulation which later was his, Armstrong and his players were greeted with noise, disrespect and constant interruptions. He tell us:

Men fought like circle saws and bottles were flying over the bandstand...with lots of just plain common shooting and cutting.[15]

Hurston was characteristically more descriptive as she reported:

Dancing the square dance. Dancing the scronch. Dancing the belly-rub. Knocking the right hat off the wrong head, and backing it up with a switch-blade....It seemed that anybody who had any fighting to do decided to settle up then and there. Switchblades, ice picks, and old fashioned razors were out....Maybe somebody stops the fight before the two switchblades go together, maybe nobody can.

Then there was the unremitting, unrelieved toil associated with the job. Playing all night in an obscure joint in a misbegotten mill camp hardly appealed to an artist's sense of aesthetics. And salaries were always subject to argument and deceit. Musicians learned to keep an eye on the man with the gate receipts lest he vanish into the night, leaving a penniless and empty-handed entertainer in the lurch. Guitarist Eddie Boyd was earning one dollar a night in the early 1930s, playing every night in the week in a murky Southern tonk. "These conditions were pretty bad," he reflected, "but hardly different from those of 20 years ago."[16]

Racial hostility always threatened the friendless artist. In an age of Jim Crow lynch laws and Black Codes, racism had a frightening way of surfacing in everyday life. No jazzman was without a war story. Wells tells of at least one musician, drummer for the Whispering Serenaders of Gold, who was castrated and died for teaching girls a dance step in Miami, Florida in the 1920s. Gene Sedric, saxophonist for Fats Waller, writes of his own hair-raising experiences:

Many times we'd come into town, check into a hotel and actually hear them in the next room planning how they were going to start the fights and shooting where we were going to play that night. Some towns had special prices that were twice as high for bands coming through.[17]

Hines is quoted in Dance's book, agreeing that prices shot up for musicians visiting these outposts. He also noted how poor and out-of-tune most pianos and other equipment were during road engagements. So bad that "I'd be playing in one key and the band would be playing in another."

Black tent shows and travelling troupes fared badly. As a child in the early 1920s, Lena Horne nearly walked into a lynching party of one black troupe outside Jacksonville, Mississippi. "Travelling blacks had no friends to protect them in strange towns," she writes, "and were always fair game for the mobs." Edmond Hall of the Claude Hopkins Orchestra remembers an incident in Birmingham, Alabama where the band was refused its job until a rope was stretched lengthwise down the center of the dance floor, tactically separating both races while dancing. Other ways of keeping races apart were more ingenious. Pianist Gus Perryman recalls one club in Gulfport, Mississippi where the band (in 1919) was suspended on a landing midway between two floors—the ground floor being for whites was smooth and tidy whereas a roughly-hewn and tattered floor was reserved upstairs for blacks.[18] Some clubs refused to deal with the issue and simply had one night for blacks and another for whites.

Partitions, indifferent audiences, violence, the possibility of being defrauded by a club owner, plus the spectre of appearing in front of white hecklers and pranksters could jolt the most indomitable. Even the friends of jazz could be worrisome. Cornetist Bunk Johnson quivered at the thought that some patrons to the Southern gin-mills "didn't bathe more than once in six months." And pianist Gavin Bushnell tells of the time he was kidnapped by an admiring but knife-threatening Louisville madam and coerced into working in her bordello for four days until he summoned up enough nerve to escape.[19]

The jazz musician before 1920 chose a profession without much social grace. Money, respectability and tolerable living arrangements were pipedreams. The vulgar surroundings which comprised his factory have already been discussed. And to middle class families of both colors, he was a leperous deviant best kept at the far end of a pole.[20] Pianist Jelly Roll Morton remarked that "black folks never had the idea they wanted a musician. In their minds a musician was a tramp." Writer Ralph Ellison's ambitions as a jazz artist in Oklahoma City of the 1920s were thwarted by respectable parents who considered it a "backward, low-class form of expression."[21] Black intellectuals, according to Nathan Huggins, long chose to ignore the achievements of jazz artists, while the *Journal of Negro History* refused to print a single article on the subject between 1916-1946 and the black newspaper *The Chicago*

Messenger ran at least one anti-jazz article in the 1920s.

Forced by reasons of poverty and racism, neglect and snobbery, jazzmen played the most disreputable places, further denigrating their image. In many cities, according to Pops Foster (as told to Tom Stoddard), musicians were under enormous pressure to discover decent accommodations before nightfall found them shivering in the cold. Prospective landladies turned thumbs-down once the secret of their vocation was out; nor could "decent women" be counted on for support. As late as the '30s the bands of Noble Sissle and Jimmy Lunceford, both successes in New York and Chicago, encountered a long line of refusals when they went on the road. Sissle's group managed to locate space in a circus compound at Terre Haute, Indiana, sleeping on firm ground with animals nervously pacing just above their bedrolls. Lunceford's orchestra "often found themselves in towns devoid of hotel and restaurant facilities for blacks."[23] After one performance in Lexington, Kentucky, Ethel Waters had to make sleeping arrangements in a horse stable.

To compound these indignities, and as a conseqence, early artists were ordered to appear wrapped in simple clown outfits. There are many photographs showing illustrious musicians rigged out in bizarre trappings—Kid Ory, King Oliver and Jelly Roll Morton, to name only three. Tom Brown's Jazz Band, a white group, was denied work until they agreed to wear gaudy shirts and overalls, straw hats and other showy costumes while squeezing their instruments in imitation of barnyard animals. Cornetist Freddie Keppard earned the bulk of his early income mocking a horse. Drummers were often called upon to stuff drumsticks in their nostrils or dangle them from their ears, looking like some kind of wild witch doctor. Other artists waddled like ducks, leered like cannibals, and in many other ways acted ridiculous. Promoters believed these antics were good for business and excited and amused an otherwise benumbed or belligerent audience. As a result, the jazz musician of 1900 was considered a "mediocre entertainer," and, as Ralph Berton describes, was "lumped in with dog acts and vaudeville hoofers." We do know that as late as 1925 the Wolverines were playing behind a trained seal act.

Sadly, the early Northern receptions were but meager improvements on what has already been said. Urban jazz musicians, like bad weather in wintertime, made friends with virtually no one. Fellow musicians fumbled around trying to copy the sound and then, failing that, feared competition for the few available jobs; highbrows disdained a music without a time-honored European pedigree; and bigots despised the end product—the intermingling of races. Social observers with little enough cultural awareness smugly labelled the music degenerate, vulgar and impure, with dire warnings forecast for the downfall of decent white women:

It was not uncommon to see white girls with colored men, especially jazz band musicians, who seemed to exert a magnetic appeal for Caucasian women all over the country.[24]

Policemen from the old school often made the most biased observations and constituted the toughest enforcers. Here is one example of a New York Irish cop's view of a downtown "black and tan":

Whatever sign of womanhood that might have been on the women's faces once is gone now.... There are no bounds to license. It takes a good deal to satisfy the best of the dull-sensed Negroes in the room. They dance until the perspiration rolls down in streams on their faces, and they drink until they are stupid.[25]

Musicians' Unions resisted fiercely and many established an endless series of roadblocks. The Chicago chapter, which through the dominance of its Irish bloc in political affairs, was a true picture of most unions at the time, called jazz "nothing but cheap and shameless," and stood resolutely opposed to its dispersion in the early years. Some unions were determined to minimize work for blacks and keep foolish whites from getting too close. Most unions were very strict toward allowing strange musicians to obtain work. The New York and Philadelphia chapters, for instance, not only had exclusionary clauses restricting the playing of jazz but campaigned actively against any places unwisely hiring these men to entertain. Out-of-towners actually faced the threat of physical reprisal from the Detroit crew who provided several test cases as warnings.[26] C. Lawrence Christensen's dated analysis exists as a study of the many silly little by-laws the unions used when restricting jobs. Such restraints were indeed successful before 1920 and before underworld employers began attacking the intolerance of these collusive restrictions.

The jazz musician's simple desire to carry on with his trade, quietly dismissing ignoble barriers, is an object lesson in integrity and commitment. The measure of his strength was so great as to withstand constant storms of fearful, deafening abuse. Indeed, only in his music could so hearty an artist escape the bondage cast by his secular surroundings. But his faith also furnishes us with two solid reasons why he chose to align himself with underworld promoters. First, because it was enough simply to play somewhere with a minimum of discomfort and confinement; these men gave him the opportunity. Second, because mobsters actually liked the music and sought out the artists as colleagues, even sharing in their electrically-charged performances. No single managerial group had ever before lent such assistance, an unexpected but gratefully received festure.

With most spectators taking little more than a passing interest in these performers, some not above reviling them with rebuke, only the more ambitious, amoral or militant black was willing to adopt the musician's avocation. He certainly knew of the desolation around him. Yet these attitudes, too, by laying down a bedrock of rebelliousness and defiance of social convention, enabled jazzmen to unthinkingly consort with underworld figures. Both had convict records to compare, and some of them had had encounters with violence. Nearly every performer, (as well as gangster,) had a grab-bag of stories replete with misdeeds and mistakes. Such similar records led artists and mobsters to accept one another almost unquestioningly.

Given the conditions of control and humiliation that plagued musicians for so long, newfound mobster patronage could hardly be shunned. And its first appearance, by our records, seems to have taken place in New Orleans in the 1870s and 1880s. At least by that time they were brought indoors and into cleaner, more cheerful surroundings. Through sheer obstinacy, the underworld sponsors began grafting the music onto a previously unexplored urban night life scene. First it was done for personal enjoyment. Later it became big business, as a wider slice of the public desired both listening to the music of gangsters and emulating these folk heroes themselves. But in the beginning it was all hunt-and-peck and a gamble fraught with risk. It now seems appropriate to examine this milieu and the early reasons why both groups managed to work so well together.

Chapter V

It All Started in New Orleans

Home of a Brash and Migratory Music

In 1896, shortly before embarking on a trip to Honduras, short story writer O. Henry paused long enough in the French Quarter of New Orleans to remark:

The Latin races are peculiarly adapted to be victims of the phonograph. They have the artistic temperament. They yearn for music and color and gaiety. They give money to the organ-grinder man...when they're months behind with the grocer.

To him Latins included the very many Sicilians who then populated the French Quarter. Indeed, no better example of the Latin's artistic peculiarities and musical gaiety can be found than in New Orleans of the late 19th century. This particular group, many of whom were Italians with ties to the underworld, blacks and Creoles, together spun common talents and musical expression around a spindle to fashion the proletarian music we have come to know as jazz. Oddly, this relationship, that is the one uniting Sicilian underworld characters and black jazz musicians, must have been common gossip at the time although little enough has been preserved in print. So little, in fact, that we are naturally inclined to consider jazz and gangsterism a phenomenon of the 1920s, along with cloche hats and raccoon coats.

But this inclination completely distorts what actually transpired and discounts historical associations that developed along intimate lines many decades before the birth of the flapper.

I have already suggested that black music, left to its own impecunious devices, would have starved to death long before the advent of its popularity. Sudden adjustments were

79

mandatory if the music was ever to survive the doldrums it found itself in by 1890 or 1900—not solely in terms of musical invention and technique but in the areas of musical promotion and presentation as well. Innovations had to take place in the way jazz was shown—not on street corners and barnyard haystacks—but in intimate surroundings that heightened its appeal and made musicians enjoy performing.

This meant changes in ownership and purveyors of nightly entertainmment. But by examining this field of endeavor one opens up a can of worms. For this unorthodox side of any city's night life—and the one in New Orleans is the best recorded—represents an uncharted and neglected field of social study. We possess simply no way of accurately gauging the extent of night life in the years preceding the rush of jazz groups generally. Still, common-sense tells us it was all important even if recorded evidence does not. Few underworld clubs either solicited publicity on an active basis or attracted people willing to admit to such. Bordellos were the leading publicists of the city's nether life, but alas pianists were frequently the only musicians these people were willing to hire, and they kept to themselves.

Precisely when and where these two groups first met is open to speculation. The Tulane University Jazz Library in New Orleans was unable to pin down a time, I contend it took place sometime before 1880. Unlike European composers, none of the early generations of post-Civil War jazzmen or Sicilian gangsters who eventually settled here kept what we could call diaries, that have been found; that is, of the relatively few who were even capable of writing. For their part, gangsters were never a storehouse of readily given knowledge. Nor were these men educated and given to dictating memoirs. What little general information we possess comes from the late 1930s when, almost as an afterthought, folk historians belatedly ferreted out musical pioneers for whatever they could remember about the foggy past. Inaccuracies and omissions notwithstanding, reporters chose not to ask questions pertinent to this study, or if they did, the venerable jazz artists quietly sidestepped answering.

Press clippings are equally one-sided and no less

unreliable. Professor Kendall wrote of these years as an era of ethnic suppression everywhere, including the press. Newspaper publishers for the eight leading local dailies employed not a single black or Italian to cover news in which they were either principal victims or assailants.[1] In their absence I have had to take from a variety of less likely elements to build my stone and mortar; criminological and musical studies, economic trends, art histories, even impressions found in guide books.

*   *   *

The previous chapter alluded to the terrible conditions a black musician encountered wandering throughout the Deep South after 1870. Many jazz histories have recorded the fact that there was abundant talent, particularly after 1890, with hundreds upon hundreds of itinerant strollers touring the provinces in search of work. Mainly they played where and as often as joints, distantly spaced, could afford them. But only in the relatively larger cities could customers demand and gambler money converge in sufficient quantities to permit the hiring of bands on anything more than a spontaneous basis. Nevertheless, even in the bigger towns, only a handful of men could survive solely on their playing, no matter how close the audience was to sharing their life's experiences. This was because in the two decades following the Civil War, traditional night life interests kept a firm grip on who played what.

New Orleans, for one city, stood ready to play its valuable part in the development of jazz. Indeed its role as midwife is ancient history and many studies dwell on this point. In part an explanation can be found in the looseness of life which the Spanish and French ushered in during the 18th century. Certainly the alternating presence of these two urbane powers, spanning 200 years, leant an atmosphere of sensual decadence to local adventurers, be they black or white. It was a city smeared with nihilistic pursuits which a Spanish Attorney-General vainly attempted to regulate in 1800. In his effort to control the mounting crime activity festering in the city's older districts, he made the closing of dance halls and niteries a matter of number one priority. Despairingly, his own notes reflect the kind of disorderly cabarets which thwarted his best efforts:

Places of riot and intoxication. . . . Open all day and night. . . and crowded with soldiers, sailors, laborers, and slaves. . .where drinking, gambling, prostitution and dancing are without end.[2]

Henry A. Kmen writes that the most lively aspects of this night life was its political nature. Inflammatory debates leading to riots were nightly happenings in the 1810s and centered chiefly on the unlikely subject of dancing: Night spots became battle zones for irate customers—English and French—who fought tooth and nail over which country's dance music would be played on a particular evening. By 1835 no fewer than 30 desegregated ballrooms and a myriad of grog shops dispensed bright music along with their nightly potions. It wasn't jazz but the moods and rhythms were getting close. This scene expanded greatly during the city's pre-War golden period of the 1850s, just before falling into shadows and disuse by war's end. For by 1865 another type of night time entrepreneur, genteel and more interested in hanging onto a dying aristocratic culture, made its appearance.[3]

So it was that two or more generations before the appearance of Sicilian immigrants and underworld figures (which we are prepared to date from 1863), wandering musicians of all races were attracted to a Delta port whose radiance, tolerance and carnival-like atmosphere leant a festive air of opportunity. Extensive criminal activities also meant quick ways of making money were near-at-hand.

The Sicilian Mobster in New Orleans

New Orleans was a city with tremendous charm and cultural beauty in 1875. It radiantly amplified its broad French heritage. George Washington Cable was a typical poetical admirer:

A city of villas and cottages. . .of umbrageous gardens. . .streets shaded by forest trees, haunted by song birds and fragrant with a wealth of flowers that never fails a day in the year.[4]

Despite the city's outer charm and fragrance, one didn't have to remain long to know it was a catchment area for many of the world's races and peoples. This fact provided a disturbing backdrop for local politics and social affairs. Some idea of its interest for immigrants can be gained from a few figures. In 1860 New Orleans ranked sixth nationally in percentage of foreign born, with little apparent change two generations later.[5] Yet regardless of wealth and station, newcomers to the city drifted into pockets unofficially demarcated for their residency, picking up the heat of rival politics from their neighbors.

Baedecker's 1893 *Guidebook* spells this out in more detail. Anglo-Americans represented 18% of the population in New Orleans and shared an uptown garden district formerly known as the Faubourg Ste. Marie, converting it into a business and residential zone. Its knowledge of black life was derived exclusively from the many visible chain gangs responsible for keeping the rambling streets clean. Germans totalled 15% and retired behind the neat and orderly Faubourg Marigny, some distance away, desirably remote owing to the city's limited transportation services. The Irish colony (14%) had been awarded the aptly-named Irish Channel area, characterized by intense gang warfare and street violence, and cruel poverty. Lastly there was the French Quarter, a district of fading Creole glamor and deteriorating tenements, lately a catchment area for outcasts. It was here that disparate groups of rural blacks, West Country Creoles, Mexican drifters, Jews and Sicilians (9% combined), and flotsam of all nationalities sought refuge.

The Sicilians were influxing noticeably. According to one report, by 1900 the city's Italian population was at an all-time high. In that year an Italian reporter wrote: "The Sicilians have always had a preference for New Orleans and their colony is regarded with pride and hope at home."[6]

The heavy influx of Sicilians can best be explained by the combination of luring job prospects abroad and violent turmoil at home. With domestic conditions so bad, many became

willing dupes to questionable employment opportunities
dangled before them by Southern plantation owners and
agents themselves climbing out of the disorder of war and
reconstruction.[7] The bait was indeed alluring, for
topographically speaking, many similarities exist between
this region of the Louisiana Basin and Sicily. In longitudinal
terms, barely a few degrees separate the two sections, both
relaxed by soft trade winds from nearby seas. Similarities like
this spurred resettlement.

Almost from the beginning these strangers presented
problems their plantation owner sponsors had failed to foresee.
Professor Cunningham writes a convincing argument that the
original intent of the Southern politicians was to lure onto
America's shores a more docile labor force than the black
workers whose belligerence was becoming extremely
uncomfortable to local aristocrats. It was thought that
Italians, poor and ignorant, would make an effective
counterbalance and aid in their own manipulation.

Whilst many Sicilians accepted the bait and left their own
impoverished country, a sizeable percentage refused to go
much beyond the port district of New Orleans; those that did
invade the upcountry provinces soon disassociated themselves
from projects designed to suppress the blacks. Cunningham's
patient article attributes this reaction to a racial animosity
simply lacking in the first waves of Sicilians; ethnic hatred like
this was a totally new experience. Roger W. Shugg says very
much the same thing.[8]

Familiar lines of urban work were soon adopted by a
people relatively uninterested in taking part in a racial chess
game. For them jobs as laborers, longshoremen, fruit peddlers,
fishermen and truck farmers were accepted with alacrity. But
refusals to endorse a role assigned them by the dominant
landed and political class inevitably led to trouble and official
retaliation was not long in coming. Employment was very
difficult to come by. And denied entry into most work spheres,
it wasn't long before most Italians found themselves being
squeezed into the squalid, black-occupied French Quarter.
Those in more desolate sectors fared even worse:

In the little town of Tallulah, Louisiana, the coming of five Sicilian

storekeepers disturbed the native whites because the Italians dealt mainly
with the Negroes and associated with them nearly on terms of equality. They
violated the white man's code. In a few years a quarrel over a goat resulted in
the lynching of all five. In another locality the whites tried to keep the color line
sharp and clear by barring Italian children from the white schools.[9]

Petty incidents everywhere fractured into examples of
pagan brutality, and we are reminded of the vigilante justice
toward many Italians in New Orleans in 1891. An unsolved
murder soon led to the lynching of 11 Italians and the jailing of
many others in a case the Court and police never could unravel.
The press was an echo of the crowd, describing "Those grimy
Sicilians...whose low, regressive countenances and slovenly
attire proclaimed their brutal natures."[10]

By 1880 the French Quarter was an immense eyesore, far
removed from what wealthy bohemians would make of it after
1928. Arnold Genthe's photographs of this area, taken in 1926,
bear witness to a dismal landscape presided over by equally
pathetic-looking inhabitants. Kendall called it an "Italian
preserve." Sidewalks were little more than crude planks and
during the rainy season the streets quickly turned into vast
muddy pools. Water left standing became the breeding grounds
for pestilent insects that introduced a variety of lethal tropical
diseases. To this was added the local custom of tossing garbage
to the area's wild dog population which roamed the streets to
forage. Morsels left by the animals soon decomposed in the hot
and steamy climate, emitting a noxious stench blanketing the
quarter for miles around. Little wonder that the highest
mortality rate in the entire Delta Basin was located in the
French Quarter. Critics knew where to apportion blame:

The worst part of this quarter is inhabited by the lower-class Sicilians, the
Mafia, and Negroes, an area of gin, cheap wine, and dope.... There were scenes
that duplicated Naples and Palermo—long lines of family wash hanging out
on once-lovely iron lacework balconies...half-naked children..old, dark, fat
men and women sleeping on their stoops...the odor of garlic and of rotten fruit
everywhere.[11]

Amidst this muck was a similar brand of politics—rotten
and corrupt to the core. Defiance of the law had been as much a

part of the city's history as the lush foliage cloistering its riverbanks. In fact, some of the worst excesses are dateable to the early 1700s. But the taste for illegality and official venality which surfaced in the years preceding the Civil War lingered on to bedevil the aspirations of newly-settling Sicilians. There is little doubt that the last 30 years of the 19th century were underscored by intensely violent and corrupt general elections, a steady waste of public monies on visibly worthless projects designed to benefit a few, and a complicated network of graft-taking—especially in the vice areas—that allowed many a magistrate and public official to spend his final days in splendor.[12]

Given such grim surroundings, the Italians suffered indignities and daily racial attacks on a par with blacks. Crime rates in both districts were much higher than elsewhere as were their general mortality rates. Like blacks, Sicilians, by being denied entry into legitimate circles, found themselves challenging the hated Irish for whatever skimpy, menial labor would be found along the wharves. The upshot was a series of convulsive skirmishes between these alley cats, squaring off for the meager spoils no one else wanted.[13]

Taking all these factors into consideration—the bigotry, the violence and hostility with the Irish (which hastened self-protection alliances), the job freezes and a general political climate that favored unsavory business dealings—we can easily understand why organized Italian crime mobs flowered in New Orleans.

In actual fact, and using the best available evidence, the initial appearance of the Mafia (or any Sicilian underworld forerunners of whatever title), is pegged at sometime during the early 1860s. Herbert Asbury spent many years probing the 19th century urban gangs and he estimated the surfacing of the Mafia in New Orleans around 1861, soon growing to an impressive size. By 1885, he claims, their inner membership totalled 300 with many more on the periphery. Asbury quotes an 1869 report by the *New Orleans Times:*

The French Quarter is infested by well-known and notorious Sicilian murderers, counterfeiters, and burglars who in the last months have formed a sort of general co-partnership or stock company for the plunder and disturbance of the city.[14]

Support for Asbury's viewpoint is both widespread and recurring. Frederic Sondern's study indicates crime societies were well-entrenched by the late 1880s and that black and Italian dockworkers colluded in refusing to unload a ship's lading without prior approval of the Mafia organizations. The Rome correspondent for the *New York Post* and a writer for *Harper's Weekly* both agreed that by 1891 New Orleans was the seat for Mafia power in America. Jackson's analysis of the city crime patterns reached this conclusion: "Mafia-related organized crime, in the form of gambling, lotteries, and prostitution, defied all efforts at regulation in the 1890s." Martin Williams claims the entire entertainment scene was under the direct thumb of the Italian societies between 1869 and 1891 while a 1939 article in *Ken* magazine attests to the tenacity of their reign: "The Mafia still controls what remains of the resorts that make New Orleans jazzy and wide-open."[15]

Italian Underworld Influence on New Orleans Night Life

This pervasiveness of the Italian crime societies over the musical scene in New Orleans before 1900 is especially important for the continuation of this study and thus requires further discussion. But before attempting this probe, the fast-changing musical and cabaret life of the city needs to be set in their historical contexts. By this approach trends can be discovered which slowly forced traditional purveyors of entertainment out and allowed underworld types to make their appearance.

Professor Kavolis has provided us with three sociological axioms of artistic creation which, when applied to this turbulent period, leads to a better understanding of its transitional importance for both jazz and its underworld promoters in New Orleans. First, he states that any large change in an economy is likely to result in strong creative influences on art styles. Dynamic forces found in free competition and active trade find their corollary in the world of art even during moments of economic depression, as was the case in New Orleans after 1870.

Post-Civil War influences on the city's night life and among the existing entrepreneurs and of its formal musical scene were sharply emphatic. Under the cumulative waves of disaster, New Orleans night life shuddered and burst. War, Federal occupation of the city, Reconstruction and the unprecedented series of economic depressions during the years 1870-1893 shook the aristocratic veneer which governed night life. High society orchestras, quadroon balls and haughty musical societies buckled under the dead weight of declining values. Along with other gaudy displays from the past, many were driven to the wall. Gone were the days when a visit to the French Quarter revealed "costly jewels, elaborate costumes, lovely women, gallant gentlemen, and magnificent music." In the words of an earlier edition of the *Daily Picayune*: "Of amusement we are likely to have a dearth.... The clubs are broken up. We shall not have many balls or parties."[16]

Almost overnight, as if by signal from some fated hand, money stopped circulating and commercial ventures in cotton, grain and slaves began plummeting. With the city's venerable staples for a good life in short demand, major banking firms refused to brace the panic. Roger W. Shugg and Charles L. DuFour paint individually drab pictures for these years which gravely affected wages, inspired a general strike and sharply constricted lending practices by the few investment and banking concerns still afloat. Corresponding to this financial lament, entertainment revenues plunged. As no class was spared, even lower class cabarets and bordellos faced bankruptcy and debtor's prison. Personal setbacks spilled over into music, affecting the players as well. The plummeting resulting fortunes of club owners led to an inadequacy of promotion, poverty, confusion and disorganization among musicians, and unsound business practices by the Old Guard which LeRoy Jones considers when he evaluates the very low quality of black music of these years. Overall standards changed little until the ascendancy of the Sicilian and Jewish underworld characters of the 1880s.

Secondly, Kavolis points to a concept he entitles "value orientation" and its link with whoever is emerging in the business world who might influence economic motivation in an art form. More particularly, Kavolis is interested in their cultural and musical persuasions. After 1880 and the decline of the less viable amusement centers, more aggressive businessmen, many of them Italian, emerged to fill gaps left in the city's night life. To a great extent this was happening in the French quarter where Italian small businessmen, criminal or otherwise, were quickly adding to their control of petty businesses, striking down nearby Irish rivals in their pursuit.[17] Thus the scene was all but set for musically-inclined Italians and Jews to invade the world of jazz as both performers and presentationists. Others feel likewise:

The importation of Italians, many of whom turned out to be first-class musicians and teachers, and the legalization of gambling in Louisiana after 1869, both gave an impetus to the musical and night life scene which aided in the later development of jazz.[18]

By 1885 a new type of investor of music had emerged, without regard for formal rules and prissy etiquette. With capital derived from unorthodox sources and underworld investments, he was in an enviable position inasmuch as his competition was limited to traditional money sources that were all but dried out. So it was the Sicilian underworld power brokers, who with their many kinship arrangements that are so typical of South European societies, were prepared to offer newer forms of night life to New Orleanians.

For traditionalists it was indeed a dark day, knowing now that proper lineage no longer could counter money earned from gambling and prostitution vices. Nor were official restrictions and surcharges adequate to stem the tide. Only the Sicilian mobs appeared willing to pay the exorbitant taxes levied against nightly pleasures after 1870 in an effort to prevent them altogether: $100 for saloons featuring music, $200 if singing was allowed, and $300 for stage shows and other pernicious divertisements.[19] Rose claims this actually had the unintended effect of eliminating the rank amateur shows put on by individuals in favor of more organized shows controlled by better organized syndicates.[20]

Little wonder that the appearance of these Mafia-backed night life operators excited feelings of wrath and rancor from the city's feudal class. The very mobility and urbane nonchalance observable in the vice lords contrasted sharply with an ethos that was fast wilting away. Applied to night clubs and saloons and other small entertainment businesses that Italians and Jews might enter without facing colossal barriers, the mobsters dramatized the assault of new men wheeling and dealing as had never been known before. Still, it was a success story not without its dangers. Not unlike the prospering Jewish class in Germany of Bismarck's time, the Mafia "became the magnet for all the malice, frustration, and resentment that festered" in New Orleans society."[21]

Kavolis's third and last insight concerns art and rapid urban growth. He says that tendencies toward experimentation and variety in art forms are closely associated with periods of rapid urban growth at the price of community cohesiveness. This surely seems true for New Orleans in the years 1865-1895. Excluding New York, the port of New Orleans developed into the largest of the country's embarcation points. Here thousands of aliens and black upcountry migrants crowded haphazardly and unplanned into the squalid, fast-degenerating French Quarter in search of shelter. To this new world these transplants brought adaptations and changes in art forms completely overturning the more staid styles in vogue. Burke, another student of this concept, discusses the importance of outsiders, social as well as geographic, as the true artistic innovators of the Renaissance.

Sicilian communities after 1865 were far from cohesive. Practically as soon as they descended the gangplanks they were hurled into the trenches, as it were, assuming roles allocated to them as part of a never-ending ethnic battle. We know little of the details, much less the number involved, but it was a common sight enacted in most American ports during this era. No sooner did Sicilian forces come to dominate territories formerly controlled by Irish than hostilities within their own ranks flared up. These were challenges anew for supremacy. For our purposes a rough period, dating around the 1870s and 1880s witnessed most of the heavy action. Not so coincidentally, its termination came almost simultaneously with the emergence of jazz on the night club scene, as if forces held in check by internecine warfare were suddenly released for more productive activities.

Three successive stages mark the introduction of a new night club scene that thrust jazz onto the New Orleans landscape. The preliminary stage occurred before 1880 and was underscored by widespread uncertainty from investors about the relevance of night clubs generally. Gradually, and with the acceptance by Sicilian factions that this form of business provided a front for other activities (gambling, prize fights, prostitution), early reservations were overcome. In addition, the high mortality rate that most clubs experienced was partly eliminated through occasional payoffs to police and other local opposition groups.

This period closed with the assassination in 1881 of an important local Mafia chieftain and the police capture of the notorious Sicilian bandit Guiseppi Esposito. Shakeups such as this, by creating slots for new leaders with new ideas, ushered in the second stage in New Orleans night club development, one that lasted until the early 1890s. This second period was marked by better organization, better demarcation zones for customers and better arrangements with the police. Operating techniques improved with less resort to violence and more attention paid to live entertainment; clubs dotted a central zone of competition rather than spreading out in random fashion; and the operator's outlooks changed. In Rose's words, they were "no longer in the nonce class."

Esposito's departure signaled the onset of devotion by his replacements to conduct affairs with less interest in blood-letting, and more attention to gambling recently made legal by the State legislature. Symbolically, the corporate board and planning room for these conceptual changes was centered in a jazz club owned by one of the beneficiaries of the Esposito removal, the Matranga clan. Henry Matranga was one of the leaders, a man whom Louis Armstrong remembered as a jazz club operator: "He treated everybody fair and black patrons loved him very much."

Under the inspirational guidance of men like the

Matranga Brothers, George Delsa (manager of Anderson's Rampart Street cafe and restaurant, an important early jazz club), Phil Lobrano, Richard Otero and Tony Battistina various underworld cliques set out to reestablish New Orleans' historical reputation as a "good time town," and still make it pay handsomely.

Aided and abetted by the semi-loose Sicilian affiliations with their underworld contacts (gamblers, ponces, fences and other sporting men), these mobsters created an attractive atmosphere that sought to extract any loose money floating around. Innovations were important for success: Slightly-raised platforms were installed to separate crowds from performers and aid in the revues; laws against women in barrooms were circumvented; jazz music was featured; and special effects—like electrical illumination in Anderson's (the first saloon to do so in America) raised customer curiosity. Safe and secure surroundings also leant their own appeal as the combined police and mob surveillance kept unsavory activities to a minimum. As a reports rose that there was a "sharp drop in crime."

Of course this area of the French Quarter has come to be known as Storyville, and the best efforts of its leading underworld figures did not go unrewarded. One source claims that for its time, Storyville generated earnings from its many cribs and night spots that were extremely handsome.[22]

The final stage in local night club development occurred during the years 1890-1912. This was a period highlighted by greater segregation of clubs than before and stronger political leverage. Less inventive rivals disappeared, prosperity shot up, allowing some owners to consolidate and expand their outlets, and jazz music flowered. Professor Stearns believes that there was a prolific number of jazz joints offering plenty of work for white as well as black artists. Rose believes the impetus for this consolidation and local expansion was generated through the three night clubs owned and operated by Sicilian mobster Peter Ciacco. Others involved in the night club expansion of jazz included Peter Lala, cabaret manager and producer of shows featuring Clarence Williams as pianist and songwriter; John Lala whose Big 25 Cafe was playground for many leading jazz musicians (Kid Ory, Freddie Keppard, Bunk Johnson and King Oliver); and Abraham and Isidore Shapiro with their 101 Ranch, "a cabaret which employed many jazz bands and was particularly famous."[23]

No simple method exists for untangling the thorny questions of how many night club owners had Mafia connections, what constituted the basis for their interaction, what was the rate of cabaret increase or decline, or how many grew wealthy in the process. Nor are simple details of daily operations available for our inspection. And we can never learn the exact number of men who held percentages in these clubs and cathouses. Rose's study of Storyville bordellos and madams highlighted the insurmountable obstacles when it came to fixing specific ownership on individuals. The same kind of problems exist here. There is no precise way of consulting land office records for ownership titles since fronts, dummy names and other subterfuges were used to keep the names of actual owners from the public eye. Perhaps leading politicians were colleagues of underworld owners inasmuch as profits were high in the salad days and favorable ties with City Hall were seen as desirable.

John Hammond sets the figure of mobster ownership at 75%. If the calculations of jazz historians Ramsey, Huber and Williams are correct, that the city supported 85 important jazz clubs, 800 saloons (some of which might have used musicians on occasion), and over 200 bordellos (employers for pianists) in 1902, then Hammond's estimate suggests a prodigious and spirited supply.[24] Even on a conservative side, activity was plentiful. (See Appendix C.)

The Sociology of Mobster and Jazz Musician

Mutual appreciation developed along several parallel lines. This was because similarities between the two groups abounded. They ranged from inadequate formal educations, legal persecution and self-segregating protectionism, rejection by the general public as potential social threats, hedonistic activities, communal work situations and associations with vice businesses.

Another parallel must surely lie in the resemblance jazz bears to music from the Old Country. Without wishing to underscore this notion too deeply, sustenance for such an argument does exist. Music critic for the *New York Tribune* Henry Edward Krebbiel, an early interest (1913) reviewer of black folk songs and blues, discerned these likenesses with music around the Mediterranean. Glancing at New Orleans he concluded:

Latin Civilization is less cruel to primitive social institutions than Anglo-Saxon; less repressive and many times more receptive.Sometimes it takes little away and gives much, as it has done with African music transplanted to its new environment.

The Sicilian approach to their peasant music offers five strong similarities to black music, sociologically if not clearly musically. First, as in New Orleans, nightly diversions kept the noisy casinos of Messina, Catania and Palermo very busy. In these darkened yet lively settings, local residents, wearied from a day of rigorous labor, drank and mingled and danced to the small bands which played a sort of improvisational, Italian-like blues. Second, as in the backroads of Georgia or Louisiana, itinerant musicians were commonplace Sicilian sights, and they entertained whomever they encountered along their desultory way, charging whatever the traffic would bear. Third, parades, brass bands and funerals were popular diversions in both locations. Fourth, Sicilians were much like black people in seeing music as a highly personalized affair, a reflection of an individual's feelings although born of a collective experience.

This was world's apart from other musical cultures even those found in Northern Italy.[25] Lastly, there are the technical aspects of the music itself. Again, without trying to draw too much of a carbon copy, distinct differences can be heard in Irish and North European music as opposed to those of Italians, Blacks, and even the music of some Jewish settlements.[26] Irish music emphasized the major melodic mode and employed seven to nine basic tonal forms, favoring the keys of C, D, G and E-flat; rhythms were also steady and uncomplicated, usually 3/4 and 6/8 time. On the other hand,

Mediterranean and African melodies were written in predominately minor modes—Cm, Dm, Fm and Gm, laced with 20 or more intricate Moorish harmonies and many times that number in syncopations. Himself an Irishman, Tom Hall confesses to the simplistic, unimaginative music he was called upon to play by Irish nationalists in the saloons he worked. Cohen remembers the difficulty he had as a musician coping with the Irish music of his Chicago youth:

My first year playing music I was doing Irish dances, filled with young Irish immigrants. All they wanted was jigs and unrhythmic steps, echoes of their country...really faraway stuff. The hippest thing was when Irish musicians used spoons and pieces of wood which had a faint African touch. But the music was thousands of years away from the jazz I knew. It was stiff and always 3/4 time.

Little remembered, many Sicilians became absorbed enough with jazz to play it on at least a semi-professional basis. This was especially true in New Orleans around the turn of the century. Indeed, such an attraction helped create a bond between black artists and the Sicilian mobsters (see Appendix D).

Leon Rappolo, clarinetist, mentioned how many white jazzmen of the early period came from Sicilian families quartered in the French District, with long familial histories of musical involvement.[27] One need only recall musician-promoter and business agent Jack Vitelle Laine whose main customers for his scores of local bands, white and black, were the mob-owned clubs. These Sicilian jazzmen, restricted by severe Jim Crow laws from getting a proper schooling from black artists, nonetheless were hired by mobs to perform, serving as a bridge between both parties. They certainly deserve more attention than has previously been accorded them.

A third closeness came from the interlocking grid of extended social associations which aided in fostering work for musicians. Halls, clubs and fraternal orders happily competed with one another in hiring bands, giving work to hundreds of sidemen. Blacks also had many social clubs and halls from which to choose. There were 226 officially listed black societies between 1862 and 1880.[28] The smart band used these jobs wisely and kept good hours and deportment. If they pleased their social directors there was no telling how far they might travel within the circuit and how many other societies would bid for their services. Buddy Bolden represents one musician whose band was assured steady work at these places by mobsters who appreciated his talents and business sense.

Bolden stands as one of the earliest known products of the marriage between jazz and organized crime in New Orleans. Dating from the mid-1880s, and for over two decades, Bolden's incredible technique as a cornetist made a lasting impression on all who heard him. His stature as a superstar of his day was best seen in the adulation women displayed to the point of fighting over who might carry his horn case. Unshakably popular, his name and dependability at keeping correct playing hours vastly impressed the mobsters who realized he guaranteed full crowds at their halls and cabarets. In return he obtained a large share of the better club dates by Italians who refused to lease their premises for engagements unless it was clear that Bolden's band would furnish the music. Eventually his band came to the attention of the Chicago gangs where, according to a devoted reviewer, "he paved the way for the Chicago's gangsters' patronage of jazz."[29]

Widespread links arose not only in New Orleans but wherever other mobs were located. Memphis was one example. Blues composer W.C. Handy was impressed enough to call it the "hottest of the hot dance towns" along the Mississippi River jazz circuit. This centered on Joe Raffanti's Midway Cafe, which welcomed sporting types of all races and dispositions. According to its historian, Beale Street, the city's dominant jazz thoroughfare, was "owned largely by Jews, policed by whites, and enjoyed by Negroes."[30] Oakley claims the favorite haunts of the musicians when visiting Memphis were the clubs owned by the Italians.

A fourth reason for a musician's interest in the mobs had to do with the generosities he was shown. He may very well have received more respect and courtesy from the New Orleans underworld club owners than from whites at any time in the past. The clubs were much cleaner and better furnished than the places most musicians had previously known. Business dealings appear to have been conducted on a honorable basis with less risk of an artist being bilked. And demands were few, so long as bands were punctual and lively. One veteran musician recalls how poorly most jazzmen did at the gate prior to mobster business dealings:

Pay was never high and sometimes it was non-existent. No musician expected to be paid for "sitting in" but many times the pay for regular work was either less than promised, or the promoters of the affair would vanish before the night was over, never to be seen again. Vanish, that is, with the receipts. It would be safe to say that 90 percent of the arguments and violence, and most of the near-fatal and sometimes fatal fights had as their origin a money quarrel.[31]

It was the rare musician who hadn't at some stage been taken for all he was worth. The early period was especially bad. Club owners of the old school pitted men against one another, hiring the cheapest; it was not improbable for them to try to intoxicate a musician in the hope he would forget the terms of his playing contract; and owing to the black man's delicate legal situation, where he enjoyed few safeguards, deals were welched on with impunity. Nor did some club owners care what patrons said or did to bands so long as they continued to spend. Mobsters were very different in this respect, as noted by clarinetist George Lewis:

The gangsters and gamblers tipped the musician well and they were never offensive to the colored musicians, as were many of the patrons. In fact, they showed such open hostility to Negro-baiting or patronizing whites that the latter found themselves leaving earlier than they had intended. And it was by no means unusual for them to find, when they reached their cars, that all four tires had been neatly slit.[32]

The result, as shown in the studies of Professors Harvey and Cameron, was that jazz musicians came to sincerely admire mobsters for the many kindnesses shown. Harvey claims this was particularly true for the older artists. Cameron furnishes several reasons why jazzmen displayed minimal animosity to mobsters: their own tolerance to criminals for whom no special stigma was attached; the acceptance on both

parts to constantly experiment on what the public wants; a
suspicion of formal rules which ossify business relationships;
emphasis on the charisma of personal leadership; and a form
of apoliticism which approved of any rule or reign that
permitted their activities.[33]

But mob-owned clubs were not pushovers,and something
beyond mere horn-tooting was expected from the artist.
Underworld owners appreciated bands which were loyal to
owners. Group concepts in jazz artistry appealed to the mobs.
Swagger, gambling instincts and late-night sociability were
additional traits which caught a mobster's approving eye.
Alertness to mob practices also counted. Cohen came to learn
this in his many dealings with New Orleans and Chicago
underworld figures:

Mob practices regarding musicians have hardly changed at all over the years.
Owners liked men who were out to help the club. Musicians who avoided being
pushy in front of customers were also appreciated. Management disapproved
of jazzmen bugging the customers or flirting with women patrons.

Artists were expected to endure the long hours demanded
of them and play all reasonable requests. Looking nice
counted. So too did dependability. A musician's word, oftimes
made to a potential employer over a drink or in a back alley
behind a club during intermission, constituted the sole basis
for an agreement that underworld operators tended to respect
fully. It made sense for jazzmen to pay close attention to these
unwritten decencies since gangsters in various cities swapped
favors with one another, and accepted tips that might prove
injurious to bands whose bad judgment or audacity spelled
their own ruin. In the best interest of the mob club owners,
attempts to report on or crush undrilled bands probably
occurred often.

Bandsmen were expected to upgrade their proficiency and
creativity. Owners recognized that customers like to hear fresh
sounds and original material. By concentrating on these
points, managements screened musicians, separating out
those who were too old or intransigent and who preferred to
keep basic skills at an unspectacular level. In the long run,
standards were being devised, partly through this external

pressure, which enhanced performances. Mob leaders assumed that any man with raw talent alone, unwilling to adapt (either by reading music and making adequate chord changes in the case of musicians or similar kinds of adjustment if they were mob warriors) possessed a temperament that presented the twin risks of violence and undependability.

It should be recalled that most of these gangsters were foreigners with a knowledge of black Southern culture that barely scratched the surface and for whom appreciation was extended only so far as musicians paralleled their own mannerisms. Accommodating attitudes of musicians served to satisfy these men. And as owners tightened their requirements, the more primitive levels of skill and behavior, unrewarding in night club atmospheres, were weeded out. In any event, astute, capable and conciliatory performers had little trouble finding work.

Long before the jazz upsurge of the 1920s, blacks and Sicilians gathered together in New Orleans for the performance and promotion of jazz. For both their arrival was the direct result of conditions bordering on economic chaos.Depressions, wartime disclocations and endemic corruption and long-standing vice ruined the aristocratic operators, simultaneously presenting Italians with opportunities which aided blacks, themselves pushed off the land and into the cities. In good-time towns like Memphis and New Orleans, the necessary retreat of the Old Guard created a vacuum the jazz-enthusiasts within the mobs soon filled.

Men of Italian extraction, denied access into respectable businesses, rose to enter whatever fields remained, vice activities notwithstanding, turning them to their advantage through their kinship networks. If sociologist Howard S. Becker's standards by which musicians rate audiences are taken into consideration, another explanation for a jazzman's admiration for underworld figures lies at hand. According to Becker, musicians awarded the highest marks to audience for their own tolerance, non-conformity and creative self-expression. Devoid of serious racial hangups which affected most Southerners of the period, and which clouded and marred interracial business dealings, the racketeers appeared willing to employ, consort with and befriend black musicians, attaching no strings in the process. Both emerged strengthened by this affiliation—driven together by the bigotry and urgency of the time.

Seen in this light—the underworld's profitable invasion of the city's cultural scene—one is led to speculate on the true reasons lying behind Storyville's closing in 1917. Officially, the district was considered too hazardous by the U.S. Navy which maintained a large base at New Orleans. Personnel going ashore were felt to be endangered of losing their money to prostitutes, or their lives, as happened to one sailor in 1917 in the French Quarter. Formal closure of the district was made by the U.S. Government soon after an investigation. Considering the disruption of the city's night life and colossal cost in personal terms to those affected, the official response now seems superficial and capricious.

At no other time or place had the Government chosen to exercise their overreaching powers. Many outposts along the Navy's supply routes were far more dangerous than anything New Orleans could muster. As a crime zone, Storyville appeared to be in a junior league. So reports one contemporary magazine, struck by the astonishment of the police on how well-behaved were the crowds visiting the area's clubs. Storyville's historian claims, "There was never even a hint of a 'crime wave' or of any exceptional lawlessness."[34]

But Storyville represented the Sicilian's life line to success and recognition. Individuals were provided the only real opportunity for making money. In so doing, a few mobile and aggressive men arose thirsting for social acceptance. If the movies are to be believed, these manipulated their wealth in an assault on the inner circles of the ruling clique, and thereby lay the rub.

The city's leading citizens had to have felt threatened by this onslaught to their value system and ruling clique. Any society with a racial outlook fossilized around the habit of boycotting those who consort with blacks, as Italians were doing in Storyville dives and gin mills, must have felt uncomfortable. Racists, religious fanatics and prohibitionists all joined forces with vice crusaders in trying to suppress the red-light area for good. Indeed, such civic improvement drives had been a daily part of city life since attempts to clean up the French Quarter began in earnest in the 1890s. It is my belief that enough leverage and pressure was applied on the Government to repress commercial vice activities that a murder served as a useful pretext for shortening the reign of the many mob-owned jazz clubs.

This was certainly true for other major cities at about the same time, and Philadelphia, Baltimore, Louisville and Chicago, to name only a few, were also beset by successful reformer campaigns to abolish commercial vice. E. Feldman and E. Anderson have both noted the contrast between reformers and the swarthy immigrant vice leaders they were attempting to crush. Feldman decries their anti-urban and nativist sentiments while Anderson, describing the Chicago scene, shows the reformers to have been mainly Protestant Republicans, a majority of them over the age of 40, perhaps 90% American born, and social leaders from philanthropic families with historical roots.[35]

Despite the newer breed of night club owner who pushed jazz into prominence, he was powerless against this latest racist surge which saw the entire South changing for the worse by 1915. The movements indeed inspired blacks to trek North, and several score jazzmen made the pilgrimage. Some left for better wages and conditions, others to rid themselves of racial misery. King Oliver, for example, fled New Orleans in 1918 in an effort to avoid endless jailings which, as curfew laws began tightening up, made men of his vocation unpleasantly vulnerable.

Sadly for those who remained, the next several decades passed all too quietly, and without progress. Even the best of the orchestras, the Sam Morgan aggregation, by retaining a blind loyalty to the city of their origins, failed to attract anything like the attention showered on far less talented colleagues who went North. The 1930s saw the bottom drop out of a local cabaret market that had always demanded tourist money and gangster talent to sustain it. Shorn of the underworld promoters, many of whom had themselves gotten out, jazz musicians were the inevitable losers. For the first time

since the 1880s, jazz was freed of its early boosters, and interest
in it dwindled accordingly. Today all that remains is a second-
rate, unpublicized, elderly tourist attraction for nostalgic
listeners—its glory days having long since been swallowed up
in the sleepy bayou atmosphere of a mossy, overgrown city.

Chapter VI

Why The Gangsters Even Bothered

Musical trends simply do not materialize out of thin air. Vast amounts of consumer interest and product coordination are necessary. So, too, are investors with an apparent willingness to gamble on a long shot in a capricious market. In the case of jazz these elements came together in the 1920s, having been stimulated by the earlier successful affiliation between mobster and musician already described. Such a relationship has been shown to have been baldly important for musicians. This was because the general public remained unmoved, quite unsusceptible to the slowly transforming promotional techniques coming out of the cabarets, and hardly seemed willing to pave the way for jazz artists.

Luckily the underworld had other thoughts. This was coupled with their marked aversion for the older musical forms, such as the waltz and polka. It was an aversion that underscored serious cultural differences with other ethnic groups. Bassist Pops Foster said these men preferred "slow, dirty blues so they could dance rough and dirty... with no coats on and their suspenders down."[1]

Superficially, and with no money derived from booze and gambling concessions, cabaret owners with underworld links began hyping a music they really enjoyed. Functionally, the music could be listened to, or used as backdrop for the intense socializing that went on in these places. Clubs could also be controlled by a few, without muscular effort. No less could political alliances be cemented here as well as working ties forged with other groups. Seen in this context, cabaret owners of the 1920s transformed an otherwise lowly amusement palace into an occasionally lucrative business whose capabailities for self-promotion, in addition to showcasing jazz music, were far-reaching.

At this stage it is not unreasonable to question the motives of the many Italian and Jewish underworld characters who sought entry into the world of the jazz night club. What was it about this life that lured men of another world? Educational limitations kept most at the chicken-scratching level when it came to writing; and the majority spoke almost unintelligible English to the outsider. How could they overcome complicated business dealings? Their involvement in niteries is no less bewildering on strictly historical and cultural grounds. Lisa Appignanesi dates cabarets to Paris of the 1870s with Jewish interest in ownership coming much after 1900 in cities like Budapest, Vienna and Munich, thus affecting to a small degree only late-arrivals to American shores. For Italians, club ownership was not a sought-after profession in the Old Country, held little significance or social standing in a land of peasants and small merchants, and even so, meant contact with outcasts and social undesirables.

And what of the general risks and violence associated with conducting a business in this country, where imagined profits led to dangerous demands of extortion? Why should these newcomers invade a mercenary field only a gamble away from losing hard-earned capital particularly when the most a successful operator could hope to achieve might be a surrounding climate of envy, social notoriety, imitators and a host of unstable enemies? Something very special about this business, and its later close ties with jazz music, fed the egos and sensitivities for countless poorly educated Jews and Sicilians who, as youthful gang members, had established reputations hanging around cheap dance halls and gin mills. Possibly, these men were simply too ignorant to appreciate the dangers. Yet their optimism brought rewards by moving into this adventure at exactly the right time in the country's history.

If these questions are to be answered, then our attention must be directed backwards a few years, to discover reasons which were to lay the groundwork for the expanding grid of gangster-owned niteries that mushroomed up after 1918.

The Jewish and Sicilian Network

Cultural affinity and proximity made it easier for Jews and Italians, gangsters or not, to get on with one another. Teller writes:

They somehow took to each other. Perhaps it was because they shared many habits—loud speech, broad gestures, pleasure in food, and profound concern for the well-being of their families. Both the Jewish and Italian womenfolk worked alongside their husbands and wielded a stern matriarchical authority over their households.

Musician Sam Cohen adds his view fostered by a Chicago upbringing:

Blacks, Italians, and Jews are easily very demonstrative people, with arms and hands waving about, moving first in one direction and then another. They are also sponataneous, given to making their immediate feelings known to those around them. Many is the time a Jew might easily be mistaken for an Italian, or otherwise.

Finally, winding up this introductory reminiscing is an Italian gangster who grew up in the 1920s:

When I was growing up in the Lower East Side, there were four kinds of people. Italians, colored people, Jews, and Americans. Anybody who wasn't one of us or colored or Jewish we always talked about as an American.[2]

The time, place and manner by which these three separate groups arrived, almost simultaneously, on the doorsteps of the larger Eastern cities, swaddled in rags and fleeing pogroms and disorder, contributed to the similarities. Between 1899 and 1914, nearly 1.5 millions Jews and well over 2 million Italians (mainly from the South and Sicily) braved the victimizing journey across the Atlantic. Few brought along property worth more than $15.[3] It was very much like the black exodus previously mentioned. They gathered along Chicago's infamous South Side, Old Levee and little Italy districts—a story repeated in Detroit, Boston, Philadelphia and New York. In such hovels, Jews, blacks and Italians, among others, got under each other's feet, an irritating beginning for cultural interaction.

Partly through fear of police and legal persecution, partly

through the sheer poverty which life imposed, bondships were forged. Horne, Gold, T.J.Jones, Cahan, Ornitz and Ianni reiterate stories which bear close resemblance to this model. One Italian racketeer wrote of his hatred for sadistic police:

I grew up in New York hating the cops—watching them as a kid shaking down the little grocery store that stayed open on a Sunday to make an extra buck, watching them put the bite on the bar where maybe there was a little card game going on in the back room....Always they were looking for something out of line, so they could get their cut.[4]

The social scene replicated a grim anthill of unparalleled misery , and the photographs of Jacob Riis bear testimony to appalling conditions these immigrants shared. An early Italian observed noted:

It is impossible to depict the degradation, the dirt, the squalor, the stinking muck, the rubble, and the disorder of these neighborhoods.[5]

The Jewish actress Ruth Gordon likened this unrelieved poverty to a "dark brown taste," while Polly Adler phrased it "that clawing uncertainty." "My parents hated all this filth," wrote Michael Gold, "but it was America, one had to accept it." Cold water flats were commonplace. So were backyard communal toilets, standing row upon row, like clay targets in a shooting gallery. Musty rooms featured solitary windows gazing directly on an outside air shaft. Available work was backbreaking and little time was left for normal, pleasurable pursuits. This was the lot for those who chose to live life in traditional, legal ways.[6]

As a result many areas in the larger Eastern cities became spawning grounds for thousands of juvenile and adult gangs seeking protection, respect and profit. Vice activities preoccupied their time in much the same way as for many young immigrants from the moment they caught a whiff of local white slavery at work:

There were hundreds of prostitutes on my street. They occupied vacant stores, they crowded into flats and apartments in all the tenements. The pious Jews...tried to shut their eyes. We children did not shut our eyes. We saw and knew.[7]

Given dreary conditions like these, musical expression enabled residents to exhibit hostile feelings openly through the use of music from other cultures. Professor Kavoris notes the ease with which the arts absorbed radical strains and stresses lying around in a society very much like the American one of 1910, crippled by repression and poverty. Many Jews, blacks and Italians seemed to have tried on musical hats from cultures with similar histories of persecution. John Rublowsky makes a useful comparison when he writes of the despised Russian Jew, whose musical hobbies offset job discrimination and bitterness—passionately embracing the violin—with the black migrant, banjo in hand, fending off oppression in his own land.

Ethnic music of Jews in the early 1900s has been approached by Judd Teller who called it a "cult activity" which redirected those with daring and creativeness into grooves far more radical than could be found at home. Pointing to his own childhood on the Lower East Side around 1900, Teller mentions the many Chassidic bands who spiced up orthodox melodies with lustful snatches of ragtime and the Boikeriker Orchester, an ensemble that played for weddings in the "New Orleans style."[8]

In 1904 Thomas J. Jones did a block survey for Columbia University, selecting the Lower East Side for the site of his sociological portrait:

Of all the different amusements possible to these tenement dwellers (Italians, Jews, and blacks for the most part), there is none that appeals to both sense and emotion so strongly as dancing, especially dancing conducted to the wild music of blaring cornet and loud-beating drum, with rattling sounds from a guitar and mandolin.

Popular journalist George K. Turner claimed that by 1909 lively music infested poorer areas of the cities. There were "tens of thousands" of dancers in New York City alone, and on "Saturday and Sunday the whole East Side dances after nightfall." Turner paid close attention to the many "Casino Gardens," euphemisms for dance halls that were rallying points among young thugs and local gangs.[9]

T.E. Sullenger's 1935 study of urban change in a Mid-

Western city detected much the same trends. In his chapter on entertainment, he noted that whereas blacks were the most musically-minded of the many ethnic groups, Jews and Italians were the ones most seduced by the black forms in music and concomitant night life. Of course, nightly attractions might be many. Eddie Zeltner, a reporter for the old *New York Daily Mirror,* remembers:

Gorgeous girls used to come to Coney Island to dance in cellar clubs which were grammar schools for gangsters.[10]

Black music affected men who later became important composers. Irving Berlin recalled "soaking up songs" in the immigrant streets near his tenement. To him, "Yiddish, Italian, black, it made no difference." Singer Lois Deppe claims that Harold Arlen was "crazy over the blues," which was why he became a "whale of a torch writer" and was "always hanging around the Fletcher Henderson band."[11] George Gershwin once wrote that by the time he was seven, he had spent countless hours sitting outside Harlem jazz clubs, listening to a sound he would later introduce into his most elaborate compositions. Sam Cohen found it invaluable learning music of other cultures:

As Jews we quickly learned the music of Italians, Poles, blacks, and Irish because they interested us as street musicians—in business—cultivating terms. I'm sure this same condition existed in New Orleans, where black music was such a crossblend of different nationalities.

Some of the underworld cabaret owners were doubtless frustrated singers, composers and musicians. Cohen met several of these. So did Art Hodes. Writing of gangster Lawrence Mangano, Hodes says:

Mangano owned an expensive guitar, tuned it like a ukelele, had two professional musician brothers, and came from a musical family. He used to sing dirty songs in his own night club.[12]

As children they had been exposed to a fair amount of musical instruction from parents and talented relatives, a not uncommon phenomenon for poor Italian and Jewish offspring, especially from tension-filled or broken homes.[13] So it was that night clubs, by allowing owners to discover musicians for themselves, or sit in with the house band to sing or entertain, or merely watch leggy chorus girls in the revue, were able to assuage these frustrations. Club owner Billy Rose remembers many gangsters that liked to sing, and points to Chicago bootlegger Jerry Dugan as a leading example. "The size of his tab," Rose recounts in his autobiography, "depended on how often the night club let him sing with its band."

Almost from the moment of adolescence, musical night life made a deep impression on many immigrants who later went into the rackets. Brief mention has already been made of a situation that Gold amplifies, claiming "there were many pimps who infested the dancehalls and picked up the romantic factory girls who came after the days' work." One leading bootlegger and club owner has left us a diary of his youthful transgressions in which he records his comings and goings he and other young loafers worked to perfection:

Thursday: Went to a dance in the afternoon, went to a dance at night, and then to a cabaret. Took some girls home. Went to a restaurant and stayed there until 7 a.m.
Friday: ...met some friends in a saloon early in the evening and stayed with them until 5 a.m.
Saturday: ...went to a dance in the Bronx late in the afternoon, and to a dance on Park Avenue at night.
Sunday: Went to a dance in the afternoon and another in the same place at night. After that I went to a cabaret and stayed there almost all night.[14]

Their creed was plain and simple. "My motto," recited bootlegger Danny Ahern in his book, "was plenty of women, plenty of cabarets, and plenty of gambling, with booze on the side." Time meant little to these night owls whose very actions deliberately separated them from the mainstream of dullish, burdensome, lower class work routines. "By 4 a.m.," a racketeer wrote, "one tried to get to as many clubs as possible, and not wanting to waste time, to get onto the next place."[15] When W.F. Whyte interviewed racketeer Chick Morelli, he got a similar response:

When I was working in the bootlegging business, I had plenty of money. And I was a free spender....I went to plenty of dances.

This adolescent interest in music and dance later carried over into many a business life. Jews were not adverse to negotiations, and quite a few possessed an uncanny marketing flair or interest in talent scouting, publicity and the presentation of entertainment. Some had begun by managing prize fighters, developing mannerisms and contacts with gamblers that later came in handy when the assault into the night club field was made. Joe Glaser not only managed Louis Armstrong but also a number of Chicago heavyweights in the 1920s.

Other leading agents of the 1920s and early 1930s included Sy Weiss, Mort Nathanson, Jay Faggen, Ed Weiner, Sid Garfield and Irving Zussman, who made fortunes for night club personalities. Other promoters of jazz attractions were Ed Fox, Lee Posner, Jack Kapp, Lou Irwin, Milt Gabler, Lou Breckner, Saul Schwartzberger, Irving Mills and Ed Bloom. The Chess Brothers prowled the streets and back alleys in their search for jazz cabaret bands. John Steinberg is credited with introducing many white jazz artists to the Eastern clubs (Eddie Lang, the Dorseys and Jack Teagarden, for example), while Lew Leslie scouted his way through a legend of black performers he featured in his famous Blackbird Revue and fed in his Lower East Side apartment. The Shribman Brothers, according to one source, took each new group they discovered through a tireless series of club auditions, "supporting, patronizing, and subsidizing everyone handled...while never owning a piece of anybody connected."[16]

What is worth stressing here is that without such men, whose musical background, tolerance for diversity, and familiarity with local racketeers were cultivated in their early years living in poor immigrant neighborhoods, the great artists, the stylistic variations in jazz, the club environments which were to become so conducive to widespread creativity, and the endlessly altering personalities and shades of music and bands the public was privileged to hear would never have materialized. Even larger claims have been advanced. Walker, who was an expert on night club life of the 1920s, is convinced that Lee Posner, having introduced to the public the bands of Duke Ellington, Cab Calloway and Don Redman, among others, was solely responsible for putting Harlem on the map.[17]

It was an age when women everywhere demanded an equal voice and assimilation—similar trends may even have occurred within the homosexual and lesbian communities of the larger cities although this is an historical chapter yet to be explored. But adaptable immigrants responded to the restless mood of the nation's youth and let people decide their own morals. Needless to say, for some, as with the homosexual groups, mobs ran clubs for their amusement, extracting a healthy profit in keeping with police repression of illegal activity.

In this era of voracious new hedonistic appetites, the old Irish cliques, "befuddled by the problems of prohibition and unable to untrack themselves," as Walker phrased it, refused to make the necessary adjustments. Dr. Caroline Ware writes of a disturbing ambivalence which affected Irish saloonkeepers. Established only after a long and exhaustive struggle, most preferred to close their doors, legally if inconsolably, rather than flaunt the law after 1920. In the case of jazz their disappearance meant little, bearing in mind how Irish saloons held most kinds of musical programs in low regard.[18] Irish gangsters were no less influenced. Ruth Spanier tells me of the time Chicago bootlegger and gang leader Dion O'Banion used to stuff $50. bills into her husband's cornet in a persuasive effort to have him switch from jazz to Irish melodies about Mother.

The Mobs and the Jazz Cabaret

Most of the night clubs and cabarets in the Eastern cities fell sway to Sicilians and Jews, implicitly and by default after 1918. For the vast majority of this new crowd, their contacts with bootleggers furnishing the illegal booze, with gamblers who made up much of the high spending audience, and with other members of the musically-oriented underworld made the difference. In some regions they dominated the night club world over other ethnic rivals nine to one.[19] Angelo remembers how entry into the club business marked the end of mercenary, dangerous days for many Italians:

Clubs numbered many old-time Sicilian owners who were not gangsters; men who ended violence when entering the business. Even so, there were always those, independent-minded, who moved in and out of criminal activities as casually as walking through a hotel lobby.

To the same extent that blacks ruled the world of jazz performance and creativity, Italians and Jews held center stage of night club ownership—each group perfecting its end of the equation. Indeed, there is a sharp distinction to be made between playing the music and selling it. "No good musician can possibly watch a cash register," says Ruth Spanier. Musician Tom Hall adds:

The two don't mix. If a man is good at selling it, he isn't much good at playing it. One has to spend time either at merchandising the music or performing it.

Jews and Sicilians took 90% of the pie in some places. This left a smaller slice of which blacks probably formed the next biggest ownership group-if only because they were far from invisible and furnished many necessary items—prostitutes, chorus girls, jazz musicians, information and money—to white gangsters.[20] Many stories have circulated about the daring exploits of some of its leaders: Robert Motts, Ed Small, Henry Jones, Pony Moore, Dickie Wells, Mushmouth Morgan, "Fats" Brown and Bessie Smith's close friend, Richard Morgan. No less than the Italians did these men establish deep and personable relationships with their communities for whom they performed many acts of generosity. Wise investors in the real estate market, these men then sank money into the more hectic and insecure cabaret world.[21]

In addition to the musical aspects which attracted racketeers into the club business, there were other factors. For one, there was the prospect of large profits; also the glamor which draped itself around club life. Ease of entry without solid credentials, and the eventual prominence that fell to some operators with their widening frames of reference were further lures. Needless to say, it was highly illusory for all but the most efficient, or wealthy, or talented. As in businesses elsewhere, failures were rife even among those who seemed most suited for success in an illegal activity. No one had a monopoly on prosperity, not even racketeers.

Prospects of large profits beaconed far and wide to attract underworld investors who should have known better and who disregarded the contentions of Granlund and Angelo that prohibition agents and police officials made larger fortunes than night club owners. Ahern believed that clubs had to double their prices, inflating the charges for food and alcohol by 300%, and continually hike the cover charges, if only to offset risks and escalating bribes that went with the business.

But the public was in a generous mood after the slow start following the war and by 1924 a buoyant period was in evidence. Angelo was convinced the smarter clubs could do well but only after adding gambling concessions and after-hours diversions to their menus. So it is that many of the flamboyant and swell-headed remarks about profiteering which date from this period must be tempered with a bitter taste from the cup of experience. Billy Rose's New York niterie, the Backstage Club, completely amortized its initial outlay of $4000 on opening night. One racketeer claimed:

It was easy for a crook to open a club and in one year pay off all its obligations and show a big profit on top of it.[22]

But was this really the case for the average operator? Angelo says these were the lucky few. To his reckoning, profits from average clubs might have totalled 5% a month, 10% at best, with all the possible risks and dangers, and perhaps double that in the more expensive places where more customer credit might be given. An accurate analysis is impossible since, as he puts it, the field tolerated wide deviations and most kept their mouths shut.

Profits were but one reason for opening a club. In fact, the impression is gained from memoirs of the era that this was a secondary reason. Many racketeers already had the money: they were seeking something quite different. Glamor, for instance. Billy Rose says the only reason he went into the field was "to wear a black hat and meet some girls." Clubs held an extraordinary attraction for women, and catered to this appeal as no night time entertainment had before. Women liberated themselves from antiquated social conventions by showing up at places hitherto denied them, and gangsters were not slow to notice this trend. Club owners and musicians alike did nothing to antagonize a harvest the older Irish saloons had spent years repulsing. Elizabeth Jordan said, "women clustered around mobster owners like bees to honey."

Gangsters, even jazz artists, quickly converted this feminine reaction into liaisons and trysts, although one could never be certain who was leading whom. Socialists vied with one another for the dubious privilege of conducting affairs, the longer and stormier the better, with mobsters amazed at how some people idealized their violent backgrounds and associations. Musicians, too, took a fling at the big time of high society romance, although these instances were less frequent and under a heavy cloak of secrecy, especially where black artists were involved.

Clubs were perfect locations for racy exhibitionism that was the hallmark of the flapper-age gangster. Then everyone dressed to satisfy a press agent. "Everybody," Martin wrote facetiously, "was trying to outbigshot the others." And in an easy money era, dapper dress and a $5000 bankroll seemed appropriate. What better way for the man of humble origins to advertise his triumph than to brush past his own doorman, wearing the latest in grey-flannel suits, pussy willow silk shirts, and expensive European shoes, bestride an arm-clinging, equally modish feminine companion? For the press, it was great copy. Almost akin to home ownership, it was an urbanized approach to flashy conspicuous consumption.

Ease of entry was a third reason, the only limitation being lack of imagination. Indeed, the 1920s appear from this vantage point as the ideal time for matching an aspiring opportunist's dream with golden opportunity, inasmuch as background credentials, organizational experience and excessive capital were not required. Recommendations from former employers counted for little. Ironically, and in this wide open era, features and accompaniments such as these might even be drawbacks, wrapping an applicant in vestiges from the past, slowing down his momentum, inclining him to think in traditional terms. Friends, a few contacts with officials and suppliers, and an optimistic attitude were all the documents one needed as a ticket of admission. Denied normal access routes into the field of business, Jews and Italians were greatly benefited by such waivers. The joys of ownership were many, and getting in brought other rewards. One prospective entrant was optimistic:

It would be a lot of fun, and being always an optimist, I even say a possibility of making some money and thus avoiding the honest toil which I knew would be forced upon me someday.[23]

Another mobster saw it as a "great place to keep politicians and judges happy, offering them booze, women, and music."[24] A racketeer and club owner in Los Angeles, who featured the best of name jazz groups in the late 1930s, spoke for an entire generation of underworld operators:

Hardly a day went by that I didn't have people coming from (out of town).... A lot of these people were here on a one or two day visit... and they wouldn't want to go to your home.... Jazz clubs were a part of my way of life and a necessity in those days.[25]

To be an operator, Billy Rose felt all a person needed was to be "wacky, a big fibber, swell-headed, bull-headed, and fat-headed." Regardless, many clubs were but playhouses and fronts for quite different purposes, as gamblers and other underworld types preferred these surroundings for their own late-night activities.

Some mobsters preferred to go it alone, and this occurred frequently during the early years in New Orleans, or before jazz became accepted in New York and Chicago by the late 1920s. But the demands imposed on a cabaret owner were generally too great for any single individual to shoulder over the long haul. One authority tells us "any hoodlum always had enough money to open a night club, and if he hasn't he found another hoodlum."[26]

Since the spread required to open a club was quite broad—a point to be discussed shortly—it was conceivable for a very average person to join the game. Of course, mercenaries were not the only people interested in owning a piece of such romantic action. Sportsmen, garment manufacturers and green grocers bored with humdrum existence might take the plunge. Wealthier sorts also entered a fray where chance, a pliable value and moral system, and a variety of roles were demanded.[27] Some lenders wrote off parts of loans they had made in early days of a night club's life in exchange for a share of the operation or some other valuable commodity.

Small operations were particularly suited to the years 1915-1923, before the industry started sorting itself out, shaking out the local incompetents. Large-scale organizations were definitely in the minority until the laters years of the decade, when costs of doing business soared as increasingly extravagant revues were demanded by customers. Owners then left calling cards in profusion for additional partnerships. Louis J. Vance refers to a "cell of 5" as being a typically workable number for club shares. "Three talented men made a good mob," says Ahern, for they would be too few for the incessant bickering that ruined many a club's business. The most important contact for some was, fairly enough, the bootlegger who not only supplied funds and friends but provided a functional basis for these immigrants. In any event, this is a subject treated extensively elsewhere and will only be touched on here where it applies to actual ownership and running of clubs.

Resources might be slender but rarely did these keep interested parties from the field of battle. Clubs opened literally on shoestrings. And for some, this describes the way they were conducted throughout their usually brief lives. The very popular Hotsy Totsy Club on New York's 7th Avenue took less than $1000 for its doors to open in the mid-1920s. The Famous Door on 52nd Street was allegedly bought for $2800 and eight bottles of Scotch in 1935. And $2500 opened Billy Rose's Boston niterie in the late '30s. Prices could even scratch bottom if one had the time to ferret out a location and wasn't too particular about the surrounding neighborhood. Texas Tommy's in

Manhattan went for $800 and places in Harlem could return a
gold mine on the right investment. One Harlem club reportedly
was purchased for $180.[28] Angelo agrees with this scale of
prices and claims costs in the 1930s might even have been
lower for the owner willing to sacrifice quality in tables, chairs
and the like. Second-hand bars, pianos, even booze and the
glasses to pour it in were all available on credit. He tabulates
further costs:

Bartenders were paid $25 a week, musicians often worked for tips alone, and it
was common to pay a waiter $1 nightly, tips and food tossed in for good
measure.

Given these rates, the field might indeed attract just about
anyone, and, as it was, just about anyone dared to enter.

This does not mean that clubs were giveaways. Some were
uncommonly expensive, requiring joint efforts from a group of
backers. Ed Fox and his team purchased the Grand Terrace in
Chicago for $100,000, turning an old movie house into a
pleasure palace in 1928. Durante estimates the average
Broadway club cost $25,000 to start, with no less than $15,000
upfront money. After 1925 costs to open escalated as economic
prosperity in general, and the value of clubs in particular,
continued to spiral. It was a trend that forced most of the bigger
places to be run by three or four investors, usually taking a
quarter interest. Syndicates which were managed by the likes
of Al Capone, Dolly Weisberg and Adolph Renucci in Chicago,
or Joe Moss, Lew Leslie and the Salvin-Thompson group (with
a million dollars worth of money tied up in clubs like the
Alabam, the Royale and The Plantation) were now the rule.

Finally, and possibly the most important reason why
gangsters were attracted to clubs was by the prominence that
followed. Few sociologists of the Mafia are as insightful as
Ianni, who saw in night club ownership "a transmission of
culture." Many hats came with owning such places. The
paternalistic one came first. Clubs gave men the opportunity to
put nephews, uncles and sons on the payroll, doubling as
cashiers, bouncers, bartenders and even clean-up men. Besides
the power and prestige this allowed in the running of a large
family, it was also a cheap way of lowering costs and keeping

profits in the family. As an owner a man ceased being a
hoodlum and now entertained different, more hallowed
corridors of power. His frame of reference widened. If he were
successful, the spinoff of success might even descend upon
every member of his extended family, giving them a social
thrust as well. In addition, he might properly entitle himself
patron of the arts, talent scout, jazz promoter, civic leader,
philanthropist (which many of these men were from very early
in their dubious careers), investment and marital counsellor,
even social worker of amateur standing:

More than one hoodlum boss thought the way to stop a good saxophone player
from drinking was to hit him hard in the mouth.[29]

The stardom some men extracted from club ownership
later brought political benefits. Billy Rose claimed that once
joining the ranks, "You were no longer a highwayman, you
were a host." Bell has reported on how night club owners Frank
Costello and Joey Adonis made wise use of their night club
contacts when they entered local New York politics in the
1930s. Indeed, it was a pleasant experience for these men
whose previous lives had been filled with violence and
abrasiveness. Simply by entering these smoke-filled, noisy but
intimate and dark hovels, everybody knew them—from
waiters to musicians, from people in the show to the regulars
lining the bar—and they joined an atmosphere where jollity
and friendliness were pervasive. Not everyone did this to make
a fast buck, as Angelo warns:

Hoods got in for the limelight, the name, the notoriety, and for the young girls.
They didn't care to make money. So the rap that many were lousy night club
operators (advanced by the critic Sylvester, for one), is just not justified. They
just wanted a place to hang out and ran clubs for this purpose alone.

Some mobsters managed to acquire a veneer of culture
through the exposure their clubs received by socialites and
world travellers. Many travel books of the 1920s and 1930s,
written by English and French travellers, focus on mobster-
owned cabarets. The English author Stephen Graham

recognized that "the night resorts are not exclusively patronized by New Yorkers" and proceded to probe the jazz scene; so too did James Agate. It has been written that "Ravel gloried in the music of Harlem night clubs and in the taps of the dancers at Roxy's, even as other visiting artists and critics had done."[30] On the other hand, some gangsters toured the fashionable Paris jazz cabarets (such as Le Boeuf Sur Le Toit, home for the Jewish pianist Jean Wiener and any American jazz bands in the area) or the Amusierkabaretts of Berlin and hotspots of London, interspersing trips to museums with visits to local niteries. Larry Fay is one example who made flying tours, endlessly seeking new ways to add lustre to his own clubs.

Through this minefield of lures and baits, racketeers who should have known better took the leap and broke into a business few knew very much of at all. Sylvester believes that by any standards the majority were reckless fools. But then it has already been said that not everyone pursued this venture to make a killing; and anyway there is something faintly amusing and ironic in the notion of these men as happy, careless managers. But how does this stack up with our impression of the night club business in the 1920s? Do we assume that sheer illegality of the situation, where gambling, alcohol and other contraband were freely offered, overcame bridal innocence when it came to staying afloat? In short, do we know anything of the attrition rate, the costs of doing business illegally, or what an operator had to endure before he hired a jazz band?

Although precise estimates of losses, expenses and failings for this field are hopelessly non-existent, a few contemporary remarks and comparative figures from the world of musical theater, then experiencing a similar prosperity founded on mob money and involvement have managed to survive. They suggest that for every club providing music in 1926, two in three were barely able to keep their heads above water; only a handful paid off—possibly 25%.[31] Durante observed that the proprietor of a cabaret is easily spotted by being the only who is bald and grey "when he should be in the Don Juan class." Angelo saw it as a "lot of hard work with only pitiful returns." Profit and success obviously depended on a place remaining intact, avoiding the police padlock and being residentially stable for a reasonable period of time. In the confusion of the 1920s, clubs were often less lucky than that. Walter C.Reckless assessed the life span of the average cabaret of the early 1920s as less than 30 months and came to the conclusion that this was simply too short a time to build up a clientele, pay off debts and begin to show investors a return on their money.

As in the case for taxi-dance halls, neatly studied by Paul G. Cressey, 1924—1926 were years of persistent urban expansion which did little to assure stability. He suggests a failure rate which may have reached 25% within hours of opening. But the beat went on. For as fast as profits accrued to some, and very large returns fell into the hands of a few, the desire to join the fray went unabated.[32]

By the late 1920s club ownership entailed enormous expenses, forced on by better organizations producing more lavish entertainment. Out of the smoke of battle had come a highly complex operation. Simon Simple ventures were fast dwindling in an age of increasing boldness, with the smaller man being squeezed between the creases. As the demand for ambience grew, clubs were forced to level up to stay even, and the search for backers became an interminable annoyance. Bankers for Harlem's Cotton Club, for example, illustrate the wealth, ethnic fluidity and large-scale affiliations which became part of the top drawer clubs by 1929. These included wealthy bootlegger Owney Madden, early-day beer baron Bill Duffy, mobster Frankie Marlowe, influential playboy-gambler Arnold Rothstein, middleweight boxing champion Johnny Panica and Harry Block, owner of a string of small clubs throughout New York.

Three out of every four clubs stood a fat chance of flopping. The best of intentions may have opened them but hidden in the thickets were more than paper tigers. These factors figuring most often in the demise of the clubs were the payoff schedule, rampant and ballooning expenses, landlord greed and, of course, owner recklessness or incompetence.

Payoffs and bribes to police and other officials caused the

majority to belly-up. These were major costs and could hardly be avoided. Some clubs were forever relocating simply to find a neighborhood where official and racketeer extortion demands left room for some profit-taking by the managers and employees. The Grahams have provided us with a laundry list of shakedown artists:

The different rackets were all muscling in and forced many clubs to close; or else consider smaller shares of large profits by incorporation. The press, friends, celebrities all expected tabs. Only the mobsters paid well. The local political club demanded monthly dues; the beat cop dropped in for a drink and to ask them to join his precinct's club; and the bootlegger expected money on the generosity he gave opening night—or else. Were the Feds, the dockworkers, and the hemstitchers also to be considered?

Some mobs sold protection to smaller clubs. The most notorious of these was the Louis-Meyer Lansky-Bugsy Siegel group which preyed upon cabaret owners after 1925, and with at least one known casualty.[33] Ed Fox, owner of the Grand Terrace, home for the Earl Hines band, remembers how these operations were conducted:

Gangsters came into the place about two years after it opened. They just walked in one day. One man went to the cash register, one stood out front, and one on either side of the building. The lieutenant went to the back. "We're going to take 25 percent...you need protection," he said. "I've been doing all right for two years and I don't need protection." Fox replied, "You're going to have protection. You have a nice family and you wouldn't want anything to happen...." So they practically ran the place, and while they were there the police never came in, so I guess there was some finagling going on.[34]

Police could be far worse and less duty-bound to a code. Billy Rose says that once police got their bribes they never bothered a club except when they came in for a sandwich, dinner or a drink. But opportunities were so dazzling we would think less of police born in the days of machine politics not to have grabbed to the hilt. A 1928 investigation revealed that New York police had collected over $7500 each from 125 speakeasies along the Upper West Side alone, or over $400,000 in the years 1926-1930.[35]

Payoffs were remitted quietly and kept unrecorded—no

sense attracting bad publicity. The amount depended on who you were or who you were not. Joe Helbock, employing "dirty money," purchased the Famous Door in 1927. He writes of expenses facing the typical jazz club owner:

You stayed in business only if you had enough money and the right connections. I had a couple of pretty good ones—one was a deputy police commissioner. With them you could get the word on whom to pay and how much.[36]

Helbock's views are characteristic of the time. In my interview with Angelo, the subject of police bribes enraged him and caused his taking the most uncharitable of all his views on the subject of jazz and the underworld:

There was so much graft in the 1920s and 1930s. Every bar had to give. Irish cops controlled it and wanted no competition. They were always on the take. They protected those they liked and occasionally made small busts for appearances sake, or simply as a warning on how much power they could muster. People were usually given nominal fines. Those not playing the game would find their places padlocked and be out of business. Such an event could cost plenty and was much undesired. So you paid. Cops could be annoying simply by standing in front of a club and harassing the customers walking in. They had many useful devices for threatening. If the mobs were as united as people keep saying they were, they would have been able to control the police far better than was actually happening.

This last point bears rethinking. Vance writes similarly:

If the police and the district attorney's office was to turn square all of a sudden, there wouldn't be a crook left in the city inside of 24 hours . . . but everyone was on the take. Before any profits could be dispersed, a thick slice must be set aside for protection—an omnibus name for "everybody on the know," from rum baron to the district leader of the party to powerful and venal plainclothesmen that infested such clubs like flies.

Besides payoffs, other rampant expenses led to further closures. The costs associated with entertainment, alcohol supplies and publicity, plus the expenses incurred in renovating a brownstone townhouse for the purposes of running a speakeasy all began to mount steadily after 1920. The fact that so many racketeers sought entry did little to suppress prices despite the resultant competitive wars because so many, ignorant of general values, quickly agreed on whatever were the going rates.

The studies of Moore and Durante offer insight into an otherwise unexplored region of early cabaret costs. Taking the Les Ambassadeurs Club as an example of a smallish niterie in New York, Durante contends that orchestras might consume 35% of the expenses although I am inclined to believe that this is being too generous; staff cost 15%, a not-altogether unreasonable estimate, rent a very minimum 10% (I would quarrel here since once landlords got wind of alleged profits they would make quick rental increases to get their due), plus advertising, supplies, miscellaneous losses and the heretofore mentioned onerous bribe schedule. If the latter were high, and nothing was available to sop up other costs, fees for musicians were scaled down proportionately.

Club size was crucial in determining profits. The usual jazz club was built along fairly clean lines—long and narrow, cavernous, perhaps 20© by 100©, seating 125 customers. Optimistically, a room with these dimensions, if crowded on a nightly basis, had every reason to expect a pleasant return. Peter Dukas calculates the break-even point at roughly 50% capacity, a figure that would strain the limits for most, two or three quiet nights a week. So it was that cover charges, which received much criticism from nightgoers, might spell the difference between a limited survival or a prompt failure. Since people often brought their own booze, free access was an unreasonable demand. Harlem clubs, if assured of live business, might be in a better position to negotiate lifting the tariff, usually on an *ad hoc* arrangement. According to R.E. Cutler and Thomas Storm, the more successful places added sociable and convivial activities to free people up and their spending, drinking and dancing more, and staying longer in groups than as individuals.

Unless a club's entertainment package was extremely cheap, clubs might hover on a level where ends rarely met. This explains to some extent why many places expected musicians to play for tips: there simply was not enough profit to cover all aspects of business, especially when bribes and extortionate demands fluctuated wildly, depending on how many hands were extended each month. Landlords and their leases also caused trouble. Though rarely considered when analysing racketeers of the 1920s, this group, as much as police themselves, had the power to make or break night clubs. They also managed to reap financial wheat during this harvest time. Moore believes that rentals may have run as high as half the gate receipts, for the unlucky. Leases were a dreadful aspect that helped close doors, and it wasn't long before landlords got crafty enough to charge all that the traffic might bear.[37]

Fleeing debts, police demands and lazy landlords was not the answer. Some operators constantly hopped around town so as to avoid these entanglements, setting up shop just long enough for the vultures to make their discovery and then descend, before pulling up stakes and moving along. While this technique had its short-term attractions and advocates, business inevitably suffered. Customers lost track of clubs on the dodge. Furthermore, a considerable amount of time and energy was required for any club to spread the name of its attractions and compile a clientele that became steady. Nomadic clubs and speakeasies, by definition, severely crimped their chances; so it was that for the average owner little could be done other than to absorb the costs and hope imaginative lures might attract customers to whom the additional expenses could be passed along in an artful way. Jazz music was one very big lure.

Frankly, it need only be said that hundreds went broke because they were awful businessmen, reckless or inept. Some built reputations on splurging, and they gambled their clubs away unnecessarily. While this may have brought amusement and admiration, it also led to the hyping of costs and the ruin of skittish clubs. Clever management, not wasteful budgets, were needed but not always in stock. As a result, club operators went broke in droves. Flying in the teeth of Hollywood typecasting, the typical club closed its doors not from a fusillade of machine gun bullets but, inauspiciously, from an excessive flutter of incompetence, shoe-string budgets and cannibal-like extortionists. The lucky ones avoided these pitfalls. But what of the gangster's own internal rules as they applied to his rivals? Here was another source for success or failure.

Rules of the Game

To the urbane racketeer, owning a jazz club was not unlike owning a Dusenburg, and the self-indulgence handsomely repaid the investment. But the common garden variety weed of gangster-turned-proprietor saw his involvement as a straight-forward business proposition. In any event, with so much money, distrust and belligerence floating around an illegal unpoliced activity, the larger and smarter operators quickly realized that a standard of ethics had to be invoked. In this way an attempt was made to reduce the notoriety, limit the casualties and preserve the gains. These men tried to a large extent to free themselves from past habits and conduct a better kind of operation, as Angelo reports:

By and large these were gentlemen we are talking about. Thieves, gamblers, and connivers, yes. But nothing serious. Unruliness was downplayed. A fellow did make a decent effort to be pleasant to people.

Thus it was that a commonsensical series of game rules evolved slowly, tacitly codified, and accepted in the main. While there may have been many locational variances, the odd deviance into violence, and cases where rules were more likely to be observed by this mob or cultural group than that one, we can point to a shadow charter. The important rules included cooperation in helping to stimulate business, good manners when "out on the town," concern for customers—especially women-a code of ethics at least loosely shown to employees and a blanket policy of secrecy to thwart undesired intrusion.

1) Help Stimulate Business for Associates

In this era of windfall profits, legitimate and otherwise, it was in keeping to show a paternalistic streak in stimulating a rival owner's night club business. This ranged from verbal advertising and bountiful tips to the avoidance of tussles and the discounting of saleable merchandise where applicable. Self-respecting gangsters were also expected to avoid cheese-paring in public. This translated into buying all the cigars and

cigarettes from the coat-room girl; or routinely donating from
25 to 50% of the tab to musicians and waiters.[38] One forever
seemed to be flashing goodwill around. "A big-shot couldn't
walk in and out," reminisces one gallant racketeer, "even if he
only use the telephone, unless he spent $50."[39] Dropping large
sums brought acceptance, publicity and smiling
managements.

Honorific recognition and attention to ceremonial ritual
was particularly well received in the Italian territories. Certain
occasions, as when clubs expanded operations or held special
opening nights for new revues, required a cast of characters not
unlike a debutante's ball, with every conceivable affiliation in
the audience. Without them a club's chances for success were
nil.[40] Opening nights were always big attractions:

> For opening nights, Italian mobs always took a party, the bigger the better,
> and set up drinks all around. Whenever the check comes to you, you drop a
> couple of extra century notes alongside. It gives the new business a break and
> lets the guy know who his friends are.[41]

Mobsters could help business simply by filling out their
image in front of their public. Max Gordon, owner of the
Village Vanguard, comments:

> One thing I know, a night club guy can't live without publicity. Without
> publicity you're dead. Even hints of violence or scandal are helpful: Let
> something happen in your joint and you'll get publicity.[42]

Does this mean that violence in clubs might have been
staged? Deliberately, very little, I'm sure; but spontaneous
recreations may have been started for fun or an eye out for
publicity. Samuel Ornitz recalls a club where it was part of a
show:

> We staged riots...and displays of eroticism for customers who loved it....We
> even had three Chinese with particularly yellow and malevolent faces to sit at
> a table smoking very fancy opium pipes...their blood hostages nearby.

Of course professional courtesy was a two-way street.
Management grew accustomed to offering banquet services or

free drinks to bountiful customers, seating special patrons ringside no matter how crowded the dance floor, even going to the extent of cancelling out gambling debts to rival lords who had helped boost business.[43]

2. *Avoid Violent and Improper Conduct*

Despite the imagery cast by Hollywood films or predatory press agents out to color up their columns, violent practices outside Chicago were definitely discouraged. While patrons wishing to read about themselves in the morning press might be tempted to initiate trouble, the insides of cabarets were off-limits for mobster rough stuff. Incompetent or faulty judgment, seen in the case of occasional bombings (known in the trade as "Italian footballs"), and mayhem in clubs only brought the visitation of police wrath, a bad press, an expensive repair bill, and, most importantly, lost trade which followed when abrupt official closures caught owners napping.[44]

Racketeers were generally pretty shy in places of business and before the public since "no one is more conservative about his investment," observed Jack Kofoed, "than the fellow who makes his money in ways not countenanced by society."[45] For most mobsters the old axiom of not interfering with another guy's rackets so long as he respected yours seemed to apply.[46] But violence could take many forms. Dance writes of the Grand Terrace and Earl Hines during the early 1920s:

Guns were often drawn at the GT—even the waiters had guns—but no shots were fired because of the risk of hitting innocent customers. Rival parties from different parts of Chicago would fight sometimes, (only) to throw ice and bottles at each other.

Jordan defined a respectable club as one with "no rough stuff, no pocket pickin', no little private rooms for two, and no knock out drops." Respectability was also measured by the way a club ejected its more unruly customers. Ellington recalls the elaborate Cotton Club procedure used to quell disturbances:

Impeccable behavior was demanded in the room while the show was on. If someone was talking loud...the waiter would come over and touch him on the shoulder. If that didn't do it, the captain would come over and admonish him politely. The headwaiter would remind him that he had been cautioned. After that, if the loud talker continued, somebody would come and throw him out.

This operated for the wealthy and famous. But it was also the prevailing attitude toward customers shown by most clubs up and down the economic spectrum. Ned Williams, press agent at the time, was constantly being amazed by the ease, promptness and fastidious gentility most managements exercised in this regard.[47]

Since public opinion mattered, owners gave both staff and musicians instructions to be wary about potential trouble that could easily take place on small dance floors whern couples bumping together might be inclined to fight. Stopping these problems early, or before they even began, kept cabarets out of the red. I once read somewhere of a club which had to spend $100,000 following a fight begun by two drunken women which later spread to the entire patronage. Some places bothered to hire ex-offenders as doormen. Ostensibly this was as a service to help people into taxis, but more as another watchful, expert eye out for signs of a rumble.[48]

Ahern believed robberies should be transacted away from a club, in the many nearby alleyway passages. As it was, few incidents occurred, whether muggings or stickups, although bizarre stories have been told of violence deferred:

One night one of Capone's clubs was held up by two mercenaries carrying shotguns. Reminded of the ownership at the door, a staff member gave each of them $20. for their effort. Several days later the pair returned as customers and bought the house a round of drinks.[49]

To avoid trouble, waiters might give Mickey Finns—neatly slipped into drinks. Clubs might attract both elegant crowds and underworld types, so it was to their advantage to devise measures which insured tranquility. New York's Hunt Club on 47th Street placed a velvet curtain between the bar and the club proper, effectively separating the hoods from the night club patrons. Many people liked to carry guns, so clubs had them checked at the door and hidden in unlikely locations to again reduce potential violence. Eddie Jackson recalls hiding them in back alleys, washroom toilets and, appropriately enough, on ice in the liquor trays.[50] Gene Fowler claims the presence of the smart set dampened gangland tempers while Cohen believes managements defused violence by directing their own mobs to visit waterfront bars whenever they felt the urge to display rowdy conduct. For jazz musicians this was a vast departure from the experiences they had known in Southern tonks.

While it lasted, and until the wars of the early 1930s, clubs were universally inviolate. "As a rule," writes one club owner, "rivals sought to take trade away from each other by legitimate means."[51] This meant cutthroat price wars, the pirating of employees from one club to another, attempts to buy out competition, or derogatory remarks made to destroy a competitor's business. Yet this sort of thing is recognized as being acceptable for any endeavor at any time. But open conflict took place in lonely garbage dumps and river beds, and by men unrelated to the night club business except in a peripheral sense. As one racketeer phrased it:

The mobster has no quarrel with the public at large. He is only too anxious to see it in good health and prosperous. They are his customers . . . his livelihood.[52]

3. *Protect Women*

Whether they be patrons or employees and singers, women were protected from abusive language, demanding situations and assaultive behavior by paternalistic club owners. In fact, clubs prided themselves on keeping the women who ventured in by themselves free from annoyance. Mobsters liked beautiful women to come escorted, thus lessening possibilities for trouble. Since brawls over and by women were the single most bellicose factor for club violence, easily causing more damage than any mobster's rampage, strategies which headed off trouble were always valid:

One had to be in evening dress to get in (the night club), for Big Joe Carozzo insisted on class, and one must not be alone. The lone visitor is sometimes a husband looking for his wife.[53]

Women could also be used to as buffers in a moderating

heated argument. Racketeers were not always known for keeping cool heads in awkward situations, but having women around tended to take their thoughts off dangerous schemes. It was thus not surprising to a wide variety of indulgences installed in cabarets, all with the air of securing a large share of female patronage: lounges, restroom amenities, special decor, comfortable furnishings, a full range of cocktails, dancing space and even stairways, so fashionably-dressed women walking in could make an immediate splash. [These were vastly different from club and saloon practices of the 1900s.] Safety against purse snatchers was even guaranteed in the Harlem joints.[54] Sam Weiss, host of the Onyx Club on 52nd Street, agrees with this view:

The attitude of the mobsters, certainly the big-time mobsters, was to let the musicians alone. They were gentlemen too, when it came to the girls. They never bothered them.[55]

4. *Maintain a Code of Ethics*
    Network people, employees, musicians, even public officials, under this maxim, should not be beaten out of their tribute, fees or bribe. Customers might be treated in a cavalier fashion as they were free not to select a night club. But deceit created unwanted repercussions that could affect many clubs and consign any single joint to the trash bin overnight. It was easier and cheaper to replace bands or hire other personnel than to cheat staff outright. If anything, tales have come down implying that owners may have been a little too munificent at times, awarding employees for the most marginal of services. In the end, lavishness had dangerous implications and caused clubs to bid themselves out of the marketplace when hard times came.
    Additionally, a man should conduct both himself and his business honorably. In this context, the creed of one bootlegger-turned-owner is worth repeating at length, for it summarizes a common-sensical attitude that characterized the industry:

In my business, the same as everywhere else, you have to have nerve and vision. But along with them you need hard work, sobriety, and honesty. Give a fair profit to your producer or importer and a fair wage to your employees; then take only a fair profit from your customers and don't handle anything but the genuine goods. Don't handle dangerous overly cheap booze, and leave customers satisfied.... I won out when I began a high-toned line for high-toned customers.[56]

According to impressario Granlund:

In all the years I dealt with them, I never had a written contract with any of them and I was never gypped or given a bad deal by a gangster owner.

Ellington has fond memories of one club owner's honesty:

Barron Wilkens was a beautiful man. He had lots of money but he never hustled a customer. Of course, that was the general spirit of those times.

Thirdly, a club owner should be wary but not be afraid to integrate. Younger patrons, ganglords and certainly many entertainers in the 1920s were open on this question and far less resistant than the so-called liberated times in which they lived. Even so, the reasons for integrating were not always altrusitic, and Eastern clubs were guilty of enticing whites with the prospect of watching black men dancing with white women[57] Collectively, mobs and club owners shared no definite opinion on the issue, and were willing to be generous if the neighborhood itself was tolerant, knowing full well the dangers of running an integrated club. In some ways, however jazz clubs were synonymous in the public's mind with integration.

In the early post-war years, it was a decidedly risky affair. No fewer than two dozen race riots took place in 1919 alone, with many more to follow as the 1920s wound down. These were not always in the South, as the terrible events in Chicago were to show. But strict segregation in places like Dallas and Atlanta created sensitivities in both black and white customers that had to be considered before a club set down its roots and invited everyone to enter. Some whites refused to visit certain areas; some blacks refused to patronize places where whites were in the majority.[58] Yet where possible,

gangsters allowed black musicians and patrons to feel at
home, employing black bouncers to reduce racial tensions. Nor
were they averse to delegating authority to black managers
who gained valuable experience and financial backing in the
process. By this means some blacks, anyway, became cabaret
operators in their own right, eventually competing with white
rivals for a share of the stacks.[59] The nature of this relationship
awaits its scholar, and only speculation can be made on how
well they cooperated.

One final point needs emphasizing. For newly-purchased
gin mills and speakeasies, the code expected a man to hire his
immigrant relatives, whatever the capacity and however inept
they appeared to be, or to retain as many of the former staff as
was possible. Offering the original owner a position was
likewise viewed as adroit and best suited to protect an
investment. Reasonable terms brought their own rewards;
antagonizing or humbling a seller, if it pushed him into
seeking gleeful revenge, hardly helped a night club forge
ahead. It was also wise to keep the club's name, and the usual
services it offered, that is, unless a stigma was attached to
either, as a way of appeasing regular clients. Regretfully, these
tacit terms did not apply everywhere, and often were not to be
found in the Chicago area for reasons of local custom.
According to Cohen, Chicago's atmosphere was so lethally
charged and public officials so corrupt that names changed as
often as table linen and club practices were in a state of
constant flux. "Transfers and turnovers appeared endlessly,"
he reports, "and distribution of power, combined with
individual ego-trips led to rip-offs where all the rules were
transcended." Embodying practices such as these, the city was
established as a truly violent place with mobs ruthlessly
expropriating each other. Musicians feared such moments
which, when they did occur, found the entire staff of a cabaret
out of work with neither warning nor compensation—
dependent on promises of some erstwhile hoodlum owner for
survival.

5. *Secrecy Counts for Everything*
    A man's past was his own and had to be left alone. Black

musicians were appreciative of this policy as the white promoters, for everyone seemed to be hiding some peccadillo in those days. Musicians had families or criminal arrests they wished kept hidden; likewise for the mobsters who wished to keep many of their investments secret. There were even socially confidential situations. Drug peddling to the wealthy might be a club's secondary source of income, providing a service few wished others to know. In some cases secrecy was desired by owners or managers having affairs with prominent socialites who had been atttracted to these "men of action," or conducting some kind of nefarious transaction with a high-level politician.

The chief difficulty I experienced in conducting research for this study rests on this aspect of the code. Few musicians had any intention of breaking venerable standards and met my inquiries with stony silence. This because the code specifically prohibits speaking to outsiders whose trustworthiness is unproven. In this connection, one bootlegger catalogued an impressive list of undesirable people who would blow secrecy in a pinch:

Never hire a talker, a braggart, anyone anxious to be taken, a scrapper, a writer, a dupe, a boozer, a lady's man, an overly flashy dresser, or fellows with little noses. Men with little noses are generally little men inside.[61]

Secrecy was extended to include the physical premises of clubs. Like out of stories of pirates' dens, clubs created unusual hiding places. Escape tunnels, trap doors, false fronts behind which alcohol might be stored, buzzer alarm systems, and the old reliable—hidden, sliding panels—were part of a club's exterior and interior security, all of them adding considerably to a thoughtful joint's budget. How often these were used, and how successfully they protected their owners, we shall never know. Many police raids, of course, had been tipped off ahead of time by adequately bribed officials, so these devices appear to have been of minimal value, allowing hiding places for gangsters to use against one another.

By the mid-1920s, the Sicilian and Jewish gangsters who had embarked on a night club jazz business were personally

committed to values and practices that did their best to
establish a workable code of ethics, minimize violence and
enhance their own self-image. Money that was spent
energetically by efficient management created a productive
velocity where a dollar generated far more than that alone. On
the other side of the scale, we have countless owners who were
driven to the wall by escalating expenses, entrepreneurial
inadequacies, and a payoff system they could never come to
master. Only a small percentage were in fact forced out
through violence brought on by rival mobs. Territories were too
large and business too bountiful, at least in the 1920s to make
this necessary. Regardless, in some respects the men of this
group, failures and successes alike, were surely ahead of their
times. They may have been avaricious to some degree, but by
fighting for small measures of social justice—through hiring
practices, integrational policies, a softened attitude toward
women and young people generally, and the feeling of avoiding
moral condemnation of others—they made an effort to improve
patron pleasures in as safe and respectful an atmosphere as
possible. This in itself was a far cry from the policies found in
saloons and bars only a few years earlier.

The opportunities and salaries and attention lavished
upon jazz artists, who were all the while being provided with a
dignified setting in which to perform (at least compared to the
past), freed from concern about racial interference, were new
departures that brought a share of wealth and fame in its train.
But the extent of this bounty requires a broader survey, and to
this we now turn our attention.

Chapter VII

Counting Up the Gains of Gangster Patronage

Comedian Joe E. Lewis:

Mob courtesy? Why at the first place I worked, the boss used to shoot you goodnight.

Comedian Henny Youngman:

In those days a hood would come into a joint with a few well-armed friends, slip the bandleader a C-note, and tell him to play very loud. That way nobody knew anything happened till some guy would fall out of his chair not dead drunk, just dead.

Introduction

Thanks to the repetitiously wanton violence served up in Hollywood movies, the merest hint of gangsterism immediately conjures up scenes of one-way rides, alley-way ambushes, tommy-gun battles from speeding cars, and the inevitable finish to a mobster's career—the concrete bathing costume. Movie historian John Gabree criticizes the heavy trading Hollywood waged on this aspect:

If Capone had never existed, Hollywood screenwriters would have had to invent him. . . . Hollywood was ever ready to exploit a good thing and followed the very popular movie "Underworld" (1927) with a cycle of crime films . . . in which gangsters and policemen were killed in great numbers (influencing) an entire generation of citizens.

Such worn-out patterns for mob mentality eventually crept into television. Elliot Ness, star of the interminable "Untouchables" series, exemplifies the resolute leader of an heroic band conducting a ceaseless campaign against

135

psychotic bootlegger killers. As a result, the early movie impressions have devolved through the new medium, filling contemporary viewers with similar attitudes. I have taught gangs and group violence courses in the university where a majority of students came away with this single-most characteristic impression although I had given it secondary importance in my lectures.

So it is that studying the relationship between gangsters and musicians would flounder lest I paid particular attention to the benefits and dispensations accruing to recipients of underworld patronage. The question whether these benefits overshadowed a mob's prediliction for violence and mayhem has to be answered. It is worth recalling that many subsidizers who were on familiar terms with the artists were Italian and Jewish, seemingly ill-suited culturally to befriend jazz musicians. Irish clan loyalties and their distaste for the music kept most of their gangsters outside the orbit of jazz. Other ethnic gangs dotted around the country were equally unhelpful. The Traum gang which ran Terre Haute and Indianapolis, the Stephens mob in San Antonio, Lou Blonger's Denver outfit, the Egans of St. Louis, and the many white Protestant groups in the Southwest, surveyed in Gus Tyler's compendium, offer examples of underworld consortiums who did nothing to promote and serve the interests of jazz musicians.

This system of patronage was witness to many special and unrecorded favors or misdeeds that have disappeared from memory, leaving us with a bag of impressionable ambiguities. In many instances we think they brought benefit although the nature of this and how it was done are not exactly clear. One authority dispenses with specifics and offers up a blanket statement: "Chicago gangsters supported Joe Oliver and many other New Orleans jazzmen bountifully and in many ways."[1] But we are left guessing what those ways might have been and whether favors were excluded for non-New Orleans artists.

Mike Rowe's account of the Chess Brothers, bootleggers and cabaret owners under the Capone umbrella, hints of their impact and the personal touch they had on many Chicago

South Side jazzmen in the late 1920s and early 1930s without being more precise. This, together with the already mentioned musicians' secrecy and the impossibility of cataloging gifts and broken jaws becomes understandable. Not that any self-respecting racketeer would have donated for reasons of publicity. More likely, as Whyte points out, this kind of decency, albeit shown in crude form, was traceable to a social etiquette arising from the juvenile gang days of their youth, where generosity was expected of the leaders.

Nor can a gauge be applied to the relative abrasiveness and conflict found between two groups. Contacts by relatively uneducated, boorish, egotistical men toward outsiders by rule necessarily spurred squabbles and misunderstandings too numerous to mention. Musicians might even blame in selected instances. C.M. Fair tells us the musicians he had spoken with claimed they disliked lending money to colleagues, avoided definite appointments when they could, were unmoved by sad stories and showed little desire for worldly responsibilities and business activity.[2]

Summing up then, this author, bearing in mind all the foregoing limitations, believes the attitudes, favors and relatively few demands which mobsters placed on jazz artists vastly outweighed any negative encounters and were of utmost importance in causing jazzmen to shape their music in the way they did. Here were some of those avenues of approach:

The Plus Side

The jazz musician who paid particular attention to house rules, was treated to a virtually unlimited protective blanket of favors. Rules in this sense included keeping silent to police and strangers, keeping a lid on avarice and alcoholic abuse (or gambling), and keeping to approved standards of neatness and reliability while on the bandstand. Satisfaction of these basics led to a wide range of services, including charity, child maintenance and alimony, even family support during unexpected jail sentences, medical benefits, aid in arranging property transfers or in witnessing legal papers, or quite possibly helping settle quarrels.[3] Mobsters were even tolerant and forgiving of transgressions unless they themselves were the main victim. One confidant told me that hotel jobs were especially prized by some musicians less for the work or money than for the unrestricted opportunities for theft and burglary while they were off the podium and strolling the lobby. Limited activities in bootlegging and dope dealing also brought with them no visible reprisals from mobsters. Ellington once turned down a lucrative offer to join a major New York bootlegging distributorship, and musicians like Mezz Mezzrow were authorized to supply marijuana and the like to comrades.[4]

Whether because of these tendencies and associations, or because so many were born amidst poverty and were playing a music sullied by the unsavoriness of its locations, jazz artists were on very familiar, often unpleasant terms with the local police. Many could hardly risk leaving places of employment without encountering distrustful officers who subjected them to harassment, surveillance and, of course, instant detention.

Omnibus street arrest charges like jaywalking, gambling, loitering and vagrancy were adroitly used by officers, demanding the inevitable appearance of some gangster-employer (or his lawyer) at the precinct station, bail money or political infuence in hand, as a means of securing release for some bedraggled musician. Earl Hines developed a technique which made police arrests a little more palatable:

Chicago police would raid the Sunset and we would all have to get into the patrol wagon and go down to the police station every night. All we did was sign up and go back to finish the rest of the night. I stood up in the wagon so often on those trips, I finally decided to *run* and get a seat when the police came.[5]

Gangsters were prompt with checkbook at meeting sudden road or hotel bills, or paying railroad fares for bands they liked but had been left high and dry by unscrupulous local promoters who reneged on contracts, leaving musicians to the mercies of unknown backwater regions. And whenever it appeared destined that bands might miss opening night performances [clubs viewed these as important celebrity and social affairs,] particularly if the reasons were beyond their control, syndicates burned the midnight oil devising ways of liberating their musicians from the clutches of some rural sheriff.[6]

Easily the most appreciated and used benefit was the cash donation. This assumed a variety of shapes and sizes but the most common were for services rendered, or as a simple gift. The latter often took the form of tips. Money was an obvious benefit to jazz artists who had always known the underneath side of life. Lil Hardin, pianist for the Louis Armstrong orchestra, recalls the gross disparity between her $2.60 a night in a drab dance hall in Memphis and the earnings of $150 a week playing for the mob-owned Dreamland and Pekin Gardens in Chicago. Arnold Loycano of the Tom Brown band remembers how "they paid us at least $25 a week in Chicago in 1915 when we'd been making $1 a night" in the South. The bands of Sammy Stewart, Chick Webb and Earl Hines, to name only three, left work in obscure cities simply because money power was to be had in the better-run gangster clubs of the larger Northern cities.[7] In Dance's biography of him, Hines was very complimentary to the Jewish owner of Chicago's Elite Inn for rescuing him from provincial anonymity with a handsome financial offer.

Salaries for black jazz artists, while not on a par with what whites received, nonetheless reflected the surging buoyancy of the period. Nightclub racketeering was one of the few growth industries in the 1920s generous enough to share windfall profits with blacks who helped create them. No longer did musicians risk playing all night for "bus fare, beer, and a bucket of pigfeet."[8] Leading sidemen and leaders alike amassed colossal sums for the times, which, when set alongside the variety of fringe benefits, enabled them to join the ranks of contemporary black professionals. Mobsters freed the musicians from the tyranny of their geography and the dominance of their superiors. Shorn of this backing, "blacks faced playing in surroundings vastly inferior in terms of working conditions, wages, and demands on what must be played."[9]

Historically, musicians have been on intimate terms with one another, if for no other reason than to steer comrades toward jobs or available accommodations. It was on this issue that another avenue was created in which urban jazzmen could pick up money and favors from underworld club owners. Many gangsters believed musicians were far better judges of talent than customers and preferred to delegate some of them as talent scouts and booking agents whenever fresh faces presented themselves. Lucky Millinder, Mezz Mezzrow, Jack Laine, Red McKenzie, Ben Pollock, Charles Elgar, Dave Peyton, Bennie Moten, Tiny Parham and Jimmy Noone represent a few illustrious, resourceful scouts; but every city had its share. Millinder, for example, earned extra money filling voids in the Hines Orchestra at the Grand Terrace.[10] Sharpiro and Hentoff quote Hot Lips Page, trumpet player, on the industrious Bennie Moten:

Moten was a businessman first and last. He had a lot of connections and he was a very good friend (to the Kansas City mobs). Through contacts of this kind he was able to control all the good jobs and choice locations in and around Kansas City. He helped the Blue Devils of Walter Page immensely. Moten played in the orchestra and at times walked off the stand into the audience to join some influential people, since it was good for business.

Borrowing money free from entangling interest rates that crippled the average debtor was also within arm's reach to a munificent mobster's favorite musicians. Ralph Watkins, manager of Kelly's Stables in Chicago, claims a considerable amount of money was lent jazzmen during these years and that feeble, token payments were not only acceptable in settlement but customary so long as musicians acted and repaid in good faith.[11] Of course this was not always the case. Musicians were inveterate gamblers, normally running a high tab and possessed a plethora of personal reasons for borrowing, so unpaid debts were commonplace.

Unscrupulous chiselers soured many a mobster's loan. But gangster reaction in such matters varied considerably, from convenient forgetfulness or mock revenge to altering work arrangements to help alleviate the debt. By this method of enforced reimbursement a musician might find himself playing well beyond his normal closing date—forcing the cancellation of future contracts—while working for peanuts, or become a rum rummer and smuggler until a percentage of the loan was paid. Cohen claims that enforcement was only spasmodically applied even when artists took to the road rather than pay up. Flagrant cases rarely met with gun-to-head tactics; rather, an informal blacklisting existed as a control mechanism. Welching could quickly tarnish a musician's reputation to the point that hiring him for jobs in any large city would be unthinkable once local racketeers learned of his past misdeeds.

Gangsters loved to tip, and so gratuities was a third form of financial backing. These could be quite sizable, far surpassing salaries, union wages, even a club's nightly profits. Ruth Spanier often saw mobsters cram "wads of bills in her husband's horn." Tommy Brookins (with the Johnny Dodds band) reports how each member made $200 a week in tips alone from gangster customers, an amount three times their standard union rate. This hardly represents an isolated situation. Trumpeter Walter Fuller says "We used to make tips galore while at the Vogue in Chicago."[12]

Some underworld characters fashioned trademarks in the manner in which they dispersed tips. Volly DeFaut, reedman for NORK when it played the Friar's Inn, was a typically curious musician whenever such men entered the room:

One mobster liked to tear up $100 bills and give parts of them to different guys in the band. We had one guy in the band who'd take them home and work into the morning putting them back together.[13]

Some mobsters tossed half dollar pieces onto the podium or dance floor; others quietly tucked them into a man's instrument, as in Spanier's case, or were unduly bountiful whenever their favorite songs were played. Bandleaders could expect to be summoned to a mobster's ringside table during intermission and a weighty envelope slipped into his breast pocket. Hines recalls Capone's style:

He used to come by the club at night and if I met him by the door he might put his hand up to straighten my handkerchief, and there would be a $100 bill, or he might give me a handshake and put a $20 bill in my hand.[14]

It was easy to become spoiled by the regularity of these donations:

Underworld bosses never owed you money. They paid 2-3 weeks in advance, and we could always count on a few guys spending high and tipping well at every show.[15]

Gangsters could be a soft touch, and reputations were founded solely on flagrant generosity. Stories by Damon Runyan, for the most part written from fact not fancy, narrate this side of gangdom. The spinoff from some musician's melancholy tale might be an educational scholarship established for him or a member of his family. Al Capone was a frequent soup kitchen operator, providing food for the downtrodden during hard times or relief work in moments of personal tragedy.[16]

During moments of grief or crisis, questions were rarely asked and offers came instinctively and without delay. Deaths in a musician's family, parents in particular, brought instant financial assistance.[17] Moreover countless stories circulate casting these men in the unlikely role of social worker whose efforts spent attempting to dissuade performers from booze and narcotics were as much from friendship as for protection of their investment. Many were the tabs picked up by racketeers for innumerable cures that addicts like Billie Holliday and Charlie Parker begrudgingly underwent.

Ellington claims that mobsters were not adverse to treating treasured jazz artists to a night on the town, all expenses paid. This often happened to Willie "The Lion" Smith by his underworld sponsors. Harlem racketeer Ed Smith exemplified the humane employer as he periodically instructed members of his house band to buy automobiles on his credit, repayment to be made in $5. installments and whenever convenient. Art Hodes remembers the time when an underworld boss gave his small group not only food, drink and $100 per man following their audition, but money enough to buy a car to get to the job.[18] The giving of band instruments appears to have been a common gesture of liberality by club managements. When the Cotton Club bought its drummer

Sonny Greer drums worth more than $3000, other club owners were prodded into buying similar sets to appease their artists. One investor of musicals, gangster Arnold Rothstein, donated an $800 gold-plated, pearl-backed ruby-encrusted banjo to Elmer Snowden simply to dazzle the audience of a revue which lasted less than a week. Not to be outdone, the Grand Terrace's Ed Fox bought Earl Hines a $3000 Bechstein piano and had his own son stand guard over it on the bandstand.[19]

Underworld leaders might even consider the final resting days of their pet performers, realizing most of them had little to look forward to when their careers ended. Investments in property were made by leading mobsters and their agents, and men like the Chess Brothers and Benny Skoler made musicians beneficiaries to property. Joe Glaser is credited with helping Louis Armstrong amass one million dollars through wise and choice purchases. Drummer Sammy Cohen remembers the many occasions when racketeers offered to set him up in a drum business upon his retirement from playing.

In this connection an incident between CBS and the Cotton Club deserves repeating. In 1927 CBS approached the club about broadcasting the Ellington Orchestra although fearful that the mob owners would extract an outrageous tribute for the privilege. But lo, to their amazement, management assumed an entirely unexpected position, insisting only that the band receive the proper amount of exposure befitting its stature. Demanding a first class aircheck, the management then softened:

There's no money in it for me; it will do some good to CBS. However, it'll probably do some good for Duke too, so go ahead and we'll see what happens.[20]

Bands securing legitimate mob sponsorship, if such a phrase can be employed, were handed virtually blank checks. They were free to decide upon their repertoire, to travel at will, to exchange or adjust sideman duties without murmur from management, and to accept concurrent engagements to the number they believed they could honor. The only stipulation was a strict one: report on time to satisfy show schedules of their original backers. There is some reason to believe these leniencies were in effect with bands in the early rather than the late 1920s, for by the early 1930s we read of orchestras being locked into "virtually lifetime contracts" by strong-willed managements afraid of impending changes, of which the Earl Hines group represents one notable exception.[21]

Business opportunities for musicians might very well have been in the process of erosion even before the 1929 crash, for we learn of few multiple job arrangements which figured so prominently in the early 1920s. Volly DeFaut says that the NORK, like many bands in the 1918-1923 period on the South Side, played for no fewer than three separate engagements alternately without drawing the least comment from any of the gangster managements. From noon until 2 p.m. NORK appeared at the Canton Tea Garden, moving to the Moulin Rouge from 3-6 p.m., only to close on its regular stint at the Friars Inn from 1-6 a.m. "All of them paid well," he reports, $150 a week plus $100 in tips."[22]

Pops Foster recalls to his biographer Tom Stoddard that his band played for five different clubs daily, packing in as tightly as possible without complaint. The Wolverines Jazz Band freely accepted work to include Jewish and Italian wedddings, plus their usual nightly chores. It may have been exhausting romping across town from one club to another, but working for these gangsters had its airy moments, as bassist Quinn Wilson remembers:

The gangsters were one reason why the job. . . was fun. They always liked to play, and those guys were funny. . . and playful.[23]

Another benefit was long engagements, preferred by the mobs [as much as the musicians] or reasons of publicity and in promoting a stable entertainment package. Few owners liked abrupt, unplanned changes and carried the same faces in their house bands for years if only because it brought a sort of peace of business mind. Bands might thus play at one or two clubs for years, becoming fixtures as well as attractions. This attempt at stability brought with it three important byproducts. First it kept bands intact over the long run. Bouts of disjointed, intermittent work—reminders of the early days of jazz—had led to constant personnel changes and depreciated musical skills. On the other hand, guaranteed employment acted as a strong bracer in recruiting decent sidemen, assuring groups of the best available talent. An orchestra thus favored with a permanent membership would, in the course of time, upgrade its techniques, smooth out jagged edges in performance and, just as significantly, learn the art of showmanship. Freed from the vagaries of box office pressures, this security enabled groups to perfect the style and sound by which they became known and accepted.

Second, long engagements increased the social and business awareness of jazz bands. Acting in the capacity of business agents, paternalistic racketeers and club owners helped young musicians in leaping the barriers. Night club managers were known to view their bands like babies, taking pride in a group's progress, as if it were an infant beginning to walk. In the process, interested jazz men learned the business. They might grow more articulate and adroit in negotiations, finances and the overlapping social interaction; and unlike their Southern predecessors, who were such novices, some might even learn ways of making supplementary incomes for themselves. Careful guidance from the right legal advisers meant musicians no longer such easy prey the unscrupulous agents.

Finally, long engagements left jazz bands untampered with and free to make significant improvements and stylistic changes. Underworld cabarets allowed more musical improvisation than dance halls, taxi dances and hotels. They also featured more than music for dancing. Art Hodes points out cabarets made money when customers were seated and ordering, not twirling around the floor. It was for this reason that floor shows, revues and intermission piano players were used extensively and creatively.[24] The first use of foot cymbals took place in a Chicago gangster hangout, the Green Mill, in 1922, possibly for a revue. Erskine Tate experimented with flutes and violins at the Club Vendome, Sammy Stewart inaugurated the interplay of bassoon and bass clarinet in the jazz orchestra during his Sunset Cafe engagement, and Fletcher Henderson, while at the Club Alabam, another underworld joint, presented the first known example of a sax section capable of broad use in cabaret surroundings. This occurred as far back as 1922. Kansas City jam sessions (which mobsters underwrote) first featured the walking bass and steady guitar chord punctuations from the Bennie Moten and Count Basie bands. The lusty, abandoned, African-influenced tones, later a trademark of the era which perfected Duke Ellington's orchestra (among others),0 was also a product of long engagements and non-intervention which gangster owners practiced in their clubs. Clearly these advances didn't spring into life overnight. Ortiz Walton reminds us that Ellington first conceived the idea of a jazz orchestra (which in 1943 became the "Black, Brown, and Beige Suite") during his long Cotton Club engagement.

Thanks to these mob benefits and the recognition that soon followed, jazz artists sustained proportionately larger social and financial gains than other ghetto residents. Alain Locke writes how the jazz musicians were "almost solely responsible for dragging black culture into an assertive position within the marketplace of the world." In 1925 A.J. Rogers noted that "jazz was protest against repressions," while a recent critic, John Lax, contends that "the jazz musician was the prestigious member of the black society in the 1920s." But it was only through the auspices of mob support that his group could hope to carve out new ground.

Musicians dressed better, and often modelled themselves along the lines of their fashionably attired bosses—although there must have been quite a lot of give and take on this point. They lived far better than most ghetto residents, and probably called most of their own shots. Photographs galore show these men seated comfortably behind the steering wheels of glamorously expensive roadsters, wrapped in enormous fur coats. Seen in its own time and context, this was indeed a social revolution of the highest order, laying the groundwork for future black demands, suggesting an equality with whites that must have filled contemporary black youngsters with racial pride. Unlike the majority of whites, gangsters displayed little overt envy and did little to upset this development.

All the foregoing should not be interpreted as ignoring the

pronounced effect jazz musicians exerted on mobsters. Nor
should one overlook the possibility that underworld figures
may very well have modelled themselves on jazz artists
employed in their clubs. Quite conceivably, jazz musicians
altered and broadened, even softened to some extent, mobster
attitudes and penchants for violence. Given the very long
relationship which transpired between them, and we have
already dated this to around the 1870s, there were sufficient
contacts to appreciably influence one another. There was a
similarity in street corner habits, vices and status
consciousness that brought the groups together. So too did
their fondness for staying out late in sociable activities,
including a swaggering style, a fascination for gambling and a
leisurely approach toward life. These interdependent
structural components, as Alphons Silberman, the French
musicologist, prefers to call them, made it difficult to decide
who was influencing whom and when. The group solidarity,
toughness, comic attitudes and masculinity of jazz bands must
have appealed to young toughs. Mobsters grew attentive to
individual members, and accepted bands like extended
families; doubtless black jazz artists expressed parallel
conviviality. Claude McKay held no reservations on the
subject, despite his suspiciousness of whites generally.[25] Some
Jews and Italians were quick to sense the value of the
relationship one Jewish musician writes::

It helped open us up to our own feelings, get rid of our collective guilt, and made
us think about creative ways to explain ourselves.[26]

Friendliness and common decency which both groups held for
one another must have allowed them to cross boundaries in
adapting parts of their character to what they liked in the other
half, and there is no reason to suppose that musicians were
anything but moderating influences on men normally
predatory and wolfish.

The Minus Side

Down through the ages any number of disagreements and

tragic misunderstandings have imperiled relations between artist and patron. According to Hoefer, many of these have gone far beyond the stage of simple verbal retort, and both sides stand guilty of mischief. In effect, conflicts of this kind amount to a universal condition. So it is that in the case of jazz musicians and their underworld benefactors the grosser excesses and turmoil may explain less than we wish. Even examples of unmitigated violence and miserliness appear more the outgrowth of a particularly feisty society than of any uniquely tyrannical notions which mobsters may have had toward musicians. Nor were musicians blameless. The preceding section has already made some remarks on this point. Saxophonist Franz Jackson claims "It's not only that musicians are suspicious, but they're very flaky in their temperaments and so sensitive."[27] And in this study, one shouldn't forget the exceptions who were unreliable and indifferent to business.

While it is easy to condemn socially-harmful behavior, violence affecting jazz artists often had very little to do with gangsters. In the course of documenting this study, I uncovered few incidents that can be portrayed as gangster brutality toward the musicians. Deliberate, raw-boned bullyism was held to a minimum. There is always the possibility that it was not unlike police brutality; and if that is the situation, we shall never know the full story.

In any event, when one considers the nightly hours jazzmen played were the same ones dedicated to criminal activity, that the most dangerous kind of men frequented the clubs and the cabarets—ostensibly to relax—and that many spots were unauthorized scenes of dreadful mayhem between irate or publicity-seeking customers who challenged everyone around including the racketeers themselves, the fact that so few examples spring to mind seems little short of miraculous. Angelo remembers only two terrible acts in his fifteen years in the business: Granlund, who once witnessed the shooting of a night club operator and a chorus girl, entitled this mishap "an exception." According to him, if problems did arise they were caused by a handful of sadists, parasites and misers.

In actual fact, a case can be made that the most dangerous

places to work lay far south of the gangster-infested eastern cities. Reporters Lait and Mortimer likened Washington D.C.'s nightlife violence in the 1920s to the worst offered up in Suez and Shanghai. Home to few gangs, Dallas, Birmingham, Memphis and Louisville bore appalling crime rates.[28] Nor should we overlook what has already been said about the nasty, turbulent Southern gin mills. These often pitted musicians against customers, as in 1932, when Evan Thomas, leader of the Black Eagle band, was murdered by a jealous husband during a performance in Rayne, Louisiana.

Artie Shaw recalls a certain Kentucky dance hall job in the 1930s when his band became sandwiched between opposing mountain clans whose long-standing feud resumed on the dance floor bullets ricocheting in every direction. Pops Foster had his own close call in Beardston, Illinois, a small coal mining town. The job was in a hangout crowded with unruly miners carrying their own moonshine in huge jugs. Drinking was continuous and in generous amounts. Foster claims that one night a foul-looking miner, unshaven and filthy, sat chewing tobacco at a table directly adjacent to the band. Over and over came his request—either play "Yes We Have No Bananas," or the pistol in his lap would start barking and spitting. With monotony the request was filled, only broken when he left to visit the toilet. Foster had little doubt that the gun would have been used had they refused to play a number which went on to haunt him in the future.

Law officers could become more violent than any gangster. Polly Adler remembers the many police shakedowns of her bordellos. They were perfect excuses, she wrote in her autobiography, for sadistic cops to use violence and strong-arm tactics on those they disliked or who refused to pay up. George Brunis, an early jazz artist, recalls the many gun fights which occurred when he played the Valentine Inn in Chicago, as Federal men took to shooting at bootleggers and the local white union took to employing police in an effort to eject black bands from the local clubs along the North Southside.[29] The most dangerous location for artists was not in night clubs or in murky back alleys, but actually on the highways. *Downbeat Magazine* pointed out that simply being a jazz musician disqualified an applicant for both automobile and life insurance policies, principally because of the many highway fatalities which claimed the lives of this group.[30]

But the fact remains that musicians were an endangered species; more so in the earlier years. Kenneth Allsop characterizes the night clubs of the 1920s as places where anything might happen to anyone without a stone's throw. Racketeer Blackie Sullivan was riddled by a dozen machine-gun bullets while standing in front of the Torch Club in Chicago and Johnny Phillips was killed in 1924 in a cabaret while in the process of kidnapping two cops. Some managers were always on pins and needles. According to Art Hodes, at the least little noise, the boss of the Capital Dancing School would blaze out of his office wielding pearl-handled revolvers. Shapiro and Hentoff comment about the glory days:

In New Orleans in the early days, there were plenty of brawls in the bar business (and) its history is full of smashed words and broken promises.

Every musician of this era doubtless harbors his own wry anecdote of a dangerous encounter. Eddie Condon, for example, tells of the night his bass player's bulky instrument became the target for a hoodlum's pistol practice. The one consolation was that after blasting the wood frame into hundreds of little chips, the marksman paid handsomely for a replacement. Pops Foster recalls playing for a small-time mob in the early 1930s. At the close of the engagement the band approached the manager who refused to pay them. "We got mad...and had a battle royal," writes his biographer, "and I got knocked on the head and ended up in the hospital."[31] This occurred in 1931 and points up how late in the day it was for bands to face this kind of danger.

Personal grudges led to nasty encounters. Richard Alexis, New Orleans bass player, suffered a broken jaw on a job, and at the Famous Door, mobster Pretty Boy Amberg once belted cornetist Louis Prima for supposed insubordination.[32] One of the more frightening incidents in the East took place in the early 1920s when black bandleader James R. Europe was shot dead by a black mobster during a Boston engagement. It goes without saying, musicians could avoid physical abuse simply by ignoring a racketeer's criminal activities. Muggsy Spanier recalls witnessing a celebrated 1933 abduction of Jake the Barber by a Chicago beer-runner but never reported it. "I figured it was none of my business. I didn't want to get mixed up in it."[33]

Given the highly unpredictable nature of violence and the constant threat of shakedowns, musicians carried weapons for their own protection. Certainly this was a habit dating from their days in New Orleans. Nevertheless, and although I have no way of proving it, I managed to locate but one instance where a musician actually put weapons to use. This was Horsey Dean, an Irish piano-playing bandleader in Chicago. Shot in the neck in a pre-Prohibition saloon fight, Dean survived with life and memory intact. He forevermore carried a pistol which he later had to use on a roadhouse hoodlum who forcefully demanded that Dean's band play a request as the group was closing up for the night:

When the hoodlum pulled out a gun and again demanded, Horsey quietly whipped out his pistol and shot him dead. He was later acquitted as police saw this as a gesture in self-defense.[34]

Duke Ellington called it an era when celebrities had to carry weapons lest they be assaulted by would-be abductors, heist artists or women bent on slapping them with paternity suits. Ellington was himself victim of a 1931 kidnapping plot, and later claimed that he carried a .38 calibre revolver to avoid encounters such as the one when several thugs demanded that he part either with $500 or his life. "Inasmuch as the entire band carried weapons," he wrote, "I told them we would welcome a shoot-out." Musician Dickie Wells was more afraid of the Southern customers:

We used to run up against a lot of frightful people, drunken people...ofays would try to frighten you if somebody got out of line and wanted to beat up the band or shoot somebody. If you pull a gun there's two chances to one, the cat is going to cool down....All the bands, white and colored, used to have a stash someplace, because there'd always be some crank who wanted to mess with you.

Jelly Roll Morton not only packed a piece in his perambulations around Chicago's tough 35th Street, he advertised the fact. Because the street was so dangerous, "you had to act bad, whether you were or not."[35]

Whenever rival gangs poached on forbidden territory bent on securing talent that didn't belong to them, the hostility level immediately shot up. When Earl Hines hired away Billie Eckstine from a low-paying job at Chicago's famed Club DeLisa, two rival mobs, armed to the teeth, squared off in the middle of the Grand Terrace ready to do battle. Only after a lengthy discussion did cooler heads prevail, and the singer allowed to stay.[36] But violence could not always be avoided. Instant shoot-outs were one face-saving, life-losing technique. The famous 1913 gun battle in the Tuxedo Dancehall between two New Orleans mobs thirsting for blood provides one example of an encroachment that left five gangsters dead or wounded. Of the musicians' reactions, it has been written:

Many, many musicians continue to refer to the big gunfight. . . and each avers he was on the bandstand that night. . . although in real fact there was neither music nor dancing that night. One musician was on the premises, but only to arrange for a job the following week.[37]

This comment serves to warn us about musicians' tales of violence and their personal contributions. These artists, whose "presence amidst the hot smell of gunpowder" is less than an accurate bit of reporting, and often must be discounted. As in the case of so many other people, violence seems to have held an irresistible fascination for musicians with minds given to artful anecdote. Not that mayhem did not occur. Muggsy Spanier witnessed a bomb explosion near the Plantation Club in Chicago and left hastily for China; Jimmy McPartland was once warned to "keep playing" the night Capone's mob decided to break up a joint. "Stop, and we'll smash your heads"; and the Wolverines played an hours' worth of "China Boy" in four different keys during a 1923 New Year's Eve brawl between two rival gangs in Cincinnati's Stockton Club. Hodes recalls being on the bandstand the night of a club holdup. The band pleaded to be left alone, claiming, "Man, we're musicians, we're

always broke." Whether because the mobsters believed the
story or just liked jazz, the tale worked and Hodes' group went
unmolested.[38]

* * *

On the other hand mobsters were unusually charming in
the event of grievous errors. If musicians wound up hurt from
battle royals, an internal racketeers's code suggested
recompense galore. A few examples have already been given.
One final one will serve to conclude the topic. Drummer Ray
McKinley mentions the night he was accidentally shot and the
aftermath:

> I was playing in some club in Chicago when one night there was a shouting
> going on and I wound up in the hospital with a bullet in me. But these gangsters
> we were working for paid all my hospital bills and after I got out they put me up
> at the Palmer House and really treated me like a king.[39]

While these men were gratuitously open-handed toward
jazz artists who abided by the rules,they could just as easily
assume the role of rejected suitor and become disgracefully
ugly. After reviewing the various confrontations likely to
develop, I divine four distinct troublesome categories. Clashes
with mob bosses could occur when musicians became too
greedy, where they pursued the same woman, from contract
insubordination, or when they competed in the same
underworld rackets. Even in these situations, however,
violence took a back seat to the commonly employed
blacklisting. In a sense this speaks to the relatively high degree
of business sophistication and respect mobsters preferred to
show musicians.

Cornetist Joe Oliver represents a casualty of the first
category—the musician who benefited greatly from gangster
support but whose unmanageable egotism outstripped their
patience. Described by one authority, Elliot Paul, as "the
earliest jazz darling of the Chicago mobster set," Oliver's
youthful loyalty to them faded under the twin pressures of
stardom and financial success. These aspects of good fortune
caused him to routinely void large sections of syndicate

contracts which, when revised to his advantage, were quickly broken again.[40]

In addition, his incessant desire to take himself on tours at the most inopportune moments, coupled with his steadily escalating price tag, dismayed men who saw their patience tested to the limits. In the words of music critic Tom Stoddard, "Joe got too big in Chicago and wanted too much money for himself." His idea of payback was viewed as parochial, and when he refused to play a New York cabaret affiliated with the underworld (a place Ellington later used as his springboard to fame) which badly needed his drawing power to recoup initially high operating expenses, he was fired from his Plantation Club work in Chicago by an irate mobster who helped get him forevermore blacklisted. Unable to play, Oliver died in 1938, a toothless janitor in a Savannah pool parlor, so poor that donations were required before an unadorned headstone could be placed on his gravesite.

The second category, the duality for women, was a source of endless squabbles between the principals. Luckily for them, or perhaps not, musicians possessed a romantic appeal which drew women to them like moths to light, much of it set in the frenetic atmosphere of an underworld club. While it was considered bad form for musicians to become associated with women customers, some did it out of curiosity and impulse. Racial aspects indeed entered into some of these liaisons, and for both parties this added mystery and danger. By and large, however, the majority of club bosses cared very little whom a musician consorted with off the job, unless it was from a gangster's own preferred stock.

Here a direct challenge was being made to a sphere of influence no respectable racketeer could afford to tolerate. Unfortunately for them, and from the inferences I have picked up sifting through the evidence, many gangster "molls" were indeed attracted by the magic of the jazz artist. It was then that the wiser, less violent man played second fiddle. Here is one illustration:

One night a musician friend and me took 2 of the Derby Club (a mob-owned place outside Chicago) hostesses out with us, but they happened to be the girl friends of some tough hoodlums out there. So they questioned the girls and also beat them up. One of their family spilled everything. . . . The following night we were told by a go-between not to go in the club, that we would be killed if we did. I didn't even wait around for the next streetcar to come along. I walked all the way back to Chicago.[41]

Clarinettist Nick LaRocca chronicles a similar story, this time involving an athletic blonde lady wrestler, girl friend to a Southside mobster. Ignoring his polite commands to desist in visiting her, LaRocca only relaxed his efforts when warned that his failure to leave Chicago the next day would find him floating in the river.[42] Mezzrow's memoirs describe one love triangle that became so explosive it threatened to destroy an orchestra and seriously undermine the entire Capone organization until the chief's unexpected appearance brought warfare to a halt.

Fletcher Henderson brings us around to the third category. This was musician insubordination to gangster business demands. But as in Oliver's case, Henderson's conflict with his bosses brought on no more than a temporal blacklisting, giving lie to the currency that disregarding mob orders led to a swift watery grave.

By 1924 Henderson was master of an immensely talented band which physically rocked the Club Alabam in Manhattan. A skilled musician and arranger, Henderson was a poor businessman, failed to control his skittish band and condoned a "good deal of idleness."[43] Worse, he eschewed mob advice on how to deal with malcontents or prevent periodic band mutinies. On the matter of discipline, many underworld bosses held to the prudent hoodlum philosophy that unless leaders exerted sharp control—and the bandleaders were no exception—chaos would ensue; and that bands were like mobs for which the democratic process was unworkable.[44] Matters came to a head when the orchestra's leading reedman, Coleman Hawkins, refused to appear in the club's revue unless substantial compensation was added to his regular salary. Management immediately sought his dismissal. But Henderson's approach was to poll the band, accept their verdict to rally around Hawkins, tear up their contract and walk out. A man of mild disposition and gentlemanly manners,

Henderson was too well liked by the mobs to fear rough stuff, but word spread and the band was henceforth frozen out of engagements which would undoubtedly have thrust the orchestra into a prominence rivalling that of Duke Ellington's.[45]

The final category, of musicians-turned-racketeers, is best illustrated by Jelly Roll Morton. As clever a racketeer as he was talented a pianist, Morton assiduously competed with local mobs in their own fields of endeavor. Some of his trades, like narcotics peddling and an occasional street hustle, they countenanced. But Morton's energetic plans for a gambling casino and ornate bordello met with less enthusiasm and the crackdown was swift and resolute. With diamond-studded teeth, well-tailored and stylish clothes, Morton's self-advertising brought an equal amount of attention and rebuke:

Jelly came on the Eastern scene dressed like an old-fashioned pimp...with spats, Stetson, diamonds, and gold sock supporters. His independent and garrulous ways antagonized many, including gangsters influential on the New York and Chicago pop scene.[46]

Allsop commented about the typical mob reaction which knocked the pianist off his perch:

The mobs were too fond of his music to kill him but let the word out that it was unhealthy for other musicians to play with him.

Seen in perspective, the greatest number of gangster warnings were mere puffs of smoke, questionable efforts to intimidate traditionally unreliable, transient artists who were absurdly anarchical about business details. Night club revues, promotion campaigns, interdependent aspects of doing business and consumer interest all required regularity which jazz artists to this day have not always shown. Regardless, gangster owners had no wish to frighten the employees—some of whom they sincerely liked—and this attitude grew stronger with the years. Violence was but one card which could be played, and enough examples have already been provided to suggest that the bosses tolerated verbal abuse from some, if relegating to others a form of banishment. It was said that

Tony Parenti, New Orleans trumpet player, welched on more gambling debts than he blew notes and was forever in hot water without getting scalded; Billy Daniels recalls the time he challenged a mobster boss, unleashing a severe tirade, only to become one of the man's closest friends; and George Wettling, Walter Fuller and Mezz Mezzrow each describe club dates where band defiance and underworld threats cancelled each other out.[47]

As familiarity developed so too did a slowly perceptible level of appreciation. Most squabbles passed off quietly. Artists received on the average far better treatment from the bosses than found elsewhere or earlier in their careers. Musicians affected the voguish swagger and insouciance from mobsters they knew intimately, often speaking to people in subdued tones about "mysterious connections" they had across town. And they came to appreciate the advantages of being loosely incorporated into a syndicate's infrastructure, with healthy and regular earnings and pleasant fringe bonuses. Both groups had sustained their share of criminal charges and social deprivations and both were willing to abide by a live-and-let-live attitude. According to musician Sam Cohen:

Given a choice of playing for mob-owners or independent owners, musicians invariably leaned towards the former.

Underworld Benefits Seen in a Wider Context

Despite immense difficulty in getting started, the entry of Jewish and Italian gangs into the world of jazz and night clubs led to momentous changes of a wide nature. The study so far has considered gains made by the musicians themselves. But in addition, other contributions of a wider, non-musical nature were made and are worth recording. Significant accomplishments were made to night life and the clubs generally, toward neighborhood improvements, in the form of social responsibility, and along the whole spectrum of artistic handiwork. Burke has already recounted how "great achievement and autonomy in art and literature tend to occur not singly but in clusters." No less than to the 1520s did this observation apply to the 1920s, and not only for jazz.

The illegalities imposed by the 18th Amendment establishing liquor prohibition meant that the mobs, ever quick to capitalize on the changes in public habit, yet indifferent to legal codes and moral approbation they never accepted, were the ones best situated to challenge the law. In fact, the way they reacted led the nation into a totally unique approach to night life, one never before attempted on such a mass scale.

That the underworld mobs were flexible and resourceful and catered to innovation was eventful. It also spoke to their ability to assume risks in giving the public what it wanted even before it demonstrated a want. Mob-controlled night clubs and cabarets fulfilled their promises and kept the jazz music gay, danceable, ethnic and stylistic, and established decorative sanctuaries that heightened its presentation. This pleased both customers and performers. Moreover, these niteries ensured jazz artists of a broader, more democratic audience than had been the case in the tightly-controlled Deep South. Henceforth women, intellectuals, white musician and a more youthful crowd generally joined the party. No longer was the music so extremely limited in who was to hear it.

The introduction of women was said to have caused important innovations in interior design and in the many nice domestic touches the clubs began to display. Glassware, clean linen, china and fresh liveried waiters in a safe environment made some difference. A 1933 architectural trade journal noted the quiet revolution in night life:

The insensitive males would return to the unaesthetic barroom of yesteryear and find therein all the "atmosphere" needed for a drinking mood. But in turning neuter, the clubs and speakeasies put an end to all that sort of self-sufficiency. Not only the drinks, the quality of food and the type of entertainments, but the character of the place as well had to be alluring.[48]

What we enjoy in contemporary clubs is the end result of a whole series of experiments from this earlier period when gangsters guessed their way through the best way of presenting their attractions. They were lavishly furnished and made beautiful. Jimmy Mundy tells us even the bandstands in places like the Grand Terrace were elaborate although we can learn the same thing simply by studying the backdrops in orchestra publicity photos.[49] Cohen appreciated that many rooms attempted to improve acoustics and were aware of what this could do for a band's sound. Still other night spots devised ingenious sophisticated, yet primitive interiors, many of which, for New York anyway, caught the artist's eye in Stephen Graham. One of Billy Rose's more exciting innovations was to invite his patrons to dance on the stage of his resplendent Casino de Paree, the first theatre-restaurant in the United States. Dancers were treated to coming on both before and after the revue to the music of the Benny Goodman Orchestra in 1934.[50] This was a vast departure from the Irish places which musician Tom Hall tells us featured wooden bars and the most uncomfortable of plain furnishings to a public which was only seen for its drinking capabilities.

Neighborhood improvements were a second peripheral benefit of the underworld's interest in cabarets and the like. This was demonstrated in two ways. First, by the attempts made to self-regulate the streets around the frontiers of a cabaret or speakeasy. Not only did this appeal to police and, in turn, minimize official intervention and shutdowns; but it placated nearby merchants who were always vulnerable to crime. And, second, by restoration of the brownstone buildings, homes for so many niteries, another aid to local merchants in their effort to keep the areas from deteriorating under pressures caused by heavy immigration. The absence of these men during the late 1950s, when additional waves rolled into the large Eastern cities, contributed to the quick decline of many urban communities.

Gangsters found it in their best interest to clean up and maintain an optimistic environment both inside and beyond the clubs. This respectful desire to avoid violence paid off with widespread publicity, and patrons came knowing their safety was assured. While force was probably applied in selected instances, the end result, unlike that in the Deep South, meant a suppression of the more obvious criminal activities and the neutralization of muggers and thieves. [51] Dickie Wells was one

witness to the increased safety around clubs. Ellington reports
that Harlem was made pleasant for musicians, patrons and the
community alike, by men who exerted an effort in keeping it
that way. Law enforcement gangs, a rather dubious bit of
vigilantism, cost taxpayers and officials nothing, kept crime
rates low, and meant a minimum of need for courts and
lockups.

Mobsters enhanced neighborhoods when they began
remodelling venerable brownstones and other older places,
scooping out the insides for either homes or clubs. This was in
sharp distinction to the general building upheaval affecting
inner cities after 1925. So it was that facades, as well as ancient
durable interiors, were given new artistic life and were
tastefully redesigned for a wider public than these places had
formerly known. On this issue Robert Sylvester and others
write convincingly.[52] As we shall see in the next chapter, when
mobster power began to erode in these pockets, internal
disintegration to communities became an obvious fact. Whole
areas were laid waste and hundreds of brownstones toppled,
making way for vast tracts of office blocks, a common sight in
many Eastern cities in the 1920s and 1930s, setting a seal of
doom on some fine older neighborhoods.

A third overall benefit worth mentioning was the
underworld's indirect route toward civic responsibility and a
social welfarism. Indeed, this group helped inaugurate Federal
aid to the arts prior to its inception by government. Thousands
of tolerable jobs were created by the night club operators. And
by employing so many men and women, black and white, from
musicians, bartenders and performers to a welter of auxiliary
trades, mobsters substituted functions with social redemption
for the very many aggressive, criminal and predatorially
individual acts that had been part of city life before 1915.
Schoner says that Harlem clubs alone paid no fewer than 1500
professional male dancers and an equal number of girl singers,
plus hundreds of musicians. No one yet has even begun to
speculate what total employment was for the larger cities in the
1920s, although James Weldon Johnson, in *Black Manhattan,*
estimates that even during the worst days of the '30s, the clubs
of Harlem were able to employ well over 2000 entertainers.

Before the days of war, welfare or college admissions for blacks, work held decidedly ethnic dimensions, was laborious and dangerous, and was certainly unrewarding. Thanks to the mobs much of this was eradicated, at least for those they chose to hire. Earnings in the clubs brought sustenance while stabilizing primarily youthful communities, which was the hallmark of so many immigrant catchment areas, at a time when public agencies for their welfare were non-existent. Mob employment represented untold wealth and was siphoned back into local communities, eclipsing in sheer volume what any other single industry (before 1941 war demands) was prepared to offer. Pleasant working conditions, hot music that appealed to staff and patron equally, and fair dealings by management explain why neighborhoods viewed mobs and clubs as gold mines; indeed a man courted disaster by informing police of a cabaret, thereby hastening its closing, putting half the block in a soup line at a time which lacked competing forms of relief.[53]

Finally, let us pay tribute to mob contributions to the arts. The 1920s stand out as a spectacular era for modernization and creation in the art world. As a result of the shocking 1925 Art Modern Exhibition in Paris, the 1929 Triannual Show in Milan, the various Bauhaus presentations in Germany, and the exciting prospects promised in Bolshevistic Russia, stimulating trends in art were being unveiled and applied to everyday life. But such trends seemed only to occur in Europe. Emily Genauer provides a critical analysis of an arid America of the time, where jazz was its leading art form to excite and influence the rest of the world. Even if we overlook Bricktop's famous Harlem-like cabaret in Paris, other areas far more distant and remote were on the musical bandwagon. A 1930 travel magazine describes Bangkok with its:

...several jazz orchestras, cabarets, and 'unoriental' dance halls (that) await the tourist where tiny-bodied native hostesses will dance with you for the asking.[54]

Only American mobster niteries caught the modern spirit in art and applied it. Experiments in architecture, sculpture and interior design revealed sharp boldness and clever innovation, and many of them borrowed from the jazz scene for their themes.[55] On the other hand, clubs were receptive to new ways of displaying their wares. Clubs reflected colorfulness, joy and imaginative fancy. In cabarets the extravagant and fanciful decorations that engulfed the bands and revues were wholly in keeping. One wonders what might have transpired had the older school of taproom owner still commanded the night clubs of America in the 1920s. Not only would they have stifled the one great art form of the country, but they would have blindly refused to introduce some of the newer artistic trends into clubs.

Luckily the revolutionary spirit, symbolized by the Art Deco imprint, found its way first into the inner settings owned by the underworld, by men who appreciated the effects caused by the bizarre, surrealistic zig-zag patterns and the exoticism of the Moorish, Mayan and Mexican motifs. Despite evidence to the contrary, European trips were taken by the more cosmopolitan racketeers. Quite possibly, having viewed Berlin's satirical revues by Mischa Spoliansky and Marcellus Schiffer or the parodies of Max Reinhardt in his basement cabaret "Sound and Smoke," mobsters installed similar techniques upon return home. For Art Deco could be found not only in the backdrops behind the orchestras, and in the chairs and platforms upon which the artists sat, but in the club's furniture, walls, lobbies and detailed decorations which stared back at the admiring viewer in glittering array.[56]

Frankie Fay, mob owner of the Midtown Manhattan Follies, reputedly spent $75,000 for lush Mayan and Egyptian decorations,and was a regular traveller to Europe. According to John Hammond (in a letter to the author), "the decor at Connie's Inn was supervised by the owner's nephew, Sol Immerman, who turned out to be a first-class artist" of Art Deco style. The Cotton Club was awash in period decorations, as was the Coq Rouge, with its transparent murals and striking skyline bar; the bewildering collection of spiral bars and cocktail lounges at the International Casino, and the exotic mural panelling at Frank Cerutti's Le Mirage are other examples. Lew Leslie injected Art Deco into his revues, exemplified by the 1930 Mozambique jungle settings. Most

Broadway musicals of the time also borrowed from the surrealistic inspirations. Again, this trend was far different from pre-1920 days when art in bars meant pictures of Indian wars, nubile nudes and mythical characters in ungainly poses. To the extent that racketeers were willing to suppress older styles and favor those which more comfortably accommodated their own attitudes, they can be said to have encouraged the new art trends.

The impact of jazz in the cabarets was extremely significant for the allied arts. One musician noted:

Flush with money and powerful from coast to coast, the syndicates had good taste and stopped at nothing to get the best in entertainment.[57]

In fact the basis for the great upsurge in music during the 1930s, a very turbulent time to be sure, can be directly linked to the training writers, composers and musicians gained while in the mob-owned speakeasies and clubs of the earlier period. Clever dance routines and patterns used in Broadway and Hollywood musicals and films were copied almost exactly from what musical directors remembered seeing in the Harlem shows where men like Dan Healy were doing the choreography. Song writers acquired valuable experience in the clubs: Harold Arlen, Irving Berlin, Hoagy Carmichael, Jerome Kern, Cole Porter, Harry Warren, Jimmy McHugh and Dorothy Fields learned the ropes in the jazz clubs. Finally, serious musicians and composers were equally affected. Early in his career, George Gershwin had written a 20-minute blues opera, "Blue Monday," set in a Harlem night club and featured in George White's Scandals of 1922. European composers were also impressed. Ravel and members of the Chicago Symphony were intrigued by what they heard from Jimmy Noone's band while it played the mob-owned Apex Club in Chicago. Paul Whiteman and his arranger Ferde Grofe were frequent visitors to the Cotton Club. And Leopold Stokowski of the Philadelphia Symphony, Fritz Kreisler, Sergei Rachmaninoff, Paderewski and Serge Koussevitsky of the Boston Symphony were a few of the more serious artists who regularly learned more about modern music in the Harlem jazz sessions.[58]

And to the degree that mob money supported black authors, performers and artists generally, a fairly large and representative figure, it may be credited with having boosted black interest in its own renaissance. For it was part of the cluster effect alluded to in the opening paragraphs of this chapter, that the era was witness to a tremendous expansion in black arts. Walton writes that "Duke Ellington was much influenced by the Harlem Renaissance and also had power exerting influence on it." Indeed, his arrival in New York from Washington, as he discussed in his autobiography, was inspired from the jazz dynamics being promoted in the mob clubs. Langston Hughes' earliest visit to New York sharply contributed to his social and racial awareness and was gangster inspired: his utmost desire in New York was to see the black musical "Shuffle Along," which had considerable mobster backing.[59]

Poet Claude McKay recalls how they helped him develop his own artistic skills:

The cabarets of Harlem in 1919-1920 enthralled me more than any theatre downtown. They were so intimate...and rich in warmth and native excitement...and along the streets I received impressions like arrows piercing my nerves and [I] distilled poetry from them.[60]

This new and profound sense of cosmopolitanism which affected black artists of the time (Chester Himes is another example[61]), paved the way for a racial self-reliance and economic power few had known before. And to a large degree this was derived from the special status blacks received from gangsters, the only people these artists seemed willing to trust. For blacks this may have been the most important of all benefits bestowed.

Chapter VIII

The 1930s, A Last Gasp

The Return to Square One

By 1930 the death knell for jazz had been sounded in most of the prosperous cities capable of sustaining hundreds of individual artists and styles. And by 1930 racketeers were at last being placed on the defensive by widespread and effective reformists attacks partially induced by a severe depression which did nothing to aid musicians. For with the breakup and dissolution of night clubs, musicians were unable to locate acceptable replacements. Theaters darkened and cabarets disappeared, one by one; and so it was that black artists began reverting to an age-old activity of clustering inactively on stoops and street corners awaiting the job offers that rarely came. It was a time of sink or swim in other waters. But other waters either meant dropping out of the business altogether or fishing in the streams of arduous dangerous one-night stands through the backwaters of the country. Casualties decimated the music world. Within a few years only the most versatile, durable and nattily-dressed black orchestras and bands would survive.

What had been done for a lark in the 1920 boom years now assumed the spectre of dire necessity, a matter of utmost urgency, in the depression: college proms, barnstorming road shows, juke joints and riverboats. It was as if the hands of time had been restored to an earlier, tougher time of deprivation and harrowing experience. Musicians were again called upon to perform hack music in front of hick audiences, accompanied by the vagaries of chance, bigotry and default in payment. There is no way of gauging the number of agents who realized and exploited the jazz artists' predicament to the fullest but it must have been considerable. Little wonder the 1920s, with its

165

gangster guarantees, held fond memories for musicians. After 1929 the road for most of them was downhill all the way and few ever recovered.

In some ways the 1930s were worse than before the war. It was a time of ceaseless belt tightening. "Even though coffee was a nickel," reminisces trackstar Jesse Owens, "people didn't have a nickle."[1] And if whites, who constituted a faceless sea of poverty, were enfeebled by the times, how much worse off were the minorities, or indeed, the musicians—themselves but a disliked sub-group within a minority?

"The 1930s were empty, man," recalls trumpeter Charlie Love. "In the depression nobody played anything." Tennessee bluesman Hammie Nixon eked out an existence only by pretending he was deaf, dumb and blind.[2] Max Kaminsky claims he nearly went crazy for lack of work in Boston where jobs were all but non-existent for plumbers and electricians, let alone jazz musicians. Don Redman maintains his technically superior and exciting band found work only in the most dangerous rural sections in front of white listeners with the most provincial of musical tastes.[3] Artist Thomas Hart Benton, having observed Beale Street in 1936, called it

quiet. I was disappointed in it for I had always heard of it as an uproarious place...for abandoned Negro gaiety it was a flop.[4]

Rowdy environments, on the other hand, struck terror in a musician's heart. Lester Young associates being mugged and swindled with his encounters in the 1930s:

Those were rough times. Our Blue Devils band was getting bruised, playing to audiences of 3 people. One time all our instruments were impounded in West Virginia...and they took us out of town.... We eventually made it to Chicago, with bruises, no horns, all raggedy and dirty.[5]

Here and there night spots benefited black artists, places where they could earn a reasonable income. Benton mentions "Harlem and a half-dozen other places." But the list was dwindling every week.[6] As in the old days, a dollar a night was the going rate. One performer remembers playing the rough Southern taxi dance halls, four-plus hours of continuous music without interruption, under stifling, oppressive conditions. Playing in eight-hour shifts with irregular groups whose personnel changed nightly, George Lewis made 75¢ a night in the rough part of the French Quarter.[7] Even areas least affected went through hard times. Danny Barker speaks poorly of life in Harlem's Lenox Club:

The depression for musicians in New York—Man it was a bitch! Whatever they picked up at the cash register in the course of a night . . . they would spill out the receipts of the night on the table and give everybody an equal share. Some mornings we'd make 75¢, other mornings we'd get 25¢. Everybody cooperated because there was nowhere else to go and in fact nobody had nothin'. [8]

Radio, cinema, hotels and the rigid regulations of the local unions (which kept out transient musicians) ignored almost totally the growing plight of jazz artists. Stride pianist James P. Johnson and musicians Danny Barker and Eddie Barefield leave entertainment industry and its exclusionary policies.[9] As late as 1941 musicologist Irving Kolodin, while writing for a monthly magazine, concurred:

The outlook for black bands in hotels, theatres, and radio is not too hopeful and even a colored guest star on a dance band's radio commercial may bring angry mutterings.[10]

Inasmuch as a handful of big hotels and radio stations monopolized job opportunities for bands, and steadfastly refused to hire blacks, much of the available work went by the boards. Crippled by the depression, the musicians' own unions harkened back to time-worn practices which left most blacks in the cold and blacklisted whites who chose to protest.[11] Those who miraculously found work bowed to a tacit code which required sharing their largess with those colleagues less fortunate. Kaminsky recalls standing by the side door of a midtown Manhattan night club in the winter of 1934, distributing 50¢ pieces to unemployed artists who shivered disconsolately in near-freezing weather until he appeared during breaks.

Within a few years only an occasional pocket of jazz remained to compete with what was becoming an unsavory fleshpot entertainment scene, replete with strip-tease joints, pinball arcades, transvestite shows and minor league movie houses. Only a few streets in Chicago were alive, and barely so. The better mob places included King Tut's Tomb, Harry's New York Bar, the Derby Club, Rocco Gallo's Club 29, the Club DeLisa, The High Hat, the Hi Ho Club, The Three Deuces and Kelly's. Possibly the jewel in the crown was reserved for the Grand Terrace ballroom where between 1928 and 1940 the Earl Hines Orchestra performed. After 1934 radio broadcasts were aired with a sumptuous floorshow comparable to New York's elegant Cotton Club at its best.[12]

New Yorkers were left with but two areas, and both continued as repositories for mobster investment. First was the new 52nd Street tract, a district the mobs had helped integrate. It was a street its historian claims "never slept" and where Nat Hentoff believes the interest in small jazz combos first arose in the mid-1930s.[13] Such places included Jimmy Ryan's, the Onyx Club, Kelly's Stables, the Famous Door, the Samoa, The Three Deuces, the Downbeat and the Spotlight. About these clubs songwriter Alec Wilder says:

It was the last time an American street gave you a feeling of security and warmth and the excitement of musical friendship.[14]

The second district was, of course, Harlem. Despite the many clubs which folded in the 1930s, Harlem could still muster up enough talent to sizzle on rare moments. Some of thes jazz joints included the downstairs at 101 Club, the Hoofer's Club, the after-house musical haunt at Gregory's, Brandy Horse, Bert Hall's Rhythm Club, Big John's, Campbell's (above a funeral parlor) and the Cave, with its picaresque skeletons on the wall. The Plantation Club, Brickwoods, The Kit Kat and Dickie Wells's each offered unforgetable evenings to listeners and dancers.[15]

Downtown clubs alternated jazz and swing music on a make-shift basis. There was Frank Bonachini's Coq Rouge, Frank Cerutti's Le Mirage (with its Voodoo Dance Troupe), the Cotton Club in Times Square, The Black Cat (a black dancerie in the Village) Nick's, near Sheridan Square, where Sunday night jam sessions lured a college crowd, and, finally, in the Chelsea area, the occasionally mob-financed Cafe Society Downtown, perhaps the most carnival-like club available to the devout jazz patron in the late 1930s. Long-time home to Billie Holliday, it was a glorified cellar, according to one jazz historian, but perhaps the only club outside Harlem where black patrons felt at ease.[16]

Well, one might wonder, in view of what has already been said about the progress of jazz after 1900, how could such an unmitigated disaster have come about so abruptly? What went wrong? Can we ascribe to the depression sole blame for the plight in which jazz artists and jazz clubs found themselves by 1933? Or can we discern more subtle, less simplistic causes? And what of the racketeers' support? We have spent the bulk of this study building up a case of close bondship between both parties. Could the depression have caused the crumbling of such a long-term relationship in so short a time? Indeed, how did the underworld groups confront the depression and what were their reactions as they pertain to jazz music?

The Mobs Lose Interest

The conventional view is that the depression kicked the props of profitability from under the mob-owned clubs, making a large number of musicians expendable. This assumes that racketeers felt the pinch in the same way and to the same degree as other groups. This assumption is totally misleading. Bootleggers and other mobster operatives flinched perhaps, but their abundant financial reserves escaped jeopardy. Resembling the larger corporations, these men—immigrants with a deep respect for liquid cash over credit—were able to tap hidden reserves to stay comfortably afloat. Damon Runyan's view of the mobsters he knew in 1931 is that they weren't hurt at all:

There is little scratch anywhere and along Broadway many racketeers are wearing their last years clothes and have practically nothing to bet on the races.

On the contrary, the general scarcity of money and

deflated prices, combined with a slackening of internal competition from the small and independent club owners and the reduced number of entrants into the field meant that beguiling investment opportunities hung on trees like apples. Despite what we think of as the depression, economic aspects for recreation during these years were rosy. One Harvard study of 1937 discovered that recreation and travel were increasing in the period not only in absolute value but were also attracting an increased share of the national income. The following chart gives some indication of this rise as it affected jazz joints:

Economic Aspects of Night Clubs[17]
(in millions of dollars)

1919	1923	1927	1929	1931	1933	1935
4	22	24	22	17	25	32

Not only were earlier investments in jazz clubs hardly to be seen as bad risks, especially after 1931-32, the times did nothing to restrain drinking. Some clubs were obviously affected, particularly in case of bad management, in case of, and some required gimmicks to stay alive. Still others pared revues to the bone and curtailed the use of large orchestras in the belief that profits could still be made. Mobster Lucky Luciano claimed the appeal of Harlem's tremendous night life never waned in the 1930s, an observation given some support by the Federal Writers Project analysis of night life in New York. They estimated over 300 clubs were still in operation in Manhattan as late as 1939.[18]

Other factors also offered enrichment to the interested club owner. Despite the end of prohibition in 1933, heavy taxes on alcohol prolonged by several years the economic rewards of bootlegging. Then, too, loansharking, lottery, slot machine and horse-betting activities mushroomed in a crisis that brought out the average man's gambling instinct, and these were quietly incorporated into the operating policies of larger places. "Always when a lot of people are out of work," one racketeer points out, "gambling picks up right away."[19] Nor can it be said that the depression quenched the thirst which mobsters held for jazz music. Henny Youngman spoke of the night life on 52nd Street where "every night...hard-boiled thugs used to fill the joints. It was a carnival time." And in Kansas City, more fully described later in this chapter, local mobs not only retained a vigorous jazz policy, they extended it. The result was a steep climb not only in profits but in some legendary performances.

So what went wrong? Why did the bottom drop out of the field for jazz artists if opportunities for their underworld protectors were like sheep ready for the flocking? In some part the mobs who owned, controlled or supported the jazz clubs simply permitted it to happen through their generosity toward the rich (Cafe Society was allowed to pay nothing in return for their cultivated appearances in Eastern clubs), by becoming too conservative (they let hotels outbid them in creative styles), by being too bloodthirsty (they raised prices when they should have lowered them and they condoned a brief but violent feud in 1931, the worst possible moment) and by ignoring neighborhoods which had long been their protective shells.

Underworld night club operators allowed themselves to be driven from the field of battle. Seen from the vantage point of time, two factors distinguish this sudden removal of jazzdom's best customers for over half a century. First, mobsters, caught up in the fears of the moment, quite simply stopped taking risks and became complacent about the night club business. In the words of one racketeer: "Everybody was afraid to give up something they didn't have for sure."[20] Creativity went out the window. So, too, did commonsense toward customers. One reporter claims:

The world of the night clubs was a world unto itself. The conceit and overbearing arrogance of the operator of any successful night club was wondrous to behold. Night club owners made their own society, made their own rules, meted out their own disciplinary measures.[21]

Second, and more importantly, enormous political pressures which originated in the upheaval of the depression caused a wholesale exodus of gangsters from the night lights of the

Eastern cities for the hinterlands. In conjunction, cheap competition and increased costs in bribery and graft cut in everywhere.[22]

Mobsters were too generous to the wrong people in the '30s. They carefully hyped a clientele of wealthy kids and playboy sots. While this may have been acceptable for the 1920s, when there was enough money circulating to tolerate such luxury, it was a disastrous policy in an era when one paid his way or went nowhere. Cafe Society looked good but it was useless in a club that otherwise remained empty. According to Angelo, little attempt was made to induce other customers into the fold with special concessions, an oversight many soon lived to regret.

Mobsters let hotels into the fray and before long these replacements sparkled with creative musical presentations. With the repeal of prohibition, hotels could in fact reclaim a popularity they had lost with the advent of the speakeasies after 1915. One leading restaurateur believed this upsurge sprang from the clever imitations which hotel managements borrowed from the more successful mob-owned cabarets:

The night clubs, being more intimate and generally directed by some one person known to the customer, seem to have an edge on the hotels. It is much more satisfactory to go to a smaller place, see the proprietor about, have his personal attention, than to enter a vast room, however beautiful, conducted by some group in a business office acres away. The hotels, realizing this, have tried to answer in a number of ways, either by having in some cases personal directors of their supper rooms or by offering better food, better dance orchestras and more elaborate entertainment.[23]

Hotels had a decided advantage over clubs who refused to step with the times, for they could cover costs in a variety of ways denied club owners. High-priced entertainment could always be offset by revenues gained from banquets, conventions, even room service, while cabarets had to be content with mere alcohol sales. That is, unless the highly volatile element of gambling was added. Reentry of the hotels by their open bigotry sorely affected black jazz groups. A contemporary survey reported white bands were featured in 75% of all night club and hotel engagements (where the figure was much higher), a complete reversal of the established pattern when mobsters of night clubs were in the driver's seat, so to speak.[24]

The hard times froze movement and creativity within the underworld organizations and club ownerships. New talent intrigued with club life failed to surface in the '30s. Indeed, few racketeers later emerged from this period with well-earned reputations; top figures had earned their wings years before. This meant that innovators available for making significant adaptations of club life to keep up with trends failed to emerge.[25] Unlike the Kansas City underworld, most Eastern places simply preferred to overcharge their few remaining patrons rather than reduce budgets by making their interiors smaller and more intimate. Durante suggests this was the prime reason apartment parties did so well, siphoning off cabaret profits. Mobsters managing the clubs took to violating the contracts they had with their own creative personnel, driving them away. Billy Rose had refused to work for a New York syndicate unless they agreed not to interfere with his operation of a club and handling of the revues. But this they reneged on, firing the Benny Goodman Orchestra at the time, and pushing Rose out of the field altogether.[26]

Club owners of the early '20s showed little hesitation in investing in their clubs despite the risks, even overspending on items like bribes, revues, interior appointments and community welfare. This was hardly the situation after 1926. Revenues were more likely to be pocketed and clubs were milked for quick private gain. Little went back into clubs and neighborhoods, experiments in the presentation of jazz were minimized and nothing was done to take advantage of the reasonable rents which hungry landlords were willing to offer without leases or even signed agreements.[27] Group commitments were being replaced by men with individualistic outlooks. Appearances and materialistic growth was everything; providing musical value for money became an outmoded attitude.

Record company investments might have been one helpful gamble for artists, but mobsters were now bent on profits and clipping losses and risks. Record sales were meagre and so, as songwriter Hoagy Carmichael told me, "the hoods were not even interested in a losing market." Without even a toehold in the recording field, racketeers were powerless to promote jazz artists had this been their choice. Their absence for jazzmen was telling:

Without the mobs, bands found difficulty moving around even places like New York. Basie couldn't get into 52nd Street in the late 1930s without mob approval and desire to fight the mid-town color line.[28]

Harlem-based gangsters did little to attract radio remotes and airchecks from the various stations although the Cotton Club was one exception. Sylvester points out how radio promotions were of major significance in thrusting hotels and midtown clubs into the limelight long enough to capitalize and draw business. *Cue* magazine, "New York's Own Entertainment Guide," in a representative issue of 24 May 1938 lists only two to 28 airchecks featuring Harlem-based and/or other black jazz outfits.

Underworld club owners were also remiss in neglecting the communal side of business. Angelo told me: "You have to put some of your money back into the street if you hope to grow and keep allies." This the owners of the '30s signally failed to do. If historian Frank Pearce is correct, "that the strength of organized crime lies in its being a grass roots phenomenon," then this abject neglect hastened the demise of the clubs. Ianni has written of the contempt the younger Italians began showing toward their elders and the older neighborhoods around this time, turning their backs on a communal life style which helped enshroud the clubs in consumer protection.

The changed attitude also decreed against the open-handedness and amicability toward local merchants which had been a hallmark of the original underworld compacts. Expressing a turbulent desire for suburban life, the nouveau riche of the older families held older arrangements in low regard, burning bridges carefully erected by an earlier generation of gangsters which had been so instrumental in their success. It followed that when the tight consolidation before 1926 disappeared, when everything that was tied up in the district and slums where these men had been born disintegrated, so too did the tactics aimed at revitalizing both the clubs and the surrounding areas.[29]

Not only did the Young Turks choose the wrong time to reject those areas that had been such bags of gold, they picked the worst possible moment to challenge the older authority figures. Unfortunately, the tale of this colossal gang warfare in 1931, "the slaughter of the Sicilian Vespers," lies beyond the focus of this study. It was a feud that did little to beckon crowds to Harlem and Upper Manhattan, scenes of some of the worst violence. The confrontations for power and control also hastened the advent of political campaigns designed to stamp out vice activities. Amidst the smoke and clamor of battle, the jazz artists were a leading casualty.

Conservative retrenchment in the clubs and cabarets meant that the push for jazz music had ended in a collective sense. Clubs began dropping jazz bands like lead balloons. This general attitude, then, serves to underscore the traditional viewpoint linking all cultural activity with the depression. Racketeers, so it would be stated, vacated the cabaret scene because of economic setbacks ushered in by the financial disaster of 1929. On the contrary, my argument is quite different. The basic reason racketeers, who liked the music, failed to exploit the depression on the entertainment front had little to do with economic trends. It was the world of the politician and the moral crusader which, in the final analysis, caused the cave-in.

To properly view this well-reasoned retreat, we must again revert to the late '20s. Then, and quite unexpectedly, mobsters found themselves almost overnight swimming in shark-infested waters. But these sharks were ambitious politicians. Through their efforts, and various legal pressures, reformist groups and an interested press developed a lust for gangster-prey. It was only after these groups had commenced their war with organized crime that the shock registering from the depression had any meaning. For the calamity served to stoke the coals, enabling the press to rivet the public's attention away from a faltering economy and onto a whole series of sinister characters. In the end, a successfully clever juxtaposition of scapegoats had taken place: Mobsters rather than politicians were represented as the unseen enemies who had brought urban bankruptcy. Hoping to disengage himself from battle with patrician hordes out for scalps, the mobster expeditiously closed shop and fled the older cities. And shorn of his benefactor, the jazz artist stood alone. He could hardly diversify his occupational portfolio to any degree or advantageously relocate. And with the departure of the underworld leaders, so too did the enjoyable nightly rituals of playing for the big-time spenders and their women. It is to this single most important impetus for the withdrawal of mob money from the jazz clubs *en masse* that we now turn our attention.

The Pain of Inflicting Pleasure

Wealthy, conservative upstate New York Republicans have long enduldged themselves in a pastime which, for lack of a better label, could be called "Purging New York City Government." Every state has its own variants; downstate Illinois and Southern California are good examples. To be especially effective, the game must be spaced from fifteen to twenty years apart and take place around election time. The exercise gains momentum if crack investigative teams are able to expose glaring corruption and misconduct. Big cities are the best targets; so too are local Democrats. In this study the Tammany mob was a prime pigeon. Victories were assured Republicans so long as voters equated the Democrats with mother hens, jealously protecting and pampering those infernal minorities, immigrants, and criminal lords. In point of fact, so effectively had this untiring game been conducted that Democrats had been sent reeling ever since the mayoralty of Fernando Wood in the 1850s. Other successful campaigns occurred during the Tweed era of the 1870s, a period of alleged graft which has just recently been attacked as overdrawn,[30] in the 1890s, during the 1910 police scandals, and at the time of the 1923 "Red Scare."

So it was that the 1930s inaugurated a fresh assault. The latest pound of flesh came from the Jewish and Italian urban racketeers and bootleggers, men whose reputations and pompish behavior served their assailants and the press well.

By 1928 gears set in motion consequent to the Republican investigation into city government had revealed the usual rotten stumps. Moreover, indications abounded that it was only the tip of an iceberg that had been exposed and that the catch, in terms of prominent Democratic politicians and their crooked hangers-on would be worth the effort. One small quirk remained to complete the ageless scenario. Rather than the politicians, it was those most closely affiliated through sweetheart deals, the mobsters of the fame, who would become objects of daily scorn in the press, being portrayed as the worst rats in the sewer.

Times were more opportune for the purpose. In the process of attacking gangster growth, and then linking these figures to government circles, the campaign aimed at serving two functions. First, it would topple Italians and Jews from their newly-reached social perch of urban influence. Second, the battle would unlease a rich vein of racial hatred in the nation that had for many years deplored the mere presence of these men. In some ways, the fondest wishes of the Republican National Committee was under serious attack for alleged anti-semitism. It was a frightening period for Jews and Italians as many articles appeared in the press aimed at underscoring their invidiousness in loal politics.

Seen from the standpoint of those who would cover the trials between 1930-1935, many of the practices employed in the Criminal Courts were designed to elicit the widest possible press coverage at the risk of distorting the truth. John Gunther was an early critic of this approach. He was aware that faulty and inflammatory reporting could only stimulate bitter anti-immigrant feelings which had been aflame since the turn of the century and were taking on vigorous life in several fascistic European countries. He also noted that such vituperous attacks would only promote laws like the Brownell Amendment of 1935, which gave police wide discretionary powers of harassment toward individuals they adjudged were "public enemies."

Needless to say, the racketeers were not left unaffected by

this swirl of events or the eventual 71 convictions recorded by a high-powered group of investigators from questionable practices. Gosch and Hammer have quoted Lucky Luciano's quick realization of the dangers:

All of us were worried—the whole bunch of us spent more time havin' meetin's to discuss the changing legal events than takin' care of business.

Like kittens tossed into a tub of water, racketeers began flying in every direction seeking safety. By 1937 one leading mobster, Louis Lepke, had had enough. "Things are getting too hot here," he told a confederate. "I'll have to lam. Be careful."[31]

Thousands of witnesses were sworn in as the elaborate and ceremoniously dignified crime-busting crews swung into action from 1930 to 1936. As early as 1931 the *New York Times* was reporting the findings of the investigations which tied the underworld to night clubs. Leading cabaret and jazz club sponsors, along with a constellation of lesser stars, were summoned before the Bench and interrogated about their business and political arrangements, legal and otherwise. Eventually, and despite high costs, lengthy Court proceedings and unscrupulous legal manoeuvres, the lawyers managed to rake in a land-office business in convictions. It was a bewildering array of charges to consider, from tax evasion and vice activities to simple charges of vagrancy.

Thomas E. Dewey, as assistant deputy attorney for New York County, emerged from the entanglements a staunch opponent of the mobs, exploiting press headlines throughout the campaign in establishing himself as an important political power. It should not be overlooked that Dewey, relative of the famous admiral, was the son of an upper class Michigan newspaper publisher whose tutelage of his son on press tactics was an instant success. Nor did Dewey give an inch. Toward his racketeering opponents he was typically sharp:

As we look over the racket situation, it often seemed to me that the Mafia was worse than the rest of the underworld. There was no honor among this breed of thieves, gunmen, robbers...or racketeers. The whole lot of them were not merely anti-social. They were slimy, cheating savages....They were members of the human race, but with few redeeming qualities.

So it was that many top celebrity gangsters felt the cutting edge of the blade. Men found guilty and sentenced included Louis Lepke, Jacob Shapiro, Dutch Schultz, Jack Guzik, Henry Margolis, Lucky Luciano, Abe Weinberg, Morris Kleinman, Rocco DiLarmi, the Capone Brothers, Moe Margolese, Waxey Gordon and at least 58 others; George Weinberg committed suicide rather than submit to the unusual hearings staged against these men.[32]

While there is little need to applaud the criminal careers of this group, almost all of them Italians and Jews, or to necessarily rationalize their behavior, there is something worth noting in that racketeers bore the brunt of criminal indictments and convictions during the 1930s. A whole welter of governmental and financial figures escaped even a tinge of dishonor for the greater roles they played in the scandals and corruption associated with the depression. Moreover, these sentenced racketeers might also have come out of the fray unscathed had it not been for the illegal, discriminatory and unethical Court proceedings before a bench indifferent to this line of argument. Gunther's meticulous study of the trials cites countless unconstitutional indiscretions used in the trials. He suggests that some of them were illegal phone taps, bugging, exorbitant bail, civil rights violations, fraudulent and trumped-up evidence, dubious testimony and confessions extracted under the duress of fear—devices inconceivable against stockbrokers and bankers who appeared before Senate subcommittees on a multitude of white collar crimes.[33] Gunther summarizes the whole affair by comparing it with "Star Chamber proceedings...the means of which...were rarely questioned and never challenged."

A second reason for the Republicans' attack on gangsterism eliciting healthy support from the press was to implicate as many Democrats as possible in the scandal. If Democrats could be shown to be even partly guilty, hopes might be raised that internecine party warfare would ensue and an irreparable split occur amongst Democrats just before the 1932 elections. Republicans needed just this sort of diversion, considering the economic mess which boded ill for them. The fact that the investigations destroyed the political

careers of two leading Democrats (New York's Mayor Jimmy
Walker and a local Tammany leader, Jimmy Hines), both of
whom were close friends of presidential aspirant Franklin
Delano Roosevelt (the State's Governor), gave the attackers
fresh reason for optimism. One astute political writer noted the
Democrats' dilemma in 1932:

Any investigation of this kind was supposed to put F.D.R. in a hole. If he broke
with Tammany he would forfeit its support for the election. . . . If he didn't
crack the whip, his national prestige would dwindle because of the Republican
charges that he condoned the corruption.[34]

Locating dissatisfied Democrats willing to climb aboard
the anti-gangster bandwagon was easy. One leading spirit was
the Democratic Judge Samuel Seabury. Since 1894 Seabury, a
wealthy, influential barrister of baronial pretensions who
lived in a squire's dream in Southampton, had fought
Tammany tooth and nail. His swashbuckling approach soon
cost him his party's favor and he lost a bid to become a
governor. It was Seabury, as chief counsel, who had brought
some measure of success to the Republican-controlled and
directed Hofstadter Committee inquiring into local corruption
in the late 1920s. Their victory was his also, and gave him a
stature for pursuing the presidency in 1932, hoping to discredit
Roosevelt in the process.[35]

Other prominent Democratic crusaders included the
elegant Secretary of the Treasury, Henry Morgenthau, Jr.,
Roosevelt's neighbor at Hyde Park and close political ally who
had seen fit to protect several bankers in a recent stock
exchange investigation; Harry F. Gugenheim, diplomat, Yale
graduate and mining executive who chaired the LaGuardia
appointed Committee for the Control of Crime in 1936; and
Democratic Governor Herbert H. Lehman who, in 1935, called
upon the "racket-ridden and exploited to support Dewey's
investigations into vice."[36] On the periphery, and without
party labels stood two Morgenthau appointees: J. Edgar
Hoover of the Federal Bureau of Investigation and Harry
Anslinger, Chief of the Narcotics Bureau, perpetually fighting
one another for press coverage in crime busting.

The lone significant Republican was Fiorello LaGuardia.

Well-known for his dedication as a crime fighter and opponent of Tammany politics, LaGuardia's career was successfully managed from this point by the adroit Seabury. Not only did the judge help get him elected mayor of New York City in 1934, partially on the success which was being made against the racketeers, but LaGuardia's oath of office was administered in Seabury's fashionable townhouse on Fifth Avenue. Within a year of his assumption of office, LaGuardia had become famous for his extra-legal, "muss 'em up" order to the police. The result was even more corruption:

Cops used the 1930s, Dewey, and the investigations to step up demands in graft, protection money....It always happens when there is a clean-up campaign going on it costs more money to operate every time you turn around.[37]

As suggested earlier, Republicans seeking the return of President Hoover to office in 1932 recognized the merits of a law and order issue as an effective smokescreen for their own ineptitude at launching a first-class depression. Trials against hoodlums would deflect a nation's attention from its own financial woes. In addition, by investigating, throttling and imprisoning mobsters, the Courts would be seriously weakening the trade union movement which had taken on new meaning after 1929. There is no doubt that many leading union officials were racketeers under indictment in various Courts. Not without good cause, Republicans envisaged the destruction of the whole union effort, and events of the 1930s furnished them with every reason to hope. It was indeed a period of extreme industrial action, much of it illegal, by the large corporations, with many examples illustrating an industry-police conspiracy designed to suppress lawful union activities. In this we can only assume the early Court actions on prominent union leaders furnished fuel for the fires of anti-union vigilantism.

Encouraged by these results, reformists in no fewer than 60 cities adopted similar anti-Jewish, -black, and -Italian warcries. As part of a broad policy, ordinances to sharply curtail jazz clubs and harass the artists received full reformist backing, and men who Dewey claimed had "no redeeming qualities" were under vicious attack. It was an effective campaign, and the number of jazz outlets began drying up. Together with the general policy of outlawing the musicians, it was likely if trends continued that the music in many areas would be driven to extinction.

Estimates suggest that the abrupt departure of gangsters as patrons and proprietors led to the direct shutdown of perhaps 80% of the jazz clubs, ruining opportunities for livelihood for two in every three jazz groups.[38] This occurred by the mid-1930s, and we have some reason to believe that business improved only slightly once the worst was over. One racketeer analyzes the New York scene:

The heat went off once Dewey had made his reputation. The only difference was things had to be run quiet.[39]

Repressive campaigns were not exclusively small-town in impact, but managed to break into the bigger cities like Boston, Baltimore, Chicago, Cleveland and Los Angeles, among others. Until events stabilized, clubs in these cities were put on the block to anyone willing to invest in a dying business. When few prospects turned up, owners had little choice but to turn off the lights, lock the doors and consign the reputation of their hot spots to posterity.

Ed Joblonski has written one post mortem for a dying club. This was the famous Cotton Club, and his analysis illustrates what withdrawal of gangster patronage meant for jazzmen. His narrative traces the highs and lows of a club which had been home to Duke Ellington, Cab Calloway, Jimmy Lunceford, Ethel Waters, Adelaide Hall and Bill Robinson, to mention but a few of the black stars who not only appeared there but afforded a rare treat for black artists of the period: radio coverage on both the CBS and NBC Blue networks. Jablonski points out that the most critical years occurred between 1932 and 1934, when the club still had a chance of surviving. But with owners and some of the club's best customers sent packing by the unrelenting legal pogroms of the 1930s, few people showed up each night to pay for the niterie's expensive revues and musicians. It was only a question of time, Jablonski writes, and after 1935 the writing was clearly on the wall: doors closed in February 1936.

Much the same trend could be observed in Chicago. Al Capone's departure for a Federal prison in 1931 marked the slide of local jazz into oblivion. And the arrest of his brother Ralph not long afterwards slashed employment for artists almost overnight. One artist recalls how the underworld leaders could dispel bad times solely through the force of their personality, their presence and their conviviality:

One night Ralph Capone came in with a large party, obviously ready to spend money and enjoy. Judging by the cheer, excitement, and tossing around of money, "you would have thought the depression was over" right then and there. But when men like Capone fled the scene, the bottom for musicians dropped out.[40]

Walter Barnes, whose band had been well paid for years at the Cotton Club in Cicero, Illinois (a Ralph Capone joint), is one musician who paid tribute to these men, carefully noting the agonies his band suffered in the South when reformers closed club doors in the mid-30s.[41]

The intention here is not to recount the many occupational ventures, legitimate and otherwise, which underworld characters pursued following their ejection from the cabaret limelight. Nor can it be said that all of them fled the night club business. Even after the Capones had departed, Chicago had the likes of the Fischetti Brothers, the Mangano clan, Cherry-Nose Gioe, Paul Ricca, Tough Tony Capezio and Louis "Little New York" Campagna operating clubs and jazz joints. Suffice it to say, however, that in this era of repressive anti-union activity, every dollar invested by racketeers with non-musical objectives was money taken away from jazz artists and their fans.

Only one large city seemed prepared to run counter to this trend—Kansas City. Kansas City of the 1930s literally bristled with jazz vitality. Yet here again my contention remains unflawed: For Kansas City was an underworld haven, and wherever this existed, and whenever mobsters promoted a pro-jazz policy, the music flourished like orchids in a hothouse. At least until 1940, Kansas City was the darling of the jazz world, capable of side-stepping external reformist pressures against its night life. And so it was that until anti-crime crusades succeeded in severing the umbilical cord that stretched between musicians and mobsters, the city helped establish a haven for great musical invention.

Kansas City: Jazz Darling of the Mid-West

Despite reactionary events being recorded elsewhere, the drought in jazz music luckily bypassed Kansas City, Missouri. It alone acted as a tiny beacon of musical radiance in a nation fast converting to more commercialized popular music being created by the larger record companies. Ironically, the music's highwater mark occurred after 1932, and only with mob endorsement, far from Harlem, in this sleepy little town (1920 population, 101,000). Rarely discussed in the histories of underworld activity, Kansas City and its night life was unashamedly piloted by a full compliment of Sicilians in conjunction with, and appoval of the Irish-controlled machine of bootlegger-politician Tom Pendergast and his family. One source has written:

People supposedly in the know say that it was in Kansas City the Mafia came closest to achieving power on a grand scale.[42]

Local historian Lyle W. Dorsett confirms this view of the mobs, without whom jazz would never have ripened:

Most of the underworld activities which flourished...had roots in the Italian section of KC's Northside (near the black section). This was part of the (city's changing scene) since the turn of the century.

Organized crime and jazz blended well in Kansas City; it was a marriage made in musical heaven. Extending from the late 1920s, its golden reign, it paralleled the departure of mobsters from the East and lasted until 1939. This last date coincided with the indictment of Pendergast for tax evasion, a charge that whisked him away to prison. His timely presence cannot be overlooked for our study. Driggs comments:

Pendergast encouraged gambling and night life. Clubs appeared during his years of power in vast proliferation and all had music of one sort or another. Many could house full bands and many of the owners had political connections. It is of significance that nearly all the developments in Kansas City music took place during Pendergast's reign.[43]

At its peak the town dispensed a brilliant blend of jazz and blues within a drab parochial sea, spreading thousands of miles in every direction, of musical mediocrity. Kansas City itself glistened with an enticing array of cabarets, gambling casinos, dance pavillions, brothels and gin joints. Customers were drawn from an enormous territory which encompassed several Midwestern states. Wealthy cattlemen, oilmen, ranchers and salesmen on a spree mixed it up, disgorging large sums of money for nightly pleasures that might eclipse otherwise hard lives on the range. Many ranching jobs were seasonal. Because of this Kansas City was host to periodic celebrations of Mardi Gras proportions, when the lid on spending was blown off. One satisfied customer extolled: "If you want to see some sin, forget about Paris and go to Kansas City."[44]

The presence of the mobs was essential but not the sole reason for the growth of jazz in the area. The city's amiability and charm and relative tolerance, like that of an earlier New Orleans, held attractions of its own. In a city devoid of rampant prosperity the other places had known in the carefree days of the 1920s, the ability to withstand a terrible depression came easier. Nor could a tourist be critical of the warm climate and cheap standard of living available in Kansas City. These were ingredients to entice anyone, much less musical and criminal outcasts fleeing officialdom elsewhere. John Hammond told me that while a musician of the stature of Count Basie knew the Eastern musical scene inside and out, he was far more content to play organ in a small pit theater by day and a Kansas City cabaret at night.

New York gangsters were known to pop in, partaking of a night life no longer viable back home. They also must have given advice to their counterparts on ways of improving business. Their arrival often triggered special nights of whirlwind performances, much like opening night at the Met. According to one adage of the time: "When the underworld flocked to Kansas City, it has to be entertained on a wild and lavish scale."[45]

Of course this commentary implies the existence and relative sophistication of a local Sicilian and Jewish mobster network. Of the latter there were few; but the durability, size and skills of the Italian contingent quickly redressed the loss. Italian immigrants, 85% of whom were Sicilians, had been late arrivals to town. The result was a political and economic retardation which kept them constantly dependent on the older power blocs, of which the Pendergast family was one of the largest. Yet lateness brought its own blessing. For while political and unsavory alliances came late, these at least occurred within an orbit unmarked by the violence which infected other regions and brought such counterproductive resistance. Resisting a wholesale bloodbath, events within the Sicilian community nevertheless did not advance without hostility as it began ironing its own laundry.

Throughout the 1920s Johnny Lazia, Charlie "the Wop" Corollo, Chee Chee DeMayo, Charlie Binaggio, Joe "Scarface" DeGiovanni and Tony Gisso, representing various factions, struggled amongst themselves for supremacy. Only afterwards could they hope to challenge the Irish who controlled the town's redlight and amusement centers. But unlike the East, the Pendergasts promoted a policy of caution and accommodation. For they were keenly aware of how gang wars had toppled empires in Chicago and ruined everyone. Mutually acceptable pacts in the areas of vice, gambling and night life were hammered out, with Pendergast's distribution of alcohol to hundreds of clubs throughout the DiGiovanni network, symbolizing the merger of the two underworlds.[46] Jazz critic Dave Dexter claims the policy included leaving the musicians alone:

No matter how loud the jazz, there was no police interference. Many cops who had seen the inside of the (mob-controlled) Sunset Club enjoyed the music.

Jazz was triumphant because the promotions were well-suited to the time and place. Bone-paring during the 1930s was unnecessary in a town which had never been persuaded towards large revues, that lacked socialites and celebrities who expected spectacles, and whose clubs were intimately small and lacked amenities to increase overhead costs. Some even resembled shacks, a far cry from the oceanliner type of club only an Eastern clientele could afford. But what they offered came in generous doses, and dissatisfaction was rarely expressed. It was a shame that Eastern mobsters came to town bent on giving instruction in the running of night clubs rather than appreciating the differences and adjusting their own outmoded jazz club policies accordingly. Hentoff believes that these little places were indeed the harbingers of jazz's future, when groups had to be small and club surroundings "homey" if the changing audiences were to be appeased. So it was that Kansas City gave us jazz groups who were able to "stretch out more" in a looser atmosphere, more congenial for listening and dancing.[47]

The jazz cabaret area in town was seductively situated for any lover of the music. It was grouped within a few short blocks near the Italian district—a fat strip of joints that pumped their infectious sounds into the still prairie night air. Within this terrain could be found the more important places under gangster tutelage, such as the Reno Club, the Tower, Main Street Theatre, Fairland Park, the Lone Star, The Sunset, the Pla-Mor Ballroom, The High Hat, the Orange Blossom, Vanity Fair, The Novelty, and the Frog Hop and El-Torreon Ballrooms. One jazz historian notes the mutual dependencies:

The musicians drifted from one of these clubs to another, checking on the action inside, welcomed by the mobs wherever they appeared.[48]

The quality of music featured caused even musicians to scratch their collective heads in disbelief. Bandleader Andy Kirk was one of the musicians freed from economic worry playing there:

Oh those years, 1933 and 1934. We were just so busy in the night clubs we didn't even have time to work our way into Chicago to cut any records.[49]

Pianist Mary Lou Williams found the city "heavenly" for jazz artists while Hentoff cites an example of one 15-hour sax contest in 1933 between Lester Young, Coleman Hawkins, Ben Webster, Dickie Wilson and Herschel Evans.[50] Despite the town's relatively small black population (roughly 10% in this period), the magnetic effect it had on musicians was supercharged. Work seemed to last three times as long as anywhere else, and living costs were so low a musician could even save a little. It was no longer only gypsy bands from throughout the Southwest that converged here. Among those that did were the jazz bands of Benny Moten, Paul Banks, Tommy Douglas, Andy Kirk, Walter Page, Jay McShann, George E. Lee, Jap Allen, Mary Lou Williams, Count Basie, Buck Clayton and Jessie Stone. Jazz artist Sam Price recalls the town's clubs encouraged jam sessions some of which were truly fabulous:

I remember once at the Subway Club I came by a session at 10 p.m. and then went home to clean up and change my clothes. I came back after 1 a.m. and they were still playing the same tune.[51]

Jazzman Buster Smith remembers how Joe Turner used to put down his cook's hat and apron and come out of the kitchen at the Cherry Blossom (run by two Italians), singing the blues.[52] And local pianist George Salisbury has his own fond recollections:

Why man, there wasn't anything like it. Kansas City was going! And when I say going, I mean our cats played around the clock 'n nobody slowed down. When a man stepped out on 12th Street—he was in it.[53]

Nevertheless, and unhappily for the artists, disregarding all the free chili or work or support the musicians received, reformist tendencies which had done so much to retard the music in other areas eventually fell on Kansas City. By 1938 sufficient evidence had been collected to the town's chief night life sponsors, including the venerable Tom Pendergast himself. Some say the reason for conviction was tax evasion;

others speculated that Pendergast had been sacrificed by the Democrats who again had to fight off attacks on President Roosevelt's alleged softness on mobsters in the wake of the 1940 presidential election.[54] Whichever the story, local committees in Kansas City derived the muscle from some source and rid themselves of Pendergast and his minions. Lacking leadership, and the termination of an active jazz policy, musicians again gathered up their belongings and sought other kinds of work as the clouds of war loomed large by 1940.

In unison, the decade and the country's widespread interest in jazz came to a close. What had begun five decades before, fostered by the Sicilian underworld new to New Orleans, was to lose prominence in America. Whatever the intentions of the racketeers afterwards, and some still stayed in the night club business to promote the music, the music became more nostalgic than prophetic. Jazz music might henceforth assume different guises and be blended into other musical patterns and shapes, or find solace in a few widely-spaced night clubs, as an art form with spacious breeding grounds and a distinct lifestyle, its days of rule, like the Plains Indians, was over. Both the cultural and criminological changes of the past thirty years have witnessed a change between mobsters and musicians that has debased the current products each now has to sell, and undermined the communal vitality which alone made their efforts worthwhile.

Chapter IX
Just Wait'll Next Year

Having come to the close of this study, perhaps a few brief, recapitulatory words are in order. Perhaps, even, a comment or two about the present state of the art and its future, although, regarding the latter, any remarks, no matter how well founded, must be seen as blowing in the wind.

If anything, previous chapters have attempted to document a bizarre relationship which called into play new forms of ethnic enterprise. By 1920 the black musician was becoming technically advanced in his art, adding sophisticated forms of business expertise into his showman's repertoire. Also, by 1920, Jewish and Italian operators were becoming pioneers in the American night club field. Despite our tracing them back over forty years, both jazz artists and jazz clubs, as urban-oriented industries, were relatively new, scarcely ten years old. As late as 1920, most of the country's young people knew next to nothing about adult night life, even less about musical entertainment, and nothing at all of black America's jazz music. Night life was for the wealthy—sterile and pretentious.

But simultaneously with the expansion of cities grew demands for more to be done at night. Growing too were immigrant groups willing to satisfy this demand. So, gradually, Jewish and Italian foreigners, most of them capable of speaking only the most flawed English, bound together by criminal associations and woes police surveillance, put their night-time hours to work more productively than their Anglo-Saxon counterparts. There was both money and recognition in night club jazz in the 1920s. Thus it would have been odd had not at least some of this ragged army sooner or later conceived the idea of entering the field. Happily, their pioneer efforts did more than just turn up loose soil; rather they cut ingenious new paths through the world of night life. They introduced a thousand and one gimmicks for commercial appeal, eliminated previously restrictive practices against blacks, women and the urban young, and by attacking the cloying 19th century bourgeois themes in music, they greatly improved popular taste. It was a wondrous process while it lasted, and it lasted until almost mid-century when conglomerates of the mighty began replacing syndicates of the poor.

Because these elements in the development of jazz prevail no longer, the music may very well be decaying. The performance of an intimately excitable, danceable art form, played before live audiences for maximum effectiveness by practitioners who controlled their product is a thing of the past. Ruined not so much from the inside, but, ironically, from without. As I have attempted to explain, my approach to understanding this music cannot depend solely on the artist. The presence of the underworld backers, as owners and listeners and friends, was instrumental in the music's very success. That both groups have gone underground is not just coincidence. And as a candle of inspiration for popular music and musicians, jazz has almost exhausted its wick.

This, of course, is not an opinion held by everyone. Back from a nine-year stay abroad, trumpet player Ted Curson believes "there's more jazz in America now than ever before."[1] In my opinion the signs for the current status of jazz are not favorable, although my pessimism is hardly a final judgment, and only future events can affirm or deny the staying power of this music.

One concerned indicator of the downward spiral has been the Schwann series of record catalogs. As a resource their limitations are obvious since one cannot assume recording bands are necessarily performing groups, or that the interior personnel are the same. But the catalogs do suggest general activity, and its extent, for this kind of music. Since 1966 Schwann Catalog lists 490 jazz bands actively recording (a lesser number earned income from clubs and college dates). By June 1973 the number had fallen to 430. Thereafter the rate plummeted alarmingly. In November 1974 it was 370, 297 in February 1975, and 236 by October 1976, prior to the big push in

disco and "cross-over music." Even allowing for a sharp
counter trend, a return to the pre-1970 rate appears unlikely. In
any event, these figures are far short of the many hundreds of
bands that performed or recorded in any single year, even
during the depths of the depression.

Time magazine pinpointed the crisis in live music as far
back as 1956. Their study of the American Federation of
Musicians discovered musical trends which were disturbing.
Starting off with a base year of 1930, when 99,000 live dates
were open to musicians, *Time* claimed opportunities by 1940
had fallen 25%, and by 1954 only 59,000 night club and dance
hall dates were available, a 40% decline in two decades.[2] If
black jazz is considered, the opportunity curve was more
startingly affected by this loss in outlets.

What remains—a hybrid cousin to the jazz of yesteryear—
now finds itself lumbering under technical rationalizations
and commercial demands more numerous than it might
reasonably support. Jazz as an expression has always required
independent, limited-based, and flexible operations to develop.
But today, with the sharp decline in small record labels, night
clubs and independent agents, jazz finds itself controlled by
huge conglomerates that shape taste and dictate styles.[3]
Today's crop of agent is far more specialized and much more
removed from his sources of creativity. Russ Sanjek at BMI
explained to me some of the rationale that affect contemporary
investors. Large financial returns, he suggests, can only
accrue to this group by narrowing significantly the range of
choices in musical groups and moods offered. This is because
commonsense tells them the public holds a dangerously short
memory when it comes to stars, and this capricious tendency is
both too expensive and risky to suit most capitalists. Better to
have a few recognized "superstars" who will repay promotions
in handsome fashion than swim around with countless
satellites who stand every chance of drowning. Since all of this
is very high finance, such restrictions limit the competition as
well. One authority claims only six "entertainment
conglomerates" account for 85% of the record business while
limiting creativity:

Costs to record and promote are so much...emphasis on the few big productions will be at the expense of new artist who may be denied exposure and backup.[4]

Promoters with ready cash for young jazz artists are now a rarity. The result, observed by a British critic, favors only the elderly:

Jazz is not dead in New Orleans but in places its getting pretty ancient.... One night (in 1978) we listened to a band whose average age was 75.[5]

External decay is helped along by dwindling numbers of night club outlets once home for so many artists; from the hyping given to the selling of flashy commercial tunes by a new breed of promoter whose relative indifference to jazz is countered by avid interest in whatever makes money; and from an inadequately developed patronage which the mobs once cultivated so assiduously.

Between 1880 and 1940, the extensive range of outlets assured bands their wares would be displayed. This aided the known as well as the unknown musician. Clubs were havens for gangsters, many of whom possessed a fine ear when it came to acknowledging lively, personable entertainment. Eastern cabarets after 1915 and Kansas City clubs after 1930 were unquestionably the best places for headstrong, audacious musicians, engaged in friendly battle to perfect their musicianship. Through nightly contests, and amidst relaxed tolerance by management and criticism by customers, jazz artists simultaneously elevated fan interest and jazz standards. Yet one cannot forget where all this took place: the friendly confines of a club. The decades after 1940, on the other hand, saw immutable changes to all this.

In the face of spiralling costs, urban disintegration and a stiff refusal to upgrade neighborhoods, club owners helped in the suppression and diffusion of local fan interest. Former fun-loving districts also began losing their intrinsic worth for musicians. And owners raced one another in vacating the industry rather than spending to improve conditions. Commitment to the area surrounding each club evaporated by 1960 as customers came away with the impression of military encampments in the center of hostile territory. So it is that famous names from San Francisco's Jazz Workshop, Blackhawk, and Matador to New York's Cafe Bohemia, Half Note, and Birdland represent countless clubs buried under the dead weight of inadequate support and insensitive policies. And with each new fatality the circumspection of jazz tightens. Henny Youngman jokingly commented on this process:

Trying to recall all the different theatres, night clubs, and hotels I've worked in, I sometimes cannot separate the real from the imaginary. Many of the theatres are now supermarkets or skating rinks or office blocks. Many of the night clubs don't exist anymore. Many of the hotels don't exist anymore. It's possible that some of the cities don't exist anymore.

Roughly two of three New York clubs open for business in 1972 no longer greet customers; less than ten current with this writing are as old (see Appendix E). In 1973 jazz organist Jimmy Smith despaired of conditions "The state of health of the clubs," he wrote, "is really bad...and the radio jocks do nothing but push rock music."[6] Local merchants, too, act as constraints. In New Orleans they were able to obtain an ordinance banning street bands from the French Quarter. Corrupt officials also pose difficulties:

In an enterprising piece of journalism the *Chicago Sun Times* bought a dilapidated tavern, ran it for 4 months and recorded all the occasions when public servants—a vast range from building inspectors to accountants and lawyers—came in and demanded bribes to allow the place to stay in business.... Virtually the only public servants not involved in the briberies were policemen.[7]

Gone are the days when musicians held a firm grip on the kind of music they wished to play. Refused in one joint they had merely to cross the street and sign on with a rival, a freedom that left both their style and self-esteem intact. Despite threats and sneers, mobsters owning these places rarely bothered to shoulder and muscle their entertainers. The remnants of that scene now feel compelled to highlight a veritable prism of unlikely musical sounds in the hope of satisfying every off-shade of musical appetite. Jazz bands appear briefly for a 2- or

3-day engagement before taking wing; lucky ones must be content with a week's stretch. Some clubs find it cheaper to simply shut down operations for "remodelling" exercises than remain open for sparse crowds and high overhead. In this atmosphere musicians are rarely pleased with their own performances. One told me he was happy if he played exceptionally well five or six times a year. Musical styles offer little solace. A check of the 1976-77 season at Greenwich Village's Bottom Line reveals only one in every six of the 245 groups that appeared there had anything to do with jazz, a bewilderment of diversity. Club owner Max Gordon is convinced that clubs

...have no image and jump around in musical styles so much as to confuse the public...who won't know what they'll find when they fall in (a joint).[8]

Jazz singer Carmen McRae, recalling her early band days listening to jazz groups at Minton's (in Harlem), believes her brand of singing is in danger of extinction for want of clubs:

They don't have those kind of clubs anymore. You know, there ought to be some place where people can get their act together—small clubs where singers (and musicians) can sharpen their instruments. But the places don't exist. Years ago people took part in jam sessions and learned. Nowadays booking agents want to know first how many records you've sold, not how well you can sing.[9]

Earfuls have replaced eyefuls. Live performances and steady work have taken a back seat to record sessions which may be the life blood of current artists but which have too much influence on the entertainment industry. In Ted Curson's words:

They're not dealing with personalities anymore. They're dealing in sound, but not personal sound. You can be exchanged for anybody. You can be imitated.[10]

Contemporary merchandising gimmicks focus on highly developed supermarket techniques in distribution. Given this climate, jazz artists appear unlikely to reach their potential. Alvin Toffler has noted that producers appreciate it is cheaper

to record a band for mass sales than place the same group in a
club setting every night for the benefit of few listeners. Yet if
bands refuse to record, they work not at all.

Agents and investors no longer share similar backgrounds
with the artists. The present college-trained, bureaucratic
agent controls people from an air-conditioned office block and
hardly sees the smoke-filled little jazz clubs where business
was once transacted in personable intimacy. Possibly, too,
alcohol and drug stimulants are less frowned upon by today's
managers than they were by the traditional mobsters, so long
as the profit margin remains healthy.

Such an air of casualness must surely affect the artists.
Young musicians appear less interested in learning diversity
in music and more in that which is most saleable. Nor is theirs
a disciplined devotion to technical skill—and the byproduct
shows it. Further, managerial skills and musical development
so highly prized by mobsters who educated musicians capable
of adroit negotiation have given way to lazy temperaments. It
is the rare musician who now knows his business from soup to
nuts. Trumpet player Dizzy Gillespie says he gets chagrined
working up a style over 20 years just to see some one else copy
and distort it, and "twist it into something that makes big
money" for others.[11]

Musical change became a matter of course when
racketeers took an active part in the social life and struggles of
the black musician. In the period under study, jazzmen tried
many ideas, exciting and otherwise, backed by men who never
relented in their admiration and enthusiasm. If no one else was
prepared to listen, at least they were; and they showed their
appreciation in ways a musician could understand: direct
payment, instant side benefits, reliable contracts and the
opportunity to control his own music. When the jazz artist
wanted to do something creative, sponsors willingly agreed.
By this process the artist was never placed in a position of
servility by an audience. Gangsters were simply not interested
in shaping the outcome of a band's style. This can hardly be
said today. Enough for a band to show up on time, play a few
requests and entertain. Alienation between the artist and the
agent was almost unknown, and certainly lacked the present

day bureaucratic excesses.

In the old days, club life was predicated on continued patronage from the regulars who came purposely to hear the music, and who identified with the musicians down to their socks and arrest records. Dickie Wells believes that musicians

...are inspired by having people dancing in front of them and play differently for a dance than at a concert.[12]

Clubs were very personal affairs. Personal, too, were the owners who fanned out into adjoining neighborhoods in search of talent.

In addition they encouraged local arts, patronized local merchants and provided welfare services generally. Today, bars, disco shops and clubs have become impersonal affairs, seeking to explore differences in people rather than their commonalities. Stylistic differences the *Village Voice* once dubbed a "study of Darwinian selection." There are black bars, gay bars and super-masculine spots, subdivided by age, inclination and fetish. Clubs exist for business types on the prowl, discos for the feverish, singles bars, bohemian haunts, lesbian locations and outlets for specialized clientele drawn from a pool of suburbanites, bikers and assorted hustlers. With a view toward mutual exclusivity, patrons ferret out their own type, where music is incidental. Juke boxes and records supersede live sound since they are cheaper and invariably subordinate to the main plot, which is the interaction of the customers themselves. In short supply, bands falter in musicianship before a sea of indifference. Mobsters and the audiences of the 1920s would have been more critical of what was being played. Jazz artist John Coltrane spoke out for the alienated artist:

Music today [1966] is directed by businessmen...who only know how to arrange the making of a profit....I like an audience that shows what they feel...and how to respond.[13]

With fewer and fewer outlets in which to perform, and fewer people willing to act as backers, jazz groups, as Schwann lists point out, are not exactly thick as flies. Eventually, one gets down to historical forces, and our veering away from this art form has shown historical constancy. Eisner's remarks from the late 1940s bear repeating:

No more than any other department of bureacraticised culture does music leave any room for freedom, or fantasy of the artist, and even when...so-called creative minds are called in, they are engaged on such terms that they either comply at once with prevailing standards or are taught by businessmen and their representatives in industry to produce, with more or less resistance what everybody else produces.[14]

Given the changes which have plagued jazz music since 1940, we might marvel at the steadfast friendship two seemingly antipodal groups established. But we have seen that mobsters and musicians were fused as the result of each mirroring the qualities possessed by the other. Mobsters were decisive, enterprising, open-handed yet grimly serious about maintaining a code of underworld ethics. Jazzmen, for their part, were adaptably fluid, spontaneous, philosophically composed at the bitterest setbacks and a whimsical spectator of life. Both yearned to exhibit their talents—one in music, the other in running a club. For each had the same flair for hedonistic adventure, egotism and showmanship that offended a racist, puritanical society. Each in his own way attracted fan worship, inspiring imitators galore, born of people sharing close dispensations and deprivations.

Under a loyalty extended by the underworld, jazzmen had wide scope in developing their music. This made all the difference in the maturation process, and allowed artists to ignore constant heckling and mockery. Mobsters reciprocated a musician's attitudes and generosities. It was an historical situation placing two pariahs on the same side of the line, where the external dangers were far more invidious than any risks each posed for the other.

But this relationship is all but over. Connections may occur, but they are now exceptions. Only occasionally do they align themselves. "The aspiring jazz musician is left to make it very much on his own," reports jazz critic Leonard Feather.[15] Sanjek forecasts a time when very few artists will survive as independents. This despite the fact that cities have become increasingly more black in complexion and outlook, and, one would think, in a more fortuitous position to aid the struggling jazz artists. Yet of all the performing arts, ethnic music (like jazz) is most deprived of funds. This is the conclusion reached by studies of government support of the arts.[16] New sources of income are mandatory, however, now that the Jewish and Sicilian investors have gone elsewhere. Ortiz Walton repeats this unhappy message in his own thoughtful analysis. His findings for 1971 suggest that a mere three-tenths of one percent of monies spent on the arts was channelled to aid jazz artists whereas European-derived music had a budget 74 times larger.

We are left to conclude that jazz has few friends in high places. This seems logical inasmuch as this group rarely has any members who originate from a background that has given us so many jazz musicians. Worse, there seems little urgency outside the ranks of the artists [themselves, and their narrow band of supporters,] to overturn this apple cart. The few grants dispensed to musicians contain countless contingencies and strings of dependency, as if one were receiving aid from relatives. Yet without a benevolent sponsor—the racketeers were a classic example—jazz is stuck in the mud. It responds best in a hothouse that is turbulent and self-indulgent, where facilities for musical expression are intimately connected with a surreal way of life, freed from concerns of the marketplace.

Among the Jewish and Italian bootleggers, gamblers and racketeers from 1880 to 1940, many willingly risked business fortunes to promote jazz and other musical entertainments. The mobsters transcended racism, public hypocrisy toward the arts and official cupidity to give jazz groups both stimulus and bandstands. Today's public cares little whether the music they listen to is mechanical in concept and style or not. In former periods, bands managed most of the important things themselves; what they overlooked, the underworld rectified.

Can today's promoters even faintly approximate the kind of atmosphere which gave jazz its liveliest years? What the bootleggers and mobsters of 1880-1940 offered was culturally stimulating, artistically creative, and exciting as well. Not only did they provide the booze and gaming tables for a people dulled by the harshness of stark reality, but they helped to integrate the entertainment capitals of the cities, while concocting a fantasy world which appealed to everyone involved. Claims and promises, immoral and illegal, they made and fulfilled.

To the poor man, whether musician or laborer, the racketeers assertively justified themselves. By doing so they vastly improved the participatory role of the lower classes in the world of art—if we consider jazz in this context—and countered the old adage about the poor lacking artistic appreciation and financial capacity to have an effect on the arts.

Perhaps there could not have been a more fortunate association for the development of jazz.

Notes for Chapter I

[1]Robert Neff and Anthony Connor, *Blues* (Boston: 1975), p. 52.

[2]Chris Albertson, *Bessie: Empress of the Blues* (London: 1975), pp. 60-63.

[3]Robert Sylvester, *No Cover Charge: A Backward Look at Night Clubs* (New York: 1956), p. 46.

[4]Dickie Wells, *The Night People* (Boston: 1971), p. 71; Bill Davidson, "Memories," *The Jazz Record,* Feb., 1946, p. 5; George Hoefer and Willie Smith, *Music on My Mind* (New York: 1964), p. 193.

[5]Earl Hines, "How Gangsters Ran the Band Business," *Ebony,* Sept., 1949, p. 41.

[6]Frank Kofsky, *Black Nationalism and the Revolution in Music* (New York: 1970), p. 157.

[7]Werner Sombart, *Jews and Modern Capitalism* (London: 1913), p. 152.

[8]Bud Freeman, *You Don't Look Like a Musician* (Detroit: 1974), p. 116.

[9]Art Hodes, "Blues for the Dago," *The Jazz Record,* Sept., 1944, p. 6.

[10]Morroe Berger, "Jazz Resistance to the Diffusion of a Culture-Pattern," *Journal of Negro History,* Jan., 1947, p. 461.

[11]*Opinion Research Corporation Survey* 105-D, April, 1940.

[12]Dorine Manners, *Scarlet Patrol* (New York: 1937), p. 108.

[13]Vincent Teresa, "A Mafioso Causes the Mafia Craze," *Saturday Review of "The Society,"* Feb., 1973, pp. 25-29.

[14]Illinois Crime Investigating Commission, *Juice Racketeers: A Report on Criminal Usury in Chicago,* June, 1970.

[15]"Angelo" was an elderly Sicilian gentleman, formerly a night club operator with direct contacts with various syndicates, who chose this alias to avoid detection by political enemies.

[16]Mark K. Hiller, "Organized Crime in Urban Sociology: Chicago in the 1920s," *Journal of Social History,* Winter 1971-72, pp. 215-16.

[17]Carey McWilliams, *A Mask for Privilege: Anti-Semitism in America* (Boston: 1948), pp. 147-48, 154.

[18]Freeman, *op. cit.,* p. 5.

[19]Donald R. Cressey, "Methodological Problems in the Study of Organized Crime as a Social Problem," *The Annals of the American Academy of Political and Social Science,* Nov., 1967.

[20]I obtained these comments either through personal interviews graciously given or by means of formal correspondence sent in reply to my inquiries.

Notes for Chapter II

[1]Rupert Hughes, *Lady's Man* (New York: 1930), p. 103; Anthony Abbot, *About the Murder of the Night Club Lady* (New York: 1931), pp. 4-5.

[2]Maria W. Lambin and Leroy S. Bowman, "Evidences of Social Relationships as Seen in the Types of New York City Dance Halls," *Social Forces,* Jan., 1925, pp. 287-89.

[3]Allon Schoener (ed.), *Harlem on My Mind* (New York; 1968), p. 80; American City Guides Series, *New York City* (New York: 1939), p. 140.

[4]Nat Shapiro and Nat Hentoff, *Hear Me Talkin' to Ya'* (New York: 1955), p. 85.

[5]See *Downbeat,* 26 Jan., 1967, p. 17; Rudi Blesh, *Combo U.S.A.* (Phila.: 1971), p. 197; and album liner notes on "Freddie Keppard Plays," Herwin Records 101.

[6]Shapiro and Hentoff, *op. cit.,* p. 168.

[7]Jack Buerkle and Danny Barker, *Bourbon Street Black* (New York: 1973), p. 163.

[8]See their RCA Victor album notes LPV 547; Edward Harvey, "Social Change and the Jazz Musician," *Social Forces,* Sept., 1967, p. 181.

[9]Kenneth Allsop, *The Bootleggers: The Story of Prohibition* (New York: 1961), p. 17; Ralph Berton, *Remembering Bix: A Memoir of the Jazz Age* (New York: 1974), p. 196.

[10]Quoted in Allsop, *op. cit.,* p. 178.

[11]Alan Lomax, *Mr. Jelly Roll* (New York: 1950), p. 183.

[12]Richard Hadlock, *Jazz Masters of the 1920s* (New York: 1965), p. 110.

[13]Elliot Paul, *That Crazy American Music* (Indianapolis: 1957), p. 197.

[14]Quoted in Hadlock, *op. cit.,* p. 122.

[15]Art Hodes, "Liberty Inn Drag," *Jazz Record,* April, 1945, pp. 8-9.

[16]Thomas J. Hennessey, "The Black Chicago Establishment," *Journal of Jazz Studies,* Dec., 1974, p. 31.

[17]See the *Amsterdam News,* 23 Oct., 1929 and the *New York Daily News,* 31 Oct., 1929.

[18]Tom Davin, "Conversations with James P. Johnson," *Jazz Review,* March/April, 1960, p. 13.

[19]Rudolph Fisher, "The Caucasian Storms Harlem," *American Mercury,* Aug., 1927, p. 394.

[20]Davin, *op. cit.,* p. 11.

[21]Fisher, *op. cit.,* p. 393.

[22]Dickie Wells, *The Night People* (Boston: 1971), p. 28.

[23]Mark K. Hiller, "Organized Crime in Urban Society: Chicago in the 1920s," *Journal of Social History,* Winter, 1971-72, p. 211.

[24]Robert Sylvester, *No Cover Charge: A Backward Look at Night Clubs* (New York: 1956), p. 45.

[25]Barry Ulanov, *Duke Ellington* (New York: 1946), p. 39.

[26]George Hoefer and Willie Smith, *Music on My Mind* (New York: 1964), p.

142; Nat Shapiro and Nat Hentoff, *Hear Me Talkin' to Ya'* (New York: 1955), p. 171.

[27]Quoted in Stanley Dance, *The World of Earl Hines* (New York: 1977), p. 138).

[28]Samuel B. Charters, *Jazz—A History of the New York Scene* (New York: 1962), p. 218.

[29]Martin Williams, *Jazz Panorama* (New York: 1962), p. 73.

[30]American City Guides, *New Orleans* (Boston: 1938), p. XL.

[31]Quoted in the *Jazz Record,* May, 1946, p. 5.

[32]Decca Records, liner notes, "The Music of Jimmy Lunceford," DL 79237.

[33]Dance, *The World of Duke Ellington* (New York: 1970), p. 165.

[34]This information came from a letter from the President of the local Hot Music Society to the San Francisco Library, dated 19 Sept., 1978, for a Black musical exhibit.

Notes for Chapter III

[1]Jimmy Durante and Jack Kofoed, *Night Clubs* (New York: 1931), p. 13.

[2]Leo Walker, *The Wonderful Era of Great Dance Bands* (Berkeley: 1964), p. 9.

[3]Quoted in Alvin Toffler, *The Culture Consumers—Art and Affluence in America* (Baltimore: 1965), p. 23.

[4]Over 2000 Italian and Jewish club owners were arrested in a 1908 sweep along the Lower East Side alone. See George Kibbe Turner, "Tammany's Control of New York," *McClure's Magazine,* June, 1909, p. 130.

[5]George Rector, *The Girl from Rectors* (New York: 1927), pp. 87-95; Samuel Ornitz, *Haunch, Paunch, and Jowl* (New York: 1923), p. 246.

[6]Herbert Asbury, *The Great Illusion, An Informal History of Prohibition* (New York: 1968), p. 12.

[7]Jim Marshall, *Swinging Doors* (Seattle: 1949), p. 61.

[8]H.C. Brown, *In the Golden 90s* (New York: 1928), p. 143; Marshall, *op cit.,* pp. 12-13; Al Rose, *Storyville, New Orleans,* (Tuscaloosa: 1974), p. 15.

[9]Alvin F. Harlow, *Old Bowery Days* (New York: 1931), p. 406.

[10]Marshall, *op. cit.,* pp. 103, 111.

[11]See the David Pittman studies; also Stephen Longstreet, and Asbury's *Great Illusion, op. cit.,* where this phenomenon is detailed at great length.

[12]Albert S. Crockett, *Old Waldorf Bar Days* (New York: 1931), p. 17.

[13]Gene Fowler, *Schnozzola* (New York: 1951), p. 26.

[14]Quoted in Maurice M. Milligan, *The Missouri Waltz* (New York: 1948), p. 52.

[15]George W. Walling, *Recollections of a New York Chief of Police* (New York: 1887), p. 487.

[16]Jack Lait and Lee Mortimer, *Chicago Confidential* (New York: 1950), pp. 124-26; Stephen Longstreet, *Chicago—An Intimate Portrait of its People, Pleasures and Power: 1860-1919* (New York: 1973), pp. 205-212.

[17]Gus Tyler (ed.) *Organized Crime in America* (Ann Arbor: 1971), p. 141.

[18]H.O. Brunn, *The Story of the Original Dixieland Jazz Band* (Baton Rouge: 1960), p. 46.

Notes for Chapter IV

[1]Cliffton Johnson, *Highways and Byways of the South* (New York: 1905), pp. 335-36.

[2]H.C. Brearley, *Homicide in the United States* (Chapel Hill: 1932), p. 99.

[3]Raymond O. Gastil, "Homicide and a Regional Culture of Violence," *American Sociological Review,* June, 1971, p. 412.

[4]Lorenzo J. Greene and Carter G. Woodson, *The Negro Wage Earner* (Washington, D.C.: 1930), p. 250; Louise V. Kennedy, *The Negro Peasant Turns Cityward* (New York: 1930), p. 66.

[5]Giles Oakley, *The Devil's Music: A History of the Blues* (London: 1976), p. 79.

[6]*Downbeat,* 6 August 1970, p. 14.

[7]Robert Neff and Anthony Connor, *Blues* (Boston: 1975), pp. 12, 167.

[8]*Ibid.,* p. 45.

[9]Nat Shapiro and Nat Hentoff, *Hear Me Talkin' to Ya'* (New York: 1955), p. 306.

[10]Library of Congress Records, V, "Dance Music," LCM 2082; also RCA Victor, "Leadbelly," LPV 505.

[11]Dickie Wells, *The Night People* (Boston: 1971), p. 43.

[12]*Downbeat,* 14 Dec., 1967, p. 5; also Oakley, *op. cit.*

[13]*Rayne Tribune* (Louisiana), 27 Nov., 1931.

[14]Perry Bradford, *Born with the Blues* (New York: 1965), p. 18.

[15]Louis Armstrong, *Satchmo: My Life in New Orleans* (New York: 1954), p. 150.

[16]Paul Oliver, *Conversations with the Blues* (New York: 1965), p. 72.

[17]Shapiro and Hentoff, *op. cit.,* p. 325.

[18]*Ibid.,* p. 326; Irene E. Cortinouis, "Jazz on the Riverboats, the Way a Player Tells it," *Journal of Jazz Studies,* June, 1974, p. 74.

[19]Alan Lomax, *Mr. Jelly Roll* (New York: 1950), p. 55; Gavin Bushness and Nat Hentoff, "New York Jazz in the 1920s," *Jazz Review,* April, 1959, p. 17.

[20]Lena Horne and Richard Schickel, *Lena* (Garden City: 1965), pp. 48-49.

[21]Shapiro and Hentoff, *op. cit.,*p. 30; Nat Hentoff, *The Jazz Life* (New York: 1961), p. 35.

[22]Nathan Huggins, *Harlem Renaissance* (New York: 1971), p. 9; See *The Chicago Messenger* of 3 March 1924, p. 71; also Chadwick Hansen, "Social Influence in the Jazz Style in Chicago: 1920-1930," *American Quarterly,* Winter 1971-72, p. 503.

[23]Samuel B. Charters, *Jazz in New Orleans: 1885-1963* (New York: 1963), p. 36; H.O. Bruun, *The Story of the Original Dixie-Land Jazz Band* (Baton Rouge: 1960), p. 28.

[24]Jack Lait and Lee Mortimer, *Washington Confidential* (New York: 1951), p. 39.

25George W. Walling, *Recollections of a New York Chief of Police* (New York: 1887), p. 487.

26Columbia Records, "Jazz Odyssey II," C3L-32; Ralph Berton, *Remembering Bix: A Memoir of the Jazz Age* (New York: 1974), p. 22; and Leo Walker, *The Wonderful Era of Great Dance Bands* (Berkeley: 1964), p. 38.

Notes for Chapter V

1John Smith Kendall, "New Orleans Newspapermen of Yesterday," *Louisiana Historical Quarterly,* July, 1946, p. 433.

2Henry A. Kmen, *Music in New Orleans: The Formative Years: 1751-1841* (Baton Rouge: 1966), p. 30.

3A.A. Foster, *New Orleans—The Glamour Period: 1800-1840* (New Orleans: 1957), p. 161; Hodding Carter (ed.) *The Past as Prelude: New Orleans: 1718-1968* (New Orleans: 1968), pp. 210-212.

4Karl Baedeker, *United States Guidebook* (Leipzig: 1893), p. 368.

5Joy J. Jackson, *New Orleans in the Gilded Age: Politics and Urban Progress—1880-1896* (Baton Rouge: 1969), p. 11.

6Sarah Searight, *New Orleans* (New York: 1973), pp. 92-99; Jackson, *op. cit.,* p. 18; J.W. Mario in *The Nation* (London), 28 March, 1900, p. 7.

7Carl Schurz, *Report on the Condition of the South* (New York: 1865), p. 40.

8George E. Cunningham, "Italians Hindrance to White Solidarity, 1890-1898," *Journal of Negro History,* Jan., 1965, p. 23; Roger W. Shugg, *Origins of the Class Struggle in Louisiana,* (Baton Rouge: 1939), p. 259.

9Quoted in John Higham, *Strangers in the Land: Patterns of American Nativism: 1860-1925* (New York: 1969), p. 169.

10Quoted in Cunningham, *op. cit.,* p. 24.

11Quoted in Robert Tallant, *The Romantic New Orleanians* (New York: 1950), pp. 308-309.

12Frederic Ramsey, Jr., and C.E. Smith, *Jazzmen* (New York: 1939), p. 31; Jackson, *op. cit.,* p. 233; American City Guides, *New Orleans* (Boston: 1938), pp. 31-32.

13John W. Blassingame, *Black New Orleans: 1860-1880* (Chicago: 1973), pp. 162-164; Earl F. Niehaus, *The Irish in New Orleans: 1800-1860* (Baton Rouge: 1965), pp. 51, 60, 59-70.

14Herbert Asbury, *The French Quarter* (New York: 1935), p. 406.

15*House Executive Documents*, Foreign Relations of the United States for 1896, p. 706; Frederick Sondern, Jr., *Brotherhood of Evil* (New York: 1959), p. 58; The Rome correspondent is mentioned by John Smith Kendall in "Who Killa de Chief," *Louisiana Historical Quarterly,* April, 1939, p. 504—Kendall, by the way, dates the first Mafia-related crime to 1878; Joy J. Jackson, "Crime and the Consciousness of a City," *Louisiana History,* Summer, 1968, p. 243; Martin Williams, *Jazz Masters of New Orleans* (New York: 1967), p. 16; *Ken,* 11 May 1939.

16City Guide, *op. cit.,* p. 141; *New Orleans Daily Picayune,* 16 Nov., 1862.

17Francis A. J. Ianni, *A Family-Business-Kinship and Social Control of*

Crime (New York: 1972), p. 1.

[18]City Guide, *op. cit.*

[19]Jim Marshall, *Swinging Doors* (Seattle: 1949), p. 85.

[20]Al Rose, *Storyville, New Orleans* (Tuscaloosa: 1974), p. 73.

[21]Fritz Stern in *Times Literary Supplement,* 5 Nov., 1976, p. 1389.

[22]Tom Stoddard, *The Autobiography of Pops Foster* (Berkeley: 1971), p. 25; Rose, *op. cit.,* pp. 31, 70.

[23]Marshall Stearns, *The Story of Jazz* (New York: 1958), p. 58.

[24]Ramsey and Smith, *op. cit.,* p. 185; Leonard V. Huber, *New Orleans: A Pictorial History* (New York: 1971), p. 206; Williams, *op. cit.,* p. 18; Shugg, *op. cit.,* p. 103; Ken, *op. cit.*

[25]Will S. Monroe, *Sicily: The Garden of the Mediterranean* (London: 1909), pp. 231-231; Louise Caico, *Sicilian Ways and Days* (New York: 1910), pp. 150-151.

[26]Velvel Pasternak, *Songs of the Chassidim* (New York: 1968), p. 294; J.B. Lampe, *Songs of Ireland* (New York: 1916).

[27]Wingy Manone, *A Trumpet on The Wing* (New York: 1948), pp. 3-11.

[28]Frank Gillis and John W. Miner, *Oh, Didn't He Ramble—The Life Story of Lee Collins* (Urbana: 1974), p. 40; Blassingame, *op. cit.,* p. 147.

[29]Elliot Paul, *That Crazy American Music* (Indianapolis: 1957), pp. 171-76.

[30]Arna Bontemps (ed.), *Father of the Blues—W.C. Handy* (London: 1957), pp. 91-92; George L. Lee, *Beele Street* (New York: 1934), p. 22; Leo Walker, *The Wonderful Era of Great Dance Bands* (Berkeley: 1964), p. 23.

[31]Quoted in Ann Fairbairn's *Call Him George* (New York: 1961), p. 149.

[32]*Ibid.,* p. 194.

[33]Edward Harvey, "Social Change and the Jazz Musician," *Social Forces,* Sept., 1967, p. 37; William B. Cameron, "Sociological Notes on the Jam Session," *Social Forces,* Dec., 1954, p. 181.

[34]*Collier's Weekly,* 29 Feb., 1908; Rose, *op. cit.,* p. 64.

[35]Egal Feldman, "Prostitution, the Alien Woman, and Progressive Imagination—1910-1915," *American Quarterly* (19) 1967, pp. 196-97; Eric Anderson, "Prostitution and Social Justice, Chicago, 1910-1915," *Social Service Review,* June, 1974, pp. 217-218.

Notes for Chapter VI

[1]Tom Stoddard, *The Autobiography of Pops Foster* (Berkeley: 1971), p. 41.

[2]Francis A.J. Ianni, *A Family Business-Kinship and Social Control of Crime* (New York: 1972), p. 78.

[3]Richard Gambino, *Blood of My Blood* (New York: 1974), p. 113; Hutchins Hapgood, *Spirit of the Ghetto: Studies of the Jewish Quarter of New York* (New York: 1902), p. vii.

[4]Anonymous, *I, Mobster* (New York: 1951), p. 10.

[5]Arrigo Petaccio, *Joe Petrisino—The True Story of a Tough Turn-of-the-Century New York Cop* (New York: 1974), p. 16.

[6]Samuel Ornitz, *Haunch, Paunch, and Jowl* (New York: 1923), p. 28.

[7]Michael Gold, *Jews Without Money* (New York: 1930), pp. 14-15.

[8]Judd Teller, *Strangers and Natives: Evolution of an American Jew from 1921 to the Present* (New York: 1968), p. 86; Albert Goldman, *Ladies and Gentlemen—Lenny Bruce* (New York: 1971), p. 111; Village Voice, 18 June 1979, p.54.

[9]George K. Turner, "Criminals of New York," *McClure's Magazine*, Nov., 1909, p. 55.

[10]Quoted in Burton B. Turkus and Sid Feder, *Murder, Inc.* (New York: 1960), p. 179.

[11]Michael Freedland, *Irving Berlin* (New York: 1974), p. 17; David Ewan, *Panorama of American Popular Music* (Englewood Cliffs: 1957), p. 180; Stanley Dance, *The World of Earl Hines* (New York: 1977), p. 137.

[12]Art Hodes, "The Rainbow Cafe," *Jazz Record,* Oct., 1943, p. 4.

[13]Willhelm Sjobert, "Social Characteristics of Entertainers," *Social Forces,* Oct., 1958, pp. 73-74.

[14]Quoted in Herbert Asbury, *Gangs of New York* (New York: 1927), pp. 346-347.

[15]J.B. Martin, *My Life in Crime* (New York: 1952), p. 138.

[16]Duke Ellington, *Music is My Mistress* (New York: 1973), p. 99.

[17]Stanley Walker, *The Night Club Era* (New York: 1933), p. 253.

[18]L.H. Whittemore, *The Man Who Ran the Subways* (New York: 1968), p. 15; Alvin F. Harlow, *Old Bowery Days* (New York: 1931), p. 404.

[19]Herbert Asbury, *Gem of the Prairie: An Informal History of the Chicago Underworld* (New York: 1942), pp. 325-326; Ralph Salerno and J.S. Thompkins, *The Crime Confederation* (New York: 1969), p. 107; Chris Albertson, *Bessie* (New York: 1972), p. 75; Mark K. Hiller, "Organized Crime in Urban Sociology: Chicago in the 1920s," *Journal of Social History,"* Winter, 1971-72, p. 219.

[20]Hiller, *op. cit.,* p. 221.

[21]Carl Van Vechten, *Nigger Heaven* (New York: 1926), p. 254; Willard K. Smith, *Bowery Murder* (Garden City: 1929), p.222; Curtis Lucas, *Lila* (New York: 1955), p.127.

[22]Martin, *op. cit.,* p. 131.

[23]Carroll and Garrett Graham, *Whitey* (New York: 1931), p. 151.

[24]Anonymous, *op. cit.,* p. 77.

[25]Mickey Cohen and John P. Nugent, *In My Own Words* (Englewood Cliffs: 1975), pp. 59, 75.

[26]Robert Sylvester, *No Cover Charge: A Backward Look at Night Clubs* (New York: 1956), pp. 174-75.

[27]Sjoberg, *op. cit.,* pp. 74-76.

[28]The Grahams, *op. cit.*

[29]Sylvester, *op. cit.,* p. 88.

[30]James Agate, *An Anthology* (New York: 1961), pp. 161, 167; Verna Arvey, *Choreographic Music* (New York: 1941), p. 280.

[31]Thomas G. Moore, *The Economics of the American Theatre* (Durham: 1968), pp. 7-9; W.A. Johnston, "Structure of the Motion Picture Industry," *Motion Picture Industry Annals* (128), 1947, pp. 20-30; Patricia Bronte, *Vittles and Vice* (Chicago: 1952), p. 15.

[32]"In the early days of Prohibition, there was much disorganization and plenty of new gangs pushing in," says the racketeer Anonymous, *op. cit.*, p. 62.

[33]Turkus and Feder, *op. cit.*, p. 232; Anon., *op. cit.*, p. 168.

[34]Dance, *World of Earl Hines, op. cit.*, p. 58.

[35]*New York Times* for 17 and 28 Feb., 1931.

[36]Quoted in Arnold Shaw, *The Street that Never Sleeps* (New York: 1971), p. 55.

[37]Jerry Stagg, *The Brothers Shubert* (New York: 1968), pp. 238-39.

[38]Vincent Teresa, *My Life in the Mafia* (New York: 1973), p. 119.

[39]Martin, *op. cit.*, p. 38.

[40]Jimmy Durante and Jack Kofoed, *Night Clubs* (New York: 1931), p. 136.

[41]Anonymous, *op. cit.*, p. 77.

[42]Interviewed in the *Village Voice*, 11 Sept., 1978, p. 65.

[43]Claude McKay, *Harlem: Negro Metropolis* (New York: 1940), p. 118.

[44]Salerno and Tompkins, *op. cit.*, p. 99; Sylvester, *op. cit.*, p. 195; Iannia, *op. cit.*, p. 11; Kenneth Allsop, *The Bootleggers: The Story of Prohibition* (New York: 1961), p. 49.

[45]Durante and Kofoed, *op. cit.*, p. 29.

[46]Mark K. Hiller, "Organized Crime in Urban Sociology: Chicago in the 1920s," *Journal of Social History*, Winter 1971-1972, p. 216.

[47]Nat Shapiro and Nat Hentoff, *Hear Me Talkin' to Ya'* (New York: 1955), p. 235.

[48]Bud Freeman, *You Don't Look Like a Musician* (Detroit: 1974), p. 75.

[49]Freeman, *op. cit.*, p. 116.

[50]Durante, *op. cit.*, p. 172.

[51]Durante, *op. cit.*, p. 156.

[52]Simeon Strunsky, *No Mean City* (New York: 1944), p. 215.

[53]Edward J. Doherty, *The Broadway Murders: A Night Club Mystery* (New York: 1929), p. 3.

[54]Arnold Shaw, *op. cit.*, p. 197.

[55]Arnold Shaw, *op. cit.*, p. 114.

[56]Anonymous, *The Real Story of a Bootlegger* (New York: 1923), p. 5.

[57]Ethel Waters, *His Eye is on the Sparrow,* (New York: 1950), p. 134; Lena Horne describes very much the same thing. Also see Chicago Commission in Race Relations, *The Negro in Chicago* (Chicago: 1922), pp. 323-24.

[58]Konrad Bercovici, *Manhattan Sideshow* (New York: 1931), p. 73; Max Jones and John Chilton, *Louis: 1900-1971* (Boston: 1971), p. 58.

[59]Ross Russell, *Jazz Style in Kansas City and the South-West* (Berkeley: 1971), p. 10.

[60]Lucas, Op. cit., p. 127.

[61]Anonymous, . . . *Bootlegger. op. cit.*, pp.106-107.

Notes for Chapter VII

[1]Elliot Paul, *That Crazy American Music* (Indianapolis: 1957), p. 194.

[2]C.M. Fair, "Requiem for a Living Art," in William Phillips and Philip Rahv (ed.), *The Avon Book of Modern Writing* (New York: 1953), p. 275.

[3]Ralph Salerno and J.S. Tompkins, *The Crime Confederation* (New York:

1969), p. 117; Stanley Dance, *The World of Earl Hines* (New York: 1977), p. 212.

⁴Barry Ulanov, *Duke Ellington* (New York: 1946), pp. 113-117. Mezzrow's autobiography mentions this role quite often.

⁵Quoted in *Village Voice*, 4 July 1977, p. 58.

⁶Mezz Mezzrow and Bernard Wolfe, *Really the Blues* (New York: 1946), p. 120; Henry "Buster" Smith and Don Gazzaway, "Conversations," *Jazz Review*, (11) Dec., 1959, p. 22 and (1) Jan. 1960, p. 19.

⁷Nat Shapiro and Nat Hentoff, *Hear Me Talkin' to Ya'* (New York: 1955), p. 81.

⁸Dave Dexter, *Jazz Story: From the 90s to the 60s* (Englewood Cliffs: 1964), p. 37.

⁹Jack Buerkle and Danny Barker, *Bourbon Street Black* (New York: 1973), pp. 105-106.

¹⁰Richard Hadlock, *Jazz Masters of the 1920s* (New York: 1965), p. 62.

¹¹Arnold Shaw, *The Street that Never Sleeps* (New York: 1971), p. 196.

¹²Henry E. Barnes, *Battling the Crime Wave* (Boston: 1931), p. 113; Stanley Dance, *op. cit.*, p. 167.

¹³*Downbeat*, 1 Dec., 1967, p. 22.

¹⁴Dance, *op. cit.*, p. 61.

¹⁵Dickie Wells, *The Night People* (Boston: 1971), p. 28.

¹⁶Allon Schoener (ed.), *Harlem on My Mind* (New York: 1968), p. 59.

¹⁷Dance, *op. cit.*, p. 168.

¹⁸Art Hodes, "Memories," *Jazz Review*, March, 1944, p. 4.

¹⁹Albert McCarthy, *Big Band Jazz* (London: 1975), p. 41; Stanley Dance, *The World of Duke Ellington* (New York: 1970), p. 67; Stanley Dance, *The World of Swing* (New York: 1974), p. 57; Dance ___*Hines, op. cit.*, p. 61.

²⁰Robert Sylvester, *No Cover Charge: A Backward Look at Night Clubs* (New York: 1956), p. 55.

²¹*Village Voice*, 12 Dec., 1977, p. 34.

²²*Downbeat*, 1 Dec., 1967, p. 22.

²³Dance, ___*Hines, op. cit.*, p. 172.

²⁴Art Hodes, "The Rainbow Cafe," *Jazz Review* Oct., 1943, p. 7.

²⁵Claude McKay, *A Long Way from Home* (New York: 1937), p. 321.

²⁶Quoted in J.C. Thomas, *Chasin' the Trane* (Garden City: 1975), pp. 147-8.

²⁷Dance, ___*Hines, op. cit.*, p. 249.

²⁸Oliver Evans, *New Orleans* (New York: 1959), p. 209; Simeon Strunsky, *No Mean City* (New York: 1944), p. 215; and Giles Oakley, *The Devil's Music: A History of the Blues* (London: 1976), p. 145. Of the 25 cities with the worst homicide rates for 1926, the first 12 were all Southern: New Orleans was 5th, Dallas 7th, and Chicago 22nd. See also *Spectator,* 2 June 1927.

²⁹Dance, ___*Hines, op. cit.*, p. 211; George Grunis, Reel One, Track One, recorded 3 June 1958, Tulane Univ. Jazz Archives.

³⁰The names of Bessie Smith, Richie Powers, Clifford Brown, Lonnie Johnson, Cecil Irwin, Doug Watkins and Frank Teschmacher can be found in this tragic category.

³¹Tom Stoddard, *The Autobiography of Pops Foster* (Berkeley: 1971), pp.

144, 244.

[32]Al Rose and Edmond Souchon, *New Orleans Jazz* (Baton Rouge: 1967), p. 6; Arnold Shaw, *op. cit.,* p. 115.

[33]This comment is from a 1960 *Chicago American* newspaper clipping pasted into Ruth Spanier's scrapbook on her husband.

[34]Bud Freeman, *You Don't Look Like a Musician* (Detroit: 1974), p. 23.

[35]Dance, ___*Hines, op. cit.,* p. 47.

[36]Earl Hines, "How Gangsters Ran the Night Club Business," *Ebony,* Sept., 1949, . 41.

[37]Al Rose, *Storyville: New Orleans* (Tuscaloosa: 1974), pp. 68-69.

[38]Eddie Condon and Thomas Sugrue, *We Called it Music* (New York: 1947), p. 125; "Barney Bigard Plays," RCA Victor liner notes, LPV 566; *North Carolina News and Observer,* p. 15, Nov., 1970; Demester, *op. cit.,* p. 47; and Art Hodes, "Memories, " *op. cit.,* p. 5.

[39]George T. Simon, *Glenn Miller and His Orchestra* (New York: 1974), pp. 41-42.

[40]Frederic Ramsey and C.E. Smith, *Jazzmen* (New York: 1939), p. 69.

[45][1]Frank Gillis and John W. Miner, *Oh, Didn't He Ramble: The Life Story of Lee Collins* (Urbana: 1974), p. 70.

[42]H.O. Bruun, *The Story of the Original Dixieland Jazz Band* (Baton Rouge: 1960), p. 48.

[43]Liner notes from "The Fletcher Henderson Story," Columbia Records, C4L-19.

[44]Dance, ___*Swing, op. cit.,* p. 53.

[45]Liner notes, "Jazz Odyssey, Harlem," Columbia Records, C3L-33.

[46]Liner notes, "Jelly Roll Morton," RCA Victor, LPV 546.

[47]George Hoefer and Willie Smith, *Music on My Mind* (New York: 1964), p. 144; Stoddard, *op. cit.,* p. 63; Shaw, *op. cit.,* p. 196; Max Kaminsky, *My Life in Jazz* (New York: 1963), p. 39; and Dance ___*Hines, op. cit.,* p. 167.

[48]*Architectural Forum,* May 1933, p. 418.

[49]Dance, ___*Hines, op. cit.,* p. 199.

[50]Polly Gottlieb, *The Nine Lives of Billy Rose* (New York: 1969), p. 75.

[51]Duke Ellington, *Music is My Business* (New York: 1973), p. 131; A. Shaw, *op. cit.,* p. 194; and Anonymous, *The Real Story of a Bootlegger* (New York: 1923), pp. 6-7.

[52]S.S. Van Dine, *The Gracie Allen Murder Case* (New York: 1938); pp. 44-46; Louis J. Vance, *The Trembling Flame* (Phila.: 1931), p. 88.

[53]Martin Williams (ed.), *Jazz Panorama* (New York: 1962), p. 53.

[54]*Travel,* Jan., 1930, pp. 18-19.

[55]Black musicians were a commonly expressed subject in the art deco period. Examples can be found in the posters of Roger Perot, the porcelaine figurines of Robj, Dada art by Otto Dix and Marcel Janco, and upon futuristic wall murals on ocean liners *SS Manhattan* and *SS Washington.*

[56]To better appreciate this style the reader is referred to Bevis Hillier, *art deco* (London: 1970), Martin Battersby, *Decorative Twenties* (London: 1969), and Sheldon and Martha Cheney, *Art and the Machine* (New York: 1936).

[57]Hines, "How Gangsters. . . .-- *op. cit.,* p. 46.

[58]*New York Sunday News,* 8 May 1921; Mezzrow and Wolfe, *op. cit.,* p. 103; and Marshall Stearns, *The Story of Jazz* (New York: 1958), p. 134.

[59]Ben Sidran, *Black Talk* (New York: 1971), p. 223; *New York World,* 27 Nov., 1924; and Hadlock, *op. cit.,* pp. 156-57.

[60]Claude McKay, *A Long Way___, op. cit.,* pp. 49, 114.

[61]See Chester Himes, *Third Generation* (New York: 1956), pp. 254-55.

Notes for Chapter VIII

[1]*Village Voice,* 2 Dec., 1974, p. 45.

[2]Samuel B. Charters, *Jazz in New Orleans* (New York: 1963), p. 110; Robert Neff and Anthony Connor, *Blues* (Boston: 1975), p. 39.

[3]Martin Williams (ed.), *Jazz Panorama* (New York: 1962). p. 101.

[4]Thomas Hart Benton, *An Artist in America* (Columbia: 1968), p. 132.

[5]Rudi Blesh, *Combo, U.S.A.* (Phila.: 1971), p. 195.

[6]Benton, *ibid.;* Ian Whitcomb, *After the Ball is Over: Pop Music from Rag to Rock* (New York: 1972), p. 47.

[7]Charters, *ibid.;* Tom Bethell, *George Lewis: A Jazzman from New Orleans* (Berkeley: 1977), pp. 97, 102-103.

[8]Nat Shapiro and Nat Hentoff, *Hear Me Talkin' to Ya'* (New York: 1955), p. 196.

[9]Lawrence C. Christensen, *Collective Bargaining in Chicago: 1929-1930* (Chicago: 1933), p. 195; Liner notes "James P. Johnson Piano Solos," Columbia Records CL 1780; Danny Barker, "Jelly Roll Morton in New York," *Jazz Review,* May 1959, p. 12; and Frank Driggs, "Eddie Barefield's Many Worlds," *Jazz Review,* July, 1960, p. 6.

[10]Irving Kolodin, "The Dance Band Business, a Study in Black and White," *Harper's Magazine,* June, 1941, p. 80.

[11]Artie Shaw, *The Trouble with Cinderella* (New York: 1952), pp. 236-37.

[12]Frank Gillis and John W. Miner, *Oh, Didn't He Ramble: The Life Story of Lee Collins* (Urbana: 1974), p. 71.

[13]The historian is Arnold Shaw; liner notes from "Little Club Jazz and Small Groups in the 1930s," New World Records NW 250.

[14]*Ibid.*

[15]S. Middleton, *Dining, Wining and Dancing in New York:* (New York: 1938), pp. 88-104; *Esquire's* "New York for World's Fair Visitors, 1939), p. 95; Dickie Wells, *The Night People* (Boston: 1971), pp. 28-29.

[16]Milt Gabler in *Downbeat,* 29 March 1973, p. 17.

[17]Julius Weinberger,"Economic Aspects of Recreation," *Harvard Business Review,* Summer, 1937, pp. 462-463.

[18]Quoted in Martin Gosch and Richard Hammer, *The Last Testament of Lucky Luciano* (Boston: 1975), pp. 121-122; American City Guide for New York, p. 53.

[19]Anonymous, *I, Mobster* (New York: 1951), p. 111.

[20]Anonymous, *op. cit.,* p. 101.

[21] Robert Sylvester, *No Cover Charge* (New York: 1956), p. 299.

[22] Anonymous, *op. cit.*, p. 91.

[23] Middleton, *op. cit.*, p. 112.

[24] See George T. Simon's "On-Spot Reports," in *Metronome* for these years for some idea of the racial inequities; Leo Walker, *The Wonderful Era of Great Dance Bands* (Berkeley: 1964), p. 34.

[25] Thomas G. Moore, *The Economics of the American Theatre* (Durham: 1968), pp. 71-74.

[26] Polly Rose Gottlieb, *The Nine Lives of Billy Rose* (New York: 1969), pp. 74-75.

[27] Polly Adler, *A House is Not a Home* (New York: 1953), p. 162; *Village Voice*, 11 Sept., 1978, p. 64.

[28] Arnold Shaw, *The Street that Never Sleeps* (New York: 1971), p. 20.

[29] Anonymous, *op. cit.*, p. 79.

[30] Professor Leo Hershkowitz contends that Tweed, much like the gangsters of the 1920s and 1930s was victimized and scorched publicly less for his venality, in which everyone participated, than for his championing the immigrant cause of his day.

[31] Burton B. Turkus and Sid Feder, *Murder Inc.* (New York: 1951), p. 304.

[32] Turkus and Feder, *op. cit.*, pp 113-14; also see the press coverage in the *New York Times*, 11 Feb., 1931, 22 June 1933, 25 Jan., 1938 and 10 Feb., 1939, as examples of the severe attitude shown by at least one paper toward the defendants.

[33] John Gunther, *Inside U.S.A.* (New York: 1947), p. 529.

[34] Gene Fowler, *Beau James, The Life and Times of Jimmy Walker* (New York: 1949), p. 264; Lester Cohen, *The New York Graphic* (Phila.: 1964), p. 153.

[35] Edward Jablonski, *Harold Arlen: Happy with the Blues* (Garden City: 1961), pp. 53-66; Herbert Mitgant, *The Man Who Rode the Tiger* (Phila.: 1963), pp. 217-219.

[36] See the *New York Times*, 6 July 1935.

[37] Bill Brennan, *The Frank Costello Story* (Derby: 1962), p. 106; Charles Garrett's study of this reign makes good reading; Anonymous, *op. cit.*, p. 131.

[38] Moore, *op. cit.*, pp. 12, 33; Barry Ulanov, *History of Jazz* (New York: 1952), p. 230.

[39] Anonymous, *op. cit.*, p. 146.

[40] Shapiro and Hentoff, *op. cit.*, p. 288.

[41] Albert McCarthy, *Big Band Jazz* (London: 1975), p. 30.

[42] Ed Reid, *Mafia and Costra Nostra Syndicates* (New York: 1952), p. 95.

[43] Quoted in Blesh, *op. cit.*, p. 195.

[44] Ross Russell, *Bird Lives* (New York: 1973), p. 31; Maurice M. Milligan, *The Missouri Waltz* (New York: 1948), p. 12.

[45] Milligan, *op. cit.*, p. 84.

[46] Reid, *op. cit.*, pp. 99-103 for a good survey of Italian underworld growth in this era; Milligan, *op. cit.*, p. 83.

[47] See his well written liner notes for "Little Club Jazz...," *op. cit.*, NWB 250.

48Ross Russell, *Jazz Style in Kansas City and the South-West* (Berkeley: 1971), p. 10.

49Gene Ferritt, *Swing Out* (Concord: 1970), p. 79.

50NWB Records, "Little Club Jazz...," *op. cit.*

51Ben Sidran, *Black Talk* (New York: 1971), p. 88.

52Henry "Buster" Smith and Don Gazzaway, "Conversations," *Jazz Review*, Jan., 1960, p. 12.

53Russel, *Bird____, op. cit.*, p. 61.

54*Ken Magazine*, 4 May 1939.

Notes for Chapter IX

1Quoted in *San Francisco Chronicle*, 18 Feb., 1979.

2*Time* Magazine, 7 May 1956.

3Peter W. Bernstein, "The Record Business: Rocking to the Big Money Beat," *Fortune*, 23 April 1979, p. 66.

4*New York Magazine*, 26 March 1979, pp. 40-41.

5London Sunday Times, 15 Jan., 1978.

6Quoted in *Downbeat*, 10 May 1973, p. 11.

7*London Sunday Times, op. cit.*

8*Village Voice*, 11 Sept., 1978, p. 65.

9Quoted in *San Francisco Chronicle*, 2 Nov., 1977.

10Curson quote from *Chronicle, op. cit.*

11Quoted in *San Francisco Chronicle*, 2 Nov., 1977.

12Dickie Wells, *The Night People* (Boston: 1971), pp. 34-35.

13Frank Kofsky, *Black Nationalism and the Revolution in Music* (New York: 1970), pp. 226, 229.

14T.W. Adorno and Hanns Eisler, *Composing for the Films* (New York: 1947), p. 54.

15See *Genesis Magazine* for July, 1974, p. 109.

16Rockefeller Panel, *The Performing Arts—Problems and Prospects* (New York: 1965); and W.J. Baumol and W.G. Bower, *Performing Arts: The Economic Dilemma* (New York: 1966).

Appendix A:

Easily the best way of entering into the spirit sparked by this study is to listen to the kind of music featured in gangster-owned night spots of the era. Lucikly for contemporary listeners, the following albums can be obtained in most large record shops. The suggestion, I think, is worth considering since a reader's lack of knowing what this music sounded like leaves not enough to the imagination.

1. Doc Cook & his Chicago Dreamland Orchestra, Joker SM 3102.
2. Fletcher Henderson & his Connie's Inn Orch., Joker SM 3077.
3. Johnny Dodds, 1926-28, Archives of Jazz BY6 529074/24.
4. Little Club Jazz: Small Night Club Groups in the 1930s, New World Records NW 250.
5. Jive at Five: Stylemakers of Jazz—1920s to 1940s, New World Records NW 274.
6. Jammin' for the Jackpot: Big Bands & Territory Bands of the 1930s, New World Records NW 217.
7. Louis Armstrong in New York (1925-32), Biography BLP CS.
8. Black Bands, 1927-34, Historical Records HLP 35 (includes Hines, Moten, Parham, Luis Russell and the Blue Rhythm Devils).
9. New Orleans Horns, 1923-26, Milestone MLP 2014 (includes Keppard and Lanier).
10. Benny Moten's Kansas City Orchestra (1923-29), HLP 9.
11. Harlem Piano (Luckey Roberts, Willie Smith) Good Time Jazz Records S-10035.
12. Chicago South Side Jazz, Joker SM 3128.
13. New York Jazz (1928-33), Historical Records HLP 19.
14. Duke Ellington at the Cotton Club, Jazz Archives JA 12-13.
15. Count Basie (1937), Saga Pan 6903.
16. Hotsy Totsy Gang (w. Benny Goodman), 1928-30, Sunbeam SB 113.
17. A.J. Piron's New Orleans Orchestra (1923-25), Rarities 9.
18. Luis Russell & his Orchestra (1929-30), CBS 63721.
19. Kings of New Orleans: Jimmy Noone, Jazz Trip II.
20. New Orleans Rhythm Kings (1923), BYG 529057/7 and 529069/19.

Appendix B:
Jazz/Urban Population Correlations

A large urbanized black population held no guarantees for the ultimate success of local jazz. Rarely did Southern cities go out of their way to attract or publicize the music, so the importance of individual communities in the music's overall development can only be guessed at. Predictably, no black "man-about town" guide exists for the Old South, providing the necessary clues. The following Table inherits this weakness while implying that where a reasonably generous segment of Jewish, Italian, and black populations co-existed and interacted, the result favored jazz music. Philadelphia, with its ethnic diffusion and rigidly sectarian religious outlooks, stands out as the only major exception.

Selected Ethnic Populations (1927-30)
Ref: World Almanac & Book of Facts, 1927-30

Percent Black		Percent Jewish/Italian
Charleston	47	--
Memphis	38	2
Richmond, Va.	32	--
Atlanta	30	2
Washington D.C.	30	--
New Orleans***	28	4.5
St. Louis	15	1
Indianapolis	12	--
Gary, Ind.	14	--
Kansas City***	10	6
Philadelphia	10	8
Chicago***	8	8
New York***	5	18
Detroit	2	4

(*** indicates important jazz center in 1926.)

Appendix C:
Italian Jazz Clubs in New Orleans
(Circa 1905)

Matranga's	-very well-known, popular and lively spot for gangsters, their chieftains, and the scene of Louis Armstrong's first local engagement.
Spano's	-another bouncy spot patronized by the mobs.
Tranchina's	-restaurant at the lake resort Spanish Fort.
101 Ranch	-popular Jewish dive for musicians and gamblers as an after hours joint; considered the town's first legitimate cabaret according to Ramsey and Smith.
Lala's Big 25	-low, smoky room well patronized by the underworld and a gathering place for black musicians of growing stature.
Villa Cabaret	-important for larger bands.
Joe Segretta's	-same, especially for the Armstrong, Bolden alumni.
Druid's Hall	-here lodge leader Dominic Barocco hired his own and other Italian jazzmen for special festivals.
LeVida Ballroom	-home of the many violin-led dance bands, often Italian, in the early years a jitney dance hall on Canal Street.
Fern Cafe No. 2	-popular mob place known for tolerance of young artists.
Eddie Grociele's	-crowded location that sponsored the famous A.J. Piron orchestra; home of the first steady association of piano with jazz band.
Tonti's Social Club	-weekend dance hall hiring larger jazz ensembles.
Quarella's	-packed lakefront spot at Milneburg and a stronghold for early day bands.
Italian Hall	-Rampart Street social hall where earliest of local recordings were made in the mid-1920s.
Halfway House	-cabaret featuring Italian bands after 1910.
Pop's Cabaret	-Salvador Romano, gambler-owner, Rampart Street
Anderson's Annex	-headquarters for Storyville's unofficial mayor, Tom Anderson who left the hiring and club managing decisions to Gregorio Delsa; much use of 3-piece bands.
Dante's Lodge	
Toro's Cabaret	-Basin Street spot for Sam Morgan Orch.
Brick House	-roaring cabaret on Saturday nights and located across the river in lively but dangerous Gretna.
Suburban Gardens	-biggest, most successful of gambling casinos after 1918.
Tony Battistina's	
Louis Abadie Cabaret	-featured the legendary Sugar Johnny Smith on cornet in Richard M. Jones' band.

216

Appendix D:
Italian Jazz Musicians in the Early Period in New Orleans

The following list is not meant to be exhaustive, merely suggestive of the very young Italians who became ragtime and jazz musicians through being exposed to it in New Orleans. None was born after 1914, most were reared in the French Quarter/Storyville district, and each played either before or during prohibition.

Adde, Leo (d)
Alessandra, Giuseppi (tb)
Almerico, Tony (t)
Assunto, Jack (tb)
Barocco, Dominic (tb)
Barocco, Joseph (sb)
Barocco, Vincente (s)
Beninate, Johnny (cl)
Bisso, Louis (p)
Bonano, Joseph (t)
Burrella, Tony (d)
Cagnolatti, Ernie (d)
Cachina, Tony (tuba)
Capraro, Angelo (g)
Castigliola, Angelo (tb)
Catalano, Tony (t)
Cordilla, Charles (cl)
Coasta, Tony (cl)
Davila, Sid (d)
Doria, Al (d)
Federico, Frank (g)
Finazzo, Marie (tuba)
Frisco, Al (d)
Frisco, Johnny (d)
Froeba, Frank (p)
Gelpi, Rene (g)
Gerosa, Joe (g)
Giardina, Ernest (bjo)
Giardina, Tony (cl)

Guarino, Felix (d)
Heynia, Frankie (p)
Lacaze, Peter (t)
Lada, Antonia (d)
Laine, Alfred (c)
Laine, Jack (d)
Laine, Juliano (tb)
Lala, Joe (c)
Lala, John (c)
Lala, Mike (t)
LaMare, Hilton (g)
LaRocca, Dominic (c)
Leglise, Vic (d)
Lizana, Florin (cl)
Loyocano, Arnold (p)
Loyocano, Freddie (g)
Loyocano, Joe (tb)
Loyocano, John (sb)
Loyocano, Steve (g)
Maestri, Katz (d)
Mangiapane, Sherwood (sb)
Manone, Joseph (t)
Mares, Paul (c)
Margiotta, Sal (cl)
Massarini, Tony (t)
Miranda, Jack (cl)
Molierei, Ernest (cl)
Netto, Frank (sb)
Nocetti, Tony (p)

Palmisano, Angelo (g)
Papelia, Anthony (cl)
Papelia, Joe (tb)
Papelia, Steve (tb)
Parenti, Tony (cl)
Parone, Joe (sb)
Peccopia, Pete (c)
Pecora, Santo (tb)
Pecorano, Santo (d)
Pellegrini, Pete (c)
Picone, Nino (s)
Pinero, Frank (p)
Pipitone, Jack (cl)
Prima, Leon (t)
Prima, Louis (t)
Provenzano, Johnny (p)
Roffolo, Leon (cl)
Sbarbaro, Tony (d)
Scaglione, Munzio (cl)
Schiro, Angelo (d)
Schiro, Luke (cl)
Schiro, Tony (g)
Sciambra, Jacobi (sb)
Scorsone, Sal (s)
Surgi, Stanley (d)
Taranto, Joe (g)
Tortirichi, Tony (d)
Veca, Lawrence (c)
Zito, Phil (d)

Appendix E:
New York City Jazz Clubs

The following list of clubs comprise the larger, more important and patronized jazz clubs for each of the intended dates. Similar events were taking place elsewhere, such as Los Angeles where, according to *Downbeats* for 4 November 1976 and 6 April 1978, the number of clubs went from 11 to 9, and the area in which they appeared, as in New York, contracted severely.

1972 (6 left from 25)	1976 (11 left from 24)	1978 (now: 18)
Ali Baba	Ali's Alley***	Ali's Alley
Blue Book	Angry Squire	Arthur's
Boomers	Arthur's***	Axis in Soho
Bradley's	Beefsteak Charlie's***	Beefsteak Charlie's
Cellar***	Boomers	Bottom Line
Club Barron	Bottom Line***	Cookery
Cookery***	Bradley's	Condon's
Dugg's Den	Cookery***	Gregory's
Duncan's	Crawdaddy	Hooper's
Fiddle Stix	Condon's	Jazzmania Society
Five Spot	Galaxy	Larson's
		Peter Brown's
Guitar	Garris	Prescott's
Half Note	Gregory's	Red Blazer Too
Jacques	Hooper's***	Ryan's
Lost & Found	Jazzmania Society***	Studio Rivbea
My House	Michael's Pub	Sweet Basil
Needle's Eye	Mikell's	Village Gate
Jimmy Ryan's***	J. Ryan's***	Village Vanguard
Slug's	Storyville	
Stryker's	Stryker's	
Village Gates***	Sweet Basil***	
Village Vanguard***	Village Gate***	
Wells	Village Vanguard***	
West Boondock***	West End Cafe	
Weston's		

***denotes clubs still in business and featuring jazz more than one night a week.
Ref: *Downbeat*, 20 July 1972, 4 November 1976, and 6 April 1978; *New York Magazine*, 6 November 1976 and 20 March 1978.

Bibliography

Abbot, Anthony, *About the Murder of the Night Club Lady,* N.Y., Covici-Friede, 1931.

Adler, Polly, *A House is Not a Home,* N.Y., Rinehart, 1953.

Adorno, T.W., *Introduction to the Sociology of Music,* N.Y., Seabury, 1977.

——— and Hans Eisler, *Composing for the Films,* N.Y., Oxford, 1947.

Agate, James, *An Anthology,* N.Y., Hill & Wang, 1961.

Ahern, Danny, *How to Commit a Murder,* N.Y., Washburn, 1930.

Albertson, Chris, *Bessie,* N.Y., Stein & Day, 1972.

Allen, Robert (Ed.), *Our Fair City,* N.Y., Vanguard, 1947.

Allsop, Kenneth, *The Bootleggers: The Story of Prohibition,* N.Y., Arlington, 1961.

American City Guides (Federal Writers Project), *New York City,* N.Y., Random House, 1939.

American City Guides (Federal Writers Project), New Orleans, Boston, Houghton-Miflin, 1938.

Amsterdam News (New York).

Anderson, Eric, "Prostitution & Social Justice, Chicago: 1910-1915," *Social Services Review,* June, 1974.

Anonymous, *I, Mobster,* N.Y., Gold Medal, 1951.

Anonymous, *The Real Story of a Bootlegger,* N.Y., Boni & Liveright, 1923.

Appignanesi, Lisa, *The Cabaret,* N.Y., Universe, 1976.

Architectural Forum.

Armstrong, Louis, *Satchmo: My Life in New Orleans,* N.Y., Prentice-Hall, 1954.

Arvey, Verna, *Choreographic Music,* N.Y., Dutoon, 1941.

Asbury, Herbert, *The Great Illusion: An Informal History of Prohibition,* N.Y., Greenwood, 1968.

——— , *Gem of the Prairie: An Informal History of the Chicago Underworld,* Garden City, Doubleday, 1942.

——— , *The French Quarter,* N.Y., Knopf, 1935.

——— , *The Barbary Coast: An Informal History of the San Francisco Underworld,* N.Y., Knopf, 1933.

——— , *Gangs of New York,* N.Y., Knopf, 1927.

Baedeker, Karl, *United States,* Leipzig, 1893.

Barker, Danny, "Jelly Roll Morton in New York," *The Jazz Review,* May, 1959.

Barnes, Henry E., *Battling of the Crime Wave,* Boston, Stratford, 1931.

Baumol, W.J. and W.G. Bower, *The Performing Arts; The Economic Dilemna,* N.Y., 1966.

Becker, Howard S., "The Professional Dance Musician and his Audience," *American Journal of Sociology,* September, 1951.

Bell, Daniel, *The End of Ideology,* Glencoe, Free Press, 1960.

Benton, Thomas Hart, *An Artist in America,* Columbia, Missouri UP, 1968.

Bercovici, Konrad, *Manhattan Sideshow,* N.Y., Century, 1931.

Berelson, Bernard and Patricia J. Salter, "Majority and Minority Americans: An Analysis of Magazine Fiction," *Public Opinion Quarterly,* (10), 1946.

Berger, Morroe, "Jazz Resistance to the Diffusion of a Culture-Pattern," *Journal of Negro History,* January, 1947.

219

Bernstein, Peter, "The Record Business: Rocking to the Big Money Beat," *Fortune,* 23 April 1979.

Berton, Ralph, *Remembering Bix: A Memoir of the Jazz Age,* N.Y., Harper & Row, 1974.

Bethell, Tom, George Lewis: *A Jazzman from New Orleans,* Berkeley, California UP, 1977.

Blassingame, John W., *Black New Orleans: 1860-80,* Chicago, Chicago UP, 1973.

Blesh, Rudi, *Combo, USA,* Philadelphia, Chilton, 1971.

————— , *Shining Trumpets,* N.Y., Knopf, 1958.

Bontemps, Arna (Ed.), *Father of the Blues: W.C. Handy,* London, Sidgwick & Jackson, 1957.

Bradford, Perry, *Born with the Blues,* N.Y., Oak, 1965.

Brady, William A., *Showman,* N.Y., Dutton, 1937.

Brearley, H.C., *Homicide in the United States,* Chapel Hill UP, 1932.

Brennan, Bill, *The Frank Costello Story,* Derby Conn., Monzick, 1962.

Bronte, Patricia, *Vittles and Vice,* Chicago, Regnery, 1952.

Brown, Henry Collins, *In the Golden 90s,* Hastings-on-Hudson, Valentine, 1928.

Bruun, H.O., *The Story of the Original Dixieland Jazz Band,* Baton Rouge, Louisiana UP,1960.

Buerkle, Jack and Danny Barker, *Bourbon Street Black,* N.Y., Oxford UP, 1973.

Burke, Peter, *Tradition and Innovation in Renaissance Italy,* London, Fontana, 1974.

Bushnell, Gavin, and Nat Hentoff, New York Jazz in the 1920s," *The Jazz Review,* April, 1959.

Caico, Louise, *Sicilian Ways and Days,* N.Y., Appleton, 1910.

Cameron, William B., "Sociological Notes on the Jam Session," *Social Forces,* December, 1954.

Carmichael, Hoagy, *Sometimes I Wonder,* N.Y., Farrar, Straus & Giroux, 1965.

Carter, Hodding (Ed.), *The Past as Prelude: New Orleans, 1718-1968,* New Orleans, Tulane UP, 1968.

Charter, Samuel B., *Jazz in New Orleans: 1885-1963,* N.Y., Oak, 1963.

————— , *Jazz, A History of the New York Scene,* N.Y., Doubleday, 1962.

Chicago Commission in Race Relations, *The Negro in Chicago,* Chicago, UP, 1933.

Chicago Messenger.

Christensen, C. Lawrence, *Collective Bargaining in Chicago: 1929-30,* Chicago, Chicago UP, 1933.

Cohen, Lester, *The New York Graphic,* Philadelphia, Chilton, 1964.

Cohen, Mickey and John P. Nugent, *In My Own Words,* Englewood Cliffs, Prentice-Hall, 1975.

Collier's Weekly.

Committee of Fourteen, *Annual Report,* N.Y., 1928.

Condon, Eddie and Thomas Sugrue, *We Called it Music,* N.Y., Holt, 1947.

Cortinouis, Irene E., "Jazz on the Riverboats, The Way a Piano Player Tells it," *Journal of Jazz Studies,* June, 1974.

Cressey, Donald R., "Methodological Problems in the Study of Organized Crime as a Social Problem," *The Annals of the American Academy of Political & Social Science,* Nov., 1967.

Cressey, Paul G., *The Taxi-Dance Hall,* Chicago, Chicago UP, 1932.

Crockett, Albert S., *Old Waldorf Bar Days,* N.Y., Aventine, 1931.

Cue (New York).

Cunningham, George E., "Italians-Hindrance to White Solidarity, 1890-1898," *Journal of Negro History,* January, 1965.

Cutler, R.E., and Thomas Storm, "Observational Study of Alcohol Consumption in Natural Settings—The Vancouver Beer Parlour," *Journal of Studies on Alcohol,* (9) September 1975.

Dance, Stanley, *The World of Earl Hines,* N.Y., Scribners, 1977.

———— , *The World of Swing,* N.Y., Scribners, 1974.

--- , *The World of Duke Ellington,* N.Y., Scribners, 1970.

Davidson, Bill, "Memories," *The Jazz Record,* February, 1946.

Davin, Tom, "Conversations with James P. Johnson," *The Jazz Review.* March/April, 1960.

Dewey, Thomas E., *Twenty Against the Underworld,* N.Y., Doubleday, 1974.

Dexter, Dave, *Jazz Story: From the 90s to the 60s,* Englewood Cliffs, Prentice-Hall, 1964.

Doherty, Edward J., *The Broadway Murders: A Night Club Mystery,* N.Y., Groseet & Dunlap, 1929.

Dorsett, Lyle W., *The Pendergast Machine,* N.Y., Oxford UP, 1968.

Downbeat.

Driggs, Frank, "Eddie Barefield's Many Worlds," *Jazz Review,* July, 1960.

DuFour, Charles L., *Ten Flags in the Wind: The Story of Louisiana,* N.Y., Harper & Row, 1967.

Dufty, William and Billie Holliday, *Lady Sings the Boues,* N.Y., Doubleday, 1956.

Dukas, Peter, *How to Plan and Operate a Restaurant,* Rochelle Park, New Jersey, Hayden, 1973.

Durante, Jimmy and Jack Kofoed, *Night Clubs,* N.Y., Knopf, 1931.

Ellington, Duke, *Music is My Mistress,* N.Y., Doubleday, 1973.

Epstein, Abraham, *The Negro Migrant in Pittsburgh,* Pittsburgh UP, 1918.

Esquire.

Evans, Oliver, *New Orleans,* N.Y., MacMillan, 1959.

Ewan, David, *Panorama of American Popular Music,* Englewood Cliffs, Prentice-Hall, 1957.

Fair, C.M., "Requiem For a Living Art," in William Phillips and Philip Raha (Ed)., *The Avon Book of Modern Writing,* N.Y., Avon, 1953.

Fairbairn, Ann, *Call Him George,* N.Y., Crown, 1961.

Feldman, Egal, "Prostitution, the Alien Woman and Progressive Imagination: 1910-1915," *American Quarterly,* (19), 1967.

Felker, Clay (Ed.), *The Power Game,* N.Y., Simon & Schuster, 1969.

Ferrett, Gene, *Swing Out,* Concord, MI., Private Printing, 1970.

Fisher, Rudolph, *The Walls of Jericho,* N.Y., Knopf, 1928.

———— , "The Caucasian Storms Harlem," *American Mercury,* August 1927.

Fitzgerald, F. Scott, *The Great Gatsby,* N.Y., Scribner, 1926.

Foster, A.A., *New Orleans, The Glamour Period: 1800-40,* New Orleans, Pelican, 1957.

Fowler, Gene, *Schnozzola,* N.Y., Viking, 1951.

———— , *Beau James, The Life and Times of Jimmy Walker,* N.Y., Viking, 1949.

Freedland, Michael, *Irving Berlin,* N.Y., Stein & Day, 1974.

Freeman, Bud, *You Don't Look Like a Musician,* Detroit, Balamp, 1974.

Gabree, John, *Gangsters From Little Caesar to the Godfather,* N.Y., Pyramid, 1973.

Gambino, Richard, *Blood of My Blood,* N.Y., Doubleday, 1974.

Garrett, Charles, *The LaGuardia Years,* New Brunswick, Rutgers UP, 1961.

Gastil, Raymond O., "Homicide and a Regional Culture of Violence," *American Sociological Review,* June, 1971.

Genauer, Emily, *Modern Interiors: Today and Tomorrow,* N.Y., Illustrated Editions, 1939.

Genesis.

Genthe, Arnold, *Impressions of Old New Orleans,* N.Y., Doran, 1926.

Gillis, Frank and John W. Miner, *Oh, Didn't He Ramble: The Life Story of Lee Collins,* Urbana Ill., Illinois UP, 1974.

Gold, Michael, *Jews Without Money,* N.Y., Liveright, 1930.

Goldman, Albert, *Ladies and Gentleman—Lenny Bruce,* N.Y., Random House, 1971.

Gosch, Martin and Richard Hammer, *The Last Testament of Lucky Luciano,* Boston, Little & Brown, 1975.

Gottlieb, Polly Rose, *The 9 Lives of Billy Rose,* N.Y., Signet, 1969.

Graham, Carroll and Garrett, *Whitney,* N.Y., Vanguard, 1931.

Graham, Hugh D., *Violence in America: Historical and Comparative Perspectives,* Washington D.C., U.S. Printing Office, 1969.

Graham, Stephen, *New York Nights,* N.Y., Doran, 1927.

Granlund, Nils T., *Blondes, Brunettes and Bullets,* N.Y., McKay, 1957.

Greene, Lorenzo J., and Carter G. Woodson, *The Negro Wage Earner,* Washington D.C., Assoc. for the Study of Negro Life, 1930.

Gunther, John, *Inside U.S.A.,* N.Y., Harper, 1947.

Hadlock, Richard *Jazz Masters of the 1920s,* N.Y., MacMillan, 1965.

Hansen, Chadwick, "Social Influences in Jazz Style in Chicago, 1920-30," *American Quarterly,* Winter, 1960.

Hapgood, Hutchins, *Spirit of the Ghetto: Studies of the Jewish Quarter of New York,* N.Y., Funk & Wagnall, 1902.

Harlow, Alvin F., *Old Bowery Days,* N.Y., Appleton, 1931.

Harper's Weekly.

Harris, Rex, *Jazz,* Harmondsworth, Penguin, 1957.

Harvey, Edward, "Social Change and the Jazz Musician," *Social Forces,* September, 1967.

Hennessey, Thomas J., "The Black Chicago Establishment, 1919-30," *Journal of Jazz Studies,* December, 1974.

Hentoff, Nat, *The Jazz Life,* N.Y., Dial, 1961.

Hershkowitz, Leo, *Tweed's New York: Another Look,* N.Y., Doubleday, 1976.

Higham, John, *Strangers in the Land: Patterns of American Nativism: 1860-1925,* N.Y., Atheneum, 1969.

Hiller, Mark K., "Organized Crime in Urban Sociology: Chicago in the 1920s," *Journal of Social History,* Winter, 1971-72.

Hines, Earl, "How Gangsters Ran the Night Club Business," *Ebony,* September, 1949.

Hodes, Art, "The Rainbow Cafe," *The Jazz Record,* October, 1943.

——— , "My First Steady Job," *The Jazz Record,* March, 1944.

——— , "Blues for the Dago," *The Jazz Record,* April, 1945.

——— , "Facts of Life," *The Jazz Record,* September, 1945.

Hoefer, George, and Willie Smith, *Music on My Mind,* N.Y., Doubleday,

1964.

Hoffman, F.L., "Murder Rates for 1926," *Spectator,* 2 June 1927.

Horne, Lena and Richard Schnickel, *Lena,* Garden City, Doubleday, 1965

House Executive Documents, Foreign Relations of the United States, for 1896.

Huber, Leonard V., *New Orleans: A Pictorial History,* N.Y., Crown, 1971.

Huggins, Nathan, *Harlem Renaissance,* N.Y., Oxford UP, 1971.

Hughes, Langston, *The Big Sea,* N.Y., Hill & Wang, 1963.

Hughes, Rupert, *Lady's Man,* N.Y., Harper, 1930.

Huizanga, Johan, *Homo Ludens: A Study of the Play Element in Culture,* Boston, Beacon, 1955.

Hurston, Zora Neale, *Dust Tracks on a Road,* Philadelphia, Lippincott, 1942.

Ianni, Francis A.J., *Ethnic Succession in Organized Crime,* Washington D.C., Dept. of Justice, 1973.

————— , *A Family Business-Kinship and Social Control of Crime,* N.Y., Russell Sage, 1972.

Illinois Crime Investigating Commission, *Juice Racketters: A Report on Criminal Usury in Chicago,* June 1970.

Jablonski, Edward, *Harold Arlen: Happy with the Blues,* Garden City, Doubleday, 1961.

Jackson, Joy J., *New Orleans in the Gilded Age: Politics and Urban Process-1880-96,* Baton Rouge, Louisiana State UP, 1969.

————— , "Crime and the Conscience of a City," *Louisiana History,* Summer, 1968.

James, Rian, *All About New York,* N.Y., Day, 1931.

Jennings, Al, *Through the Shadows with O'Henry,* N.Y., Fly, 1921.

Johnson, Clifton, *Highways and Byways of the South,* N.Y., MacMillan, 1905.

Johnson, James Weldon, *Black Manhattan,* N.Y., Atheneum, 1930.

————— , *Autobiography of an Ex-Colored Man,* N.Y., Knopf, 1927.

Johnston, W.A., "Structure of the Motion Picture Industry," *Motion Picture Industry Annals,* (128), 1947.

Jones, LeRoi, *Blues People,* N.Y., Morrow, 1963.

Jones, Max and John Chilton, *Louis: 1900-71,* Boston, Little & Brown, 1971.

Jones, Thomas J., *The Sociology of a New York City Block,* N.Y. Columbia UP, 1904.

Jordan, Elizabeth, *The Night Club Mystery,* N.Y., Century, 1929.

Kaminsky, Max, *My Life in Jazz,* N.Y., Crown, 1928.

Kavolis, Vytautas, *Artistic Expression: A Sociological Analysis,* Ithaca, Cornell UP, 1968.

Ken.

Kendall, John Smith, "New Orleans Newspapermen of Yesteryear," *Louisiana Historical Quarterly,* July, 1946.

————— , "Old-Time New Orleans Police Reporters and Reporting," *Louisiana Historical Quarterly,* January, 1946.

————— , "Who Killa de Chief," *Louisiana Historical Quarterly,* April, 1939.

Kennedy, Louise V., *The Negro Peasant Turns Cityward,* N.Y., Columbia UP, 1930.

Kmen, Henry A., *Music in New Orleans: The Formative Years-1751-1841,* Baton Rouge, Louisiana State UP, 1966.

Kobler, John, *Capone,* N.Y., Fawcett, 1971.

Kofsky, Frank, *Black Nationalism and the Revolution in Music,* N.Y., Pathfinder, 1970.

Kolodin, Irving, "The Dance Band Business: A Study in Black and White," *Harper's,* June, 1941.

Krehbiel, Henry E., *Afro-American Folksongs Studied,* N.Y., Ungar, 1913.

Kummer, Frederic A., *Manhattan Masquerade,* N.Y., Sears, 1934.

Lait, Jack, and Lee Mortimer, *Washington Confidential,* N.Y., Crown, 1951.

————— , *Chicago Confidential,* N.Y., Cwon, 1950.

Lambian, Maria W., and Leroy S. Bowman, "Evidences of Social Relationships as Seen in Types of New York City Dance Halls," *Social Forces,* January, 1925.

Lampe, J.B., *Songs of Ireland,* N.Y., Remick, 1916.

Landesco, John, *Organized Crime in Chicago,* Chicago UP, 1929.

Lathrop, Elsie, *Early American Inns and Taverns,* N.Y., McBride, 1926.

Lavine, E.H., *Gimme-How Politicians Get Rich,* N.Y., Vanguard, 1931.

Lax, John, "Chicago Black Musicians in the 1920s—Portrait of an Era," *Journal of Jazz Studies,* June, 1974.

Lee, George L., *Beale Street,* N.Y., Ballou, 1934.

Leigh, Francis B., *10 Years on a Georgia Plantation,* London, Bentley, 1883.

Leonard, Neil, *Jazz and the White American,* Chicago, Chicago UP, 1962.

Lippman, Walter, *Early Writings,* N.Y., Liveright, 1970.

Locke, Alain, *The Negro and His Music,* Washington D.C., Association in Negro Folk Education, 1935.

Lomax, Allan, *Mr. Jelly Roll,* N.Y., Buell, 1950.

London Sunday Times.

Longstreet, Stephen, *Chicago: An Intimate Portrait of its People, Pleasures and Power,* 1860-1919, N.Y., McKay, 1973.

Lucas, Curtis *Lila* (N.Y. Lion) 1955.

Lyle, John H., *The Dry and Lawless Years,* N.Y., Dell, 1961.

Manners, Dorine, *Scarlet Patrol,* N.Y., Godwin, 1937.

Manone, Wingy, *A Trumpet on the Wing,* N.Y., Doubleday, 1948.

Marshall, Jim, *Swinging Doors,* Seattle, McCaffrey, 1949.

Martin, J.B., *My Life in Crime,* N.Y., Harper, 1952.

McCarthy, Albert, *Big Band Jazz,* London, Putnam, 1975.

McKay, Claude, *Harlem: Negro Metropolis,* N.Y., Harcourt & Brace, 1940.

————— , *A Long Way from Home,* N.Y., Furman, 1937.

————— , *Home to Harlem,* N.Y., Harper, 1928.

McWilliams, Carey, *A Mask for Privlege: Anti-Semitism in America,* Boston, Little & Brown, 1948.

Metronome.

Mezzrow, Mezz and Bernard Wolfe, *Really the Blues,* N.Y., Random, 1946.

Middleton, S., *Dining, Wining and Dancing in New York,* N.Y., Dodge, 1938.

Milligan, Maurice M., *The Missouri Waltz,* N.Y., Scribners, 1948.

Mitchell, Joseph, *McSorley's Wonderful Saloon,* N.Y., Duell, Sloan & Pearce, 1938.

Mitgang, Herbert, *The Man Who Rode the Tiger (Samuel Seabury),* Philadelphia, Lippincott, 1963.

Monroe, Will S., *Sicilty: The Garden of the Mediterranean,* London Bell, 1909.

Moore, Thomas G., *The Economics of the American Theatre,* Durham, Duke UP, 1968.

Moore, William H., *The Kefauver Committee in the Politics of Crime,* Columbia, Missouri UP, 1974.

Nation (London).

Nearing, Scott, *Black America,* N.Y., Vanguard, 1929.
Neff, Robert and Anthony Connor, *Blues,* Boston, Godine, 1975.
Ness, Eliot and Oscar Fraley, *The Untouchables,* N.Y., Popular, 1964.
New Orleans Daily Picayune.
New York American.
New York Daily News.
New York Magazine.
New York Sunday News.
New York Times.
New York World.
Niehaus, Earl F., *The Irish in New Orleans, 1800-60,* Baton Rouge, Louisiana
    State UP, 1965.
North Carolina News & Observer.
Notch, Frank K., *King Mob,* N.Y., Harcourt & Brace, 1930.
Oakley, Giles, *The Devil's Music: A History of the Blues,* London, BBC
    Publications, 1976.
O'Henry, *Cabbages and Kings,* N.Y., Doubleday & Page, 1904.
Oliver, Paul, *Conversations with the Blues,* N.Y., Horizon, 1965.
Opinion Research Corporation Survey, 105-D, April, 1940.
Ornitz, Samuel, *Haunch, Paunch and Jowl,* N.Y., Boni & Liveright, 1923.
Pasternak, Velvel, *Songs of the Chassidim,* N.Y., Bloch, 1968.
Paul, Elliot, *That Crazy American Music,* Indianapolis, Bobbs-Merrill, 1957.
Pearce, Frank, *Crimes of the Powerful,* London, Pluto, 1976.
Petaccio, Arrigo, *Joe Petrosino-The True Story of a Tough Turn-of-the-
    Century New York Cop,* N.Y., MacMillan, 1974.
Pittman, David and C.W. Gordon, *Revolving Door: A Study of the Chronic
    Police Case Inebriate,* Glencoe, Free Press, 1958.
Pittman, David and Charles Snyder (Ed.), *Society, Culture and Drinking
    Patterns,* N.Y., Wiley, 1962.
Ramsey, Frederic, Jr., and C.E. Smith, *Jazzmen,* N.Y., Harcourt & Brace, 1939.
Rayne Tribune (Louisiana).
Reckless, Walter C., *Vice in Chicago,* Chicago UP, 1933.
Rector, George, *The Girl from Rector's,* Garden City, Doubleday & Page, 1927.
Reid, Ed, *Mafia and the Costa Nostra Syndicates,* N.Y., Random, 1952.
Riis, Jacob, *How the Other Half Lives,* N.Y., Dover, 1971.
Rockefeller, Panel, *The Performing Arts-Problems and Prospects,* N.Y., 1965.
Rogers, A.J., *100 Facts About the Negro,* N.Y., Rogers, 1952.
Rose, Al, *Storyville, New Orleans,* Tuscaloosa, alabama UP, 1974.
Rose, Al, and Edmond Souchon, *New Orleans Jazz,* Baton Rouge, Louisiana
    State UP, 1967.
Rowe, Mike, *Chicago Breakdown,* N.Y., Drake, 1975.
Rublowsky, John, *Popular Music,* N.Y., Basic, 1967.
Runyan, Damon, *The Best of D. Runyan,* N.Y., Pocket, 1940.
Russell, Ross, *Bird Lives,* N.Y., Charterhouse, 1973.
————, *Jazz Style in Kansas City and the South-West,* Berkeley, California
    UP, 1971.
Salerno, Ralph and J.S. Tompkins, *The Crime Confederation,* N.Y.,
    Doubleday, 1969.
San Francisco Chronicle.
Schoener, Allon (Ed.), *Harlem on My Mind,* N.Y., Random, 1968.
Schurz, Carl, *Report on the Condition of the South,* N.Y., Arno, 1865.

Schwann Record Catalogue.
Searight, Sarah, *New Orleans,* N.Y., Stein & Day, 1973.
Shapiro, Nat and Nat Hentoff, *Near Me Talkin' to Ya',* N.Y., Dover, 1955.
Shaw, Arnold, *The Street that Never Sleeps,* N.Y., Coward & McCann, 1971.
Shaw, Artie, *The Trouble with Cinderella,* N.Y., Farrar, Straus, & Young, 1952.
Shugg, Roger W., *Origins of the Class Struggle in Louisiana,* Baton Rouge, Louisiana State UP, 1939.
Sidran, Ben, *Black Talk,* N.Y., Rineholt & Winston, 1971.
Silberman, Alphons, *The Sociology of Music,* London, Routledge, Kegan Paul, 1963.
Simon, George T., *Glenn Miller and His Orchestra,* N.Y., Crowell, 1974.
Sinclair, William A., *The Aftermath of Slavery,* Boston, Small & Maynard, 1905.
Sjoberg, Wilhelm, "Social Characteristics of Entertainers," *Social Forces,* October, 1958.
Smith, Henry "Buster", and Don Gazzaway, "Conversations," *The Jazz Review,* December, 1959 and January, 1960.
Smith, Willard K., *Bowery Murder,* Garden City, Doubleday & Doran, 1929.
Sombart, Werner, *Jews and Modern Capitalism,* London, Unwin, 1913.
Sommer, Robert, *Personal Space: The Behavioral Basis of Design,* N.Y., Prentice-Hall, 1969.
Sondern, Jr., Frederick, *Brotherhood of Evil,* N.Y., Farrar, Straus, & Cudahy, 1959.
Spectator.
Stagg, Jerry, *The Brothers Shubert,* N.Y., Crest, 1968.
Stearns, Marshall, *The Story of Jazz,* N.Y., Oxford UP, 1958.
Stoddard, Tom, *The Autobiography of Pops Foster,* Berkeley, California UP, 1971.
Strunsky, Simeon, *No Mean City,* N.Y., Dutton, 1944.
Sullenger, T.E., *Social Determinants in Juvenile Delinquency,* N.Y., Wiley, 1936.
Sullivan, Edward D., *Chicago Surrenders,* N.Y., Vanguard, 1930.
Survey.
Sylvester, Robert, *Notes of a Guilty Bystander,* Englewood Cliffs, Prentice-Hall, 1970.
————, *No Cover Charge: A Backward Look at Night Clubs,* N.Y. Dial, 1956.
Tallant, Robert, *The Romantic New Orleanians,* N.Y., Dutton, 1950.
Teller, Judd, *Strangers and Natives: Evolution of an American Jew from 1921 to the Present,* N.Y., Delacorte, 1968.
Teresa, Vincent, *My Life in the Mafia,* N.Y., Doubleday, 1973.
———— , "A Mafioso Cases the Mafia Craze," *Saturday Review of The Society,* February, 1973.
Thomas J.C., *Chasin' the Trane,* Garden City, Doubleday, 1975.
Thurmond, Wallace, *The Blacker the Berry,* N.Y., Macaulay, 1929.
Time.
Times Literary Supplement (London).
Toffler, Alvin, *The Culture Consumers-Art and Affluence in America,* Baltimore, Penguin, 1965.
Travel.
Turkus, Burton B. and Sid Feder, *Murder Inc.,* N.Y., Bantam, 1960.
Turner, George Kibbe, "Criminals of New York," *McClure's Magazine,* November, 1909.

Turner, George Kibbe, "Criminals of New York," *McClure's Magazine,* November, 1909.

——— , "Tammany's Control of New York," *McClure's Magazine,* June, 1909.

Tyler, Gus (Ed.), *Organized Crime in America,* Ann Arbor, Michigan UP, 1971.

Ulanov, Barry, *History of Jazz,* N.Y., Viking, 1952.

——— , *Duke Ellington,* N.Y., Creative Ace, 1946.

Vance, Louis J., *The Trembling Flame,* Philadelphia, Lippincott, 1931.

Van Dine, S.S., *The Gracie Allen Murder Case,* N.Y., Collier, 1938.

Van Vechten, Carl, *Parties,* N.Y., Knopf, 1930.

——— , *Nigger Heaven,* N.Y., Harper & Row, 1926.

Variety.

Village Voice (New York).

Walker, Leo, *The Wonderful Era of Great Dance Bands,* Berkeley, Howell-North, 1964.

Walker, Stanley, *The Night Club Era,* N.Y., Stokes, 1933.

Walling, George W., *Recollections of a New York Chief of Police,* N.Y., Caxton, 1887.

Walton, Ortiz, *Music-Black, White and Blues,* N.Y., Morrow, 1972.

Ware, Caroline, *Greenwich Village: 1920-30,* N.Y., Harper, 1935.

Waters, Ethel, *His Eye is on the Sparrow,* N.Y., Doubleday, 1950.

Weinberger, Julius, "Economic Aspects of Recreation," *Howard Business Review,* Summer, 1937.

Wells, Dickie, *The Night People,* Boston, Crescendo, 1971.

Whitcomb, Ian, *After the Ball is Over: Pop Music from Rag to Rock,* N.Y. Simon & Schuster, 1972.

White, Walter, *Rope and Faggot,* Private, 1928.

Whittemore, L.H., *The Man Who Ran the Subways-Mike Quill,* N.Y. Holt, Rinehart & Winston, 1968.

Whyte, William F., *Street Corner Society,* Chicago, Chicago UP, 1943.

Williams, Martin, *Jazz Masters of New Orleans,* N.Y., MacMillan, 1967.

——— , (Ed.), *Jazz Panorama,* N.Y. Crowell-Collier, 1962.

Youngman, Henny, *Take My Wife...Please!,* N.Y., Putnam, 1973.

Zeidman, Irving, *The American Burlesque Show,* N.Y., Hawthorn, 1967.

Zorbaugh, Harvey W., *The Gold Coast and the Slum,* Chicago, Chicago UP, 1929.

Interviews and correspondence were conduced with the following people, to whom my appreciation is extended: Hoagy Carmichael, Sam Cohen, Leonard Feather, Ira Gitler, Ralph J. Gleason, Benny Goodman, Norman Granz, John Hammond, Phoebe Jacobs, Shelly Manne, Jimmy McPartland, Turk Murphy, Sy Oliver, Louis Prima, Russ Sanjek, Ruth Spanier, "Angelo", and Tom Hall.

Finally, information was obtained by consulting liner notes produced by the following record companies: Herwin, RCA Victor, Saga, Columbia, New World, Library of Congress and Decca.

Index